Ballplayers on Stage

Travis Stern

Baseball, Melodrama, and Theatrical Celebrity
in the Deadball Era

Sport and Popular Culture · Brian M. Ingrassia, Series Editor

THE UNIVERSITY OF TENNESSEE PRESS · KNOXVILLE

*The Sport and Popular Culture series is designed to promote critical,
innovative research in the history of sport through a wide spectrum of works—
monographs, edited volumes, biographies, and reprints of classics.*

ALL IMAGES ARE COURTESY OF THE LIBRARY OF CONGRESS EXCEPT WHERE NOTED.

Library of Congress Cataloging-in-Publication Data
NAMES: Stern, Travis W., author.
TITLE: Ballplayers on stage : baseball, melodrama,
and theatrical celebrity in the deadball era / Travis Stern.
DESCRIPTION: First edition. | Knoxville : The University of Tennessee Press, 2024. |
Series: Sport and popular culture | Includes bibliographical references and index. |
SUMMARY: "Travis Stern explores the relationship between professional baseball and professional theater in the late nineteenth and early twentieth centuries. He argues that examining theater from this era helps us better understand baseball's development and its transformation from a strictly working-class attraction to an entertainment of the emerging middle class in the US. Stern examines case studies of five players from baseball's pre-Babe Ruth "deadball" era: Cap Anson, Mike "King" Kelly, Christy Mathewson, Ty Cobb, and Rube Waddell, with a concluding study of Babe Ruth himself. While one draw of theatrical performance was the additional profit it promised the players during the off-season, the stage also offered these men an opportunity to take a more active role in shaping their public image. Thus, this book offers not only an intersectional historical study of baseball and theater, but also insight into the creation of celebrity in early twentieth-century America"—Provided by publisher.
IDENTIFIERS: LCCN 2024008497 (print) | LCCN 2024008498 (ebook) |
ISBN 9781621908821 (hardcover) | ISBN 9781621908838 (pdf) | ISBN 9781621908890 (kindle edition)
SUBJECTS: LCSH: Baseball—Social aspects—United States—History—19th century. | Baseball—Social aspects—United States—History—20th century. | Sports and theater—United States—History—19th century. | Sports and theater—United States—History—20th century. | Anson, Adrian C. (Adrian Constantine), 1852-1922 | Kelly, Michael J., 1857-1894. | Mathewson, Christy, 1880-1925. | Cobb, Ty, 1886-1961. | Waddell, Rube 1876-1914. | Ruth, Babe, 1895-1948.
CLASSIFICATION: LCC GV867.64 .S64 2024 (print) | LCC GV867.64 (ebook) |
DDC 792.088/7963570973—dc23/eng/20240403
LC record available at https://lccn.loc.gov/2024008497
LC ebook record available at https://lccn.loc.gov/2024008498

To Dad,
WHO WAS AROUND AT THE BEGINNING
OF THIS PROJECT BUT NOT HERE AT ITS END,

and for Ellie,
WHO WASN'T AROUND FOR THE BEGINNING
BUT IS HERE NOW.

Contents

Illustrations

In Michael Lewis's memorable 2003 book *Moneyball: The Art of Winning an Unfair Game,* baseball is all about statistics, not persona. Aging scouts weighing in on youthful draft picks without paying attention to the numbers seemingly have all the self-awareness of a T-Rex lumbering around a Cretaceous-era swamp moments before the meteor smashes into the earth's crust. Sabermetricians have been telling us for at least the last two decades that teams should judge players by measures like walks, fielding percentage, and OPS, not the sweetness of their swing, the swagger of their bodies, or the cut of their jib. In the era of computer-driven analytics, why draft an Adonis when you could have Kevin Youkilis, the "Greek God of Walks"?

There is a reason, though, why baseball men may have once focused on personalities more than on numbers. As Travis Stern shows us in *Ballplayers on Stage: Baseball, Melodrama, and Theatrical Celebrity in the Deadball Era*, a number of early Hall of Famers once performed in or wrote full-length melodramatic plays, or moonlighted in vaudeville. This is a lively story. Legends that crossed over from field to stage included some of the biggest names in baseball's early history: Adrian "Cap" Anson, Mike "King" Kelly, Christy Mathewson, Ty Cobb, and Rube Waddell. All of these players are now enshrined on bronze plaques in Cooperstown, but their celebrity transcended statistics, allowing them to portray archetypical figures on the stage. While some simply played themselves, others played the stereotypical hero, villain, or fool. We find King Kelly appearing in a farce titled *A Rag Baby* and also doing dramatic readings of the 1888 poem "Casey at the Bat" (which some thought was based on Mr. Kelly himself). Meanwhile, Ty Cobb verbally ripped apart one of his detractors after a poor stage review, informing the other man that not only was he richer and a better ballplayer than the reviewer, but also a better writer and theater critic! (Could we expect any less from the aggressive and acerbic Georgia Peach?). Pitcher Rube

Waddell—perhaps the most colorful member of this lineup—not only acted in *The Stain of Guilt*, but occasionally insisted on pitching with a diamond emptied of fielders, just to prove his dominance. When it comes to baseball, what could more dramatic than that?

The Deadball Era was the period dating roughly from 1900 to 1920 when baseball's rules had more or less solidified into their modern form, yet games were still low-scoring, small-ball affairs with few home runs. It was also a progenitor of the era of sports celebrity, a time when the best ballplayers went from simple renown to actual fame. The most recognizable players gained celebrity not just due to their on-field feats but rather because of their ability and willingness to transform diamond personas into theatrical gold, a pre-Hollywood alchemy that made baseball into America's best-loved sport. By transcending genres—appearing on stages and newspaper headlines in an age before athletes ever appeared on celluloid, television screens, or internet fantasy leagues—ballplayers became celebrities. As cultural historian Warren Susman once observed in his book *Culture as History: The Transformation of American Society in the Twentieth Century,* sport celebrity was based as much on style as on substance; in their athletes, as in their automobiles, Americans wanted "color, personality, [and] crowd appeal" (1984, 142).

A key part of this story is the way modern transportation networks fueled the rise of truly national cultures of celebrity. As Stern shows us, baseball's dramatic stage emerged at a time when combination companies replaced stock companies, and traveling vaudeville shows brought a variety of entertainments to cities and towns all over America. Theater companies and vaudeville circuits were not so different from professional baseball leagues that traveled between metropolises. (Indeed, during the 1910s and 1920s, the Supreme Court of the United States heard multiple cases that hinged on the question of whether opera, vaudeville, and baseball constituted interstate commerce.) Sports leagues and dramatic circuits were analogous cultural forms, and so theatrical performances helped baseball celebrities spread their fame even farther than the games themselves. In an era when there were no big-league teams south or west of St. Louis, the right stage role could introduce baseball celebrity to any place with a proscenium.

Scripted and unscripted drama worked in synergy during the Deadball Era. While the stage offers a place where meaning is marketable, sport by contrast appeals to the crowd because it conveys meaningful yet unpredictable physicality. Assuming no game-fixing shenanigans, the result after nine innings (or four quarters, or five hundred miles) is unknown until the last strike (or final buzzer, or drop of the checkered flag). In drama, though, what happens before the curtain falls comes as no surprise to anyone with access to a script. It is not shocking that in baseball's early years, the game's most famous heroes—as well as its best-known villains and fools—played both sides of the scripted-unscripted divide, and in the process successfully worked their way into American hearts and psyches.

It is only appropriate that *Ballplayers on Stage* ends with Babe Ruth, perhaps the prototypical modern ballplayer who made a significant amount of money by selling his persona in the consumer marketplace. Many know the origin story of the Curse of the Bambino: in early 1920, Boston Red Sox owner Harry Frazee sold George Herman Ruth's contract to the upstart New York Yankees, ostensibly in an attempt to acquire funds to stage a musical called *No, No, Nanette*. (Ruth's sale may or may not have bankrolled that stage production, but it certainly did kickstart one of sport's greatest dynasties.) Ruth was then in his famous transition from pitcher to slugger, but his transformation involved more than just relocating from the pitching mound to the outfield. By moving southward—from a hidebound town famous for once banning plays to a wide-open metropolis virtually synonymous with theater—the Babe came to personify modern sport celebrity. Stern tells us the rest of the story: Anson, Kelly, Mathewson, Cobb, and Waddell became baseball celebrities, and they did not need Hollywood (or candy bars) to do it. They found their fame in large part on the early-1900s stage.

This is a well-researched and theoretically astute book, which will appeal to readers interested in baseball and the modern American stage. Take a seat and unfold the opera glasses—or sharpen the scorecard-pencil and grab a box of Cracker Jack, if you will—and discover how the early twentieth-century stage helped transform baseball heroes into celebrities.

BRIAN M. INGRASSIA
West Texas A&M University

Acknowledgments

I am indebted to the many people who helped me in a variety of ways during the course of this project, and I offer each of the following my sincere thanks for their time and energy: the fine people at the University of Tennessee Press, including Brian M. Ingrassia and Thomas Wells; Lucy Reynolds from Clare Omnia; Tim Wiles, Jim Gates, and Freddy Berowski at the A. Bartlett Giamatti Research Center; Taryn Herman and Jason Simon for their assistance at the New York Public Library; Mark Schmitt and Maureen Brunsdale at Milner Library Special Collections; Ashley Madaris and Eli van Sickel for helping me as research assistants; Ann Haugo; Andrew Gibb; Andrea Ryan; Scott Harman; Ellen Peck; and my fellow MA/PhD students at the University of Illinois at Urbana-Champaign. Additionally, I want to express gratitude to the Interlibrary Loan Department of the University Library at the University of Illinois at Urbana-Champaign and of the Cullum-Davis Library at Bradley University, the Library of Congress, the Mid-America Theatre Conference (MATC), the Society for American Baseball Research (SABR), the Ty Cobb Museum in Royston, Georgia, and the Mary Imogene Bassett Hospital ER in Cooperstown, New York.

I want to thank Esther Kim Lee, Adrian Burgos, Jr., Peter Davis, Valleri Robinson, Sean Bartley, Shannon Walsh, Sarah McCarroll, Bill Nowlin, Ron E. Kates and Warren Tormey, and Chris Woodworth for taking time to look at various pieces of this project over time. Their feedback and advice as well as their encouragement and support were more valuable than my words could possibly express. This project is considerably richer because of their insight and input.

My colleagues at Bradley University have provided continuous support to me and this project: Jeffrey Huberman, Scott Kanoff, Chad Lowell, Dan Matisa, Johanna Pershing, Becki Arnold, Sara Gauwitz, and Larry Son. I also want to thank my students at Bradley University and Illinois State University for helping me in ways they may never fully realize.

Finally, I want to thank my family for their support and understanding. In particular I want to thank my wife, Laura, and my daughter, Ellie, for so many things—not the least of which was enabling me to keep my sense of humor throughout this whole process.

Introduction

Just after the conclusion of the 1914 World Series where the National League's Boston Braves swept the Philadelphia Athletics of the American League, *New York Tribune* sports columnist Heywood Broun wrote that while having a new champion crowned every year was particularly good for the game itself, it was very bad for the stage. The sportswriter, who would become the drama critic for the paper the very next year and eventually a member of the Algonquin Round Table, noted wryly that "no sooner have the successful players learned to conduct themselves before the footlights than a shift in the championship makes it necessary to break in a new set of performers."[1]

By that point, professional baseball players had been appearing on professional theatre stages in the United States for more than twenty-five years.[2] Discussing the offseason activities of professional baseball players, historians Harold Seymour and Dorothy Seymour Mills write in their multi-volume history of the game that the most widely publicized avenue for players to earn money while not on the field in the early twentieth century was on the stage. Seymour and Mills note the theatrical appearances of nearly twenty players in the first decade and a half of the new century. Some players appeared at short curtain speeches to celebrate recent glory while others toured across the country with vaudeville acts where they sang and danced, performed in humorous skits with professional performers, recited personal anecdotes, or displayed other individual talents.[3] Several players were featured as cast members in fully formed combination companies presenting a single, unified theatre production instead of several plays in rotation.

Though the primary goal for both the baseball and theatrical professionals involved in these appearances was financial profit, the presence of players on the stage spotlights the relationship between theatre and baseball during the developing decades of the professional game. Baseball and theatre were both part of a larger and expansive entertainment landscape in the decades surrounding the turn of the twentieth century in the United States. Like most popular entertainments before the widespread availability of the phonograph and moving pictures, they were both based on a shared presence among performers and audience. The interplay between these two industries, as well as the way stories were being told in this era, influenced the development of how audiences saw the game, its players, and themselves.

This book examines some of the overlaps between professional baseball and professional theatre in the United States during the late nineteenth and early twentieth centuries by looking specifically at baseball players who were involved in professional productions of multi-act plays. The process seems straightforward: a player has success on the ballfield, so theatrical producers then put them onstage with the expectation that they would all make a little money. What did success have to look like, however, to make the player a viable possibility for appearing for an extended period on the stage? When crowds came to see the player onstage, what were they expecting to see? What was it that made players particularly appealing? What, if anything, beyond financial gain did they receive from these activities?

Beyond the players themselves, what effect did these interactions have on baseball? If historian Jules Tygiel is correct that historical analysis of baseball illustrates the American past and the broader changes of society, then how was baseball interacting with popular elements of that society?[4] These overlaps in popular entertainment, whether purposeful or undesigned, allowed audiences to see one amusement in terms of another. When players did step onstage, given the changing nature of American identity during the era with regard to shifting gender, ethnic, racial, class, and regional and national roles, what cultural tropes were at play in these productions in the roles these players performed? Using five representative players and their constructed image and persona from baseball's pre-Babe-Ruth "deadball" era as case studies to explore these questions, and concluding with a brief look at Ruth himself, I argue that baseball benefitted greatly from these interactions in a variety of ways—from how crowds conceived of players as more than athletes to how they conceived of the game of baseball itself as a performance of established cultural roles. Outside of vaudeville, players onstage were inserted into a theatre style called melodrama, which was the dominant theatre style in the United States at the time. Exploring this interplay at the early development of the sport helps us see how baseball began to be viewed in melodramatic terms with players filling the roles of heroes, villains, and fools.

In addition, understanding theatre from this era helps us in identifying baseball's development and the ways its stories and some of its players being displayed onstage indicated the larger hopes and fears about and within the industry as it sought to move away from the coarse and rugged working-class reputation it had and toward middle class respectability. Elite or otherwise notable baseball players were widely recognized to the point of celebrity. As that recognition spread, audiences increased at the ballpark. In transferring the celebrity and notoriety players had earned on the field to the stage, theaters were selling the image and presence of the baseball players themselves rather than whatever acts the players performed. While it is clear that these players were trading on the celebrity they had achieved on the field, their typical stage performances depended on and reinforced their status as professional baseball players and rarely strayed from that idea. The most interesting place to look is where the overlap was most apparent: baseball players themselves appearing onstage during this time in scripted full-length multi-act dramas where words could clearly express those hopes and fears and provide a complete and clearly defined story that offered a version of reality. Much more so than in vaudeville, where many players sought to supplement their income, these multi-act melodrama productions gave audiences clear and complete stories and, very often, new ways in which to see the world.

Baseball emerges as a sport in the United States in an era when melodrama had been popular for years. The first fully acknowledged professional ball club debuted in 1869 after years of local amateur and semi-professional teams competed with each other under various differing regional rules for "base ball." The professional Cincinnati Red Stockings traveled throughout the eastern half of the country playing against teams of local players, creating a new model of business for the game in which highly skilled players were able to showcase their abilities by touring from city to city matching themselves up against the "local nine." At these games, crowds paid to see young men they knew from the area almost always lose to the touring professionals.[5] From its outset, baseball faced the perception of widespread drunkenness and gambling, contributing to a reticence by the middle class to attend some games. Still, by the inception of the National League of Professional Baseball Clubs in 1876—and, thus, the establishment of the major leagues in professional baseball—the game had been solidified as one of many forms of popular entertainment available to the American public. With the emergence of the American League in 1901, what was considered major league baseball was available in thirteen different cities across the United States with sixteen teams. The creation of the World Series, pitting the champions of the two leagues against each other, further developed baseball's prominence as an entertainment.

The mechanics of clubs participating as a league mirrored the structure of a contemporary phenomenon in the theatrical world known as "combination companies," as the American theatre was undergoing similar changes during the post-Civil-War era. A theatrical industry had been present in the country since it was a group of colonies and had adapted to various social and economic conditions. Seen as a drain on the local economy of a community early in the nation's history, theatre had also had to overcome arguments couched in religious and moral terms that had led to legislation prohibiting it in certain cities. The gradual growth of those cities and the need to provide distraction for both an increasingly immigrant working class as well as those in the higher classes gave theatre a solid foothold as an American industry by the mid-nineteenth century. This did not necessarily mean widespread social acceptance, however. While certain stars charmed the upper classes, they still remained well below broad social respectability.

The theatre of post-Civil-War America was an industry that was heavily dependent on touring, which had been made more cost-effective through the vast number of railroad tracks laid in the eastern United States for logistical purposes during the war. American theatre practices began to transition away from a previous reliance on area stock companies that featured the same core of local actors that audiences knew performing productions in repertoire either independently or alongside an established solo touring theatrical star. Instead, the industry moved toward combination companies—productions originating typically in New York that toured as a self-contained unit. Comprising a full complement of professional performers and a variety of scenery elements in combination, these productions traveled between towns performing the same program of entertainment until moving to the next location. By the National League's first year in 1876, nearly 100 combination companies were traveling many of the same railroad routes as the professional baseball clubs, and audiences had become very familiar with how these theatre troupes told their stories.[6]

In terms of those stories, melodramas of various kinds dominated American stages during this time. Melodrama sought to evoke strong emotional reactions through compelling action and easily identifiable characters. These characters included a hero, who embodied an ideal that audiences wanted for themselves and the larger society; a villain, who may have shared some of the traits of the hero but whose opposition to and obstruction of the desires of the hero was quite apparent; and some comic relief, which didn't fall squarely into either category but indicated where the limits of acceptability lay. These character types were broad enough to permit variation and indications of individuality, but they were clear and distinct enough to be readily identified by audiences watching the stories play out in front of them. It created a narrative framework that persuaded audiences to see the issues of the world around them in simple and uncomplicated terms. Audiences, regardless of class, who were willing to empathize with the stories' victims, idolize and cheer the stories' heroes, and despise the stories' villains could enjoy melodrama. The middle class and those who aspired to join it particularly embraced melodrama as a thrilling model of how to navigate an uncertain and rapidly changing world.

Melodrama relied on both displaying big emotions for the audience and eliciting them in the audience as well. It accomplished this by employing character types that were broad enough that most in attendance could identify at least some traces in their own personal sphere. Writing separately about melodrama, both Robert Heilman and James L. Smith argue that while it is displayed onstage in a necessarily heightened way, people can easily appreciate their own lives in the terms of melodrama. Heilman believes it is the competitive nature of our lives which makes conflict external between people rather than internal.[7] Smith argues that, generally, seeing our own lives in melodramatic terms allows us to savor our victories and despair our defeats without any of the troublesome complexities brought about by whatever resolutions arise.[8] Onstage, melodrama reinforced the feelings an audience held about the world and allowed them to see the world around them in terms that were reassuring and easy to comprehend. With melodrama as the most prominent form of storytelling in the late nineteenth century, people could find comfort in looking at their world through a melodramatic frame—particularly any aspect of competition that had clearly understood winners and losers. As historian Warren Susman noted in *Culture as History* regarding the changes in how information was circulated in the 1920s, there were "new ways of knowing" that didn't originate in the printed word that reframed a rational understanding of the world for the population.[9] By that time, many Americans' emotional understanding of the world had already been largely shaped by melodrama.

Nearly all aspects of a melodramatic production were constructed to be easily comprehended at an emotional level. Costumes used design elements like line and color to indicate characters' personalities and how audiences should feel about them. The plot and dialogue were easy to follow, with the story presenting a task that must be accomplished and offering conversations in straightforward, simple terms often laden with emotional sentiment. The words were merely an excuse to present action and spectacle enhanced by the latest innovations in scenic and lighting technology to create stirring stage pictures. Plots might strain credulity at times, but the acting style was not necessarily based on presenting much in terms of subtlety. Audiences didn't have to have extensive pre-existing knowledge to appreciate what was on the stage. Just an emotional reaction was enough—particularly since the emotions were expertly engineered by the script, presentation, and performance. Writing about P. T. Barnum's successful American tour of Jenny Lind, historian LeRoy Ashby notes that middle-class audiences weren't expected to be musical experts to judge Lind's talents. Barnum preferred they express themselves the way anyone can: through feelings—"that great source of democratic knowledge."[10] Melodrama thrived on the same idea.

Still, as with any performance style, evoking the intended emotional responses to a character's portrayal required performers to adhere to some set of conventional standards. It was unmistakable which actors were believed to be good performers based on what they were able to make the audience feel. It often didn't matter what the actual lines were as long as the actors could convey they emotion and action required of the story. Actors didn't have to be believable; they just had to seem believable enough to make the audience feel something.

In his book *The Great Baseball Revolt*, Robert Ross acknowledges that baseball curiously seemed to benefit from other popular entertainments' increased popularity in the late nineteenth century.[11] I argue that a contributing factor to that boost was that audiences grew adept at seeing some of these entertainments in the terms or framework of others. For instance, baseball's popularity grew as audiences saw the game in melodramatic terms. Baseball and melodramatic theatre shared traits that made it easy to see one through the frame of the other, such as a conflict that resulted in a clear winner, visible indication of rooting interests made obvious through clothing, thrilling action to decide the contest, and, importantly, the physical presence of both performers and audience. Additionally, entertainment-focused newspapers of the time, including the *New York Clipper* and *The Sporting Life*, reported

extensively on both baseball and theatre in their pages, so readers were ac-
customed to seeing the two industries aligned. The "gee-whiz" style of jour-
nalism with vivid and laudatory descriptions that was used by sportswriters
covering and creating sports heroes, as pointed out by media historian Amber
Roessner, was also evident in the stories of performers and plays alongside
producer-generated puff pieces.[12] Putting players onstage and associating
them with highly visible professional productions within the context of melodrama further encouraged crowds to see baseball in melodramatic terms and
cast the game's players in the familiar character types of the style.

In this book, both theatre and baseball of this era are examined through
a lens of performance studies where events are not understood as discrete
and complete phenomena but as part of a larger and continuing series of
enactments. To paraphrase performance scholar Richard Schechner, the
world is not a book to be read but a performance in which to participate.[13]
Understanding baseball and its players as part of a participatory process
of their time rather than solely as a series of events provides the opportunity to understand how these players participated (to whatever extent they
may have been aware) in the performance of baseball on the field and away
from it.[14]

For players to have had a chance to make money on the stage during their
off-season, whether it was by performing in multi-act plays or by performing
in vaudeville, they would first have had to achieve some recognition within
the baseball world through their baseball persona—essentially, how the player
was known. Players established a baseball persona through a combination of
their on-field achievements and their own idiosyncratic style of play. Individual accomplishments, such as being the top hitter or pitcher in the league,
had more influence on a player's image than those achievements that were
team-based, such as being a member of a pennant-winning or world championship club. These kinds of achievements were quantifiable and clear. In
the early years of baseball, Henry Chadwick developed and popularized a
set of players' statistics that provided measurable difference between poor,
middling, and superior players. The numbers also standardized comparisons
between players by providing context between that player and the rest of
the league, thus giving a larger scale view to the fan. Jules Tygiel argues that
Chadwick was establishing a national standard that would be necessary for
fans to compare players across the country. Based on a scientific perspective, these statistics were intended to provide an understanding of players

who were not being given attention for the style with which they played the game.[15] Statistics such as batting averages and runs scored, as well as pitching wins and strikeouts, were widely reported in newspapers for individual players and often served as the primary way for fans to understand players they didn't regularly see in person. As such, public knowledge of these players' feats did not depend on proximity to the players.

This was not true, however, for an understanding of a player's particular playing style. It was often their immediate and viewable game-to-game performance that held the most meaning and won a player fans. Amber Roessner has shown that the subjective nature of newspaper reports of how a player ran, batted, or threw did influence public perception of a player.[16] By attending the games, local fans were able to discern for themselves the ways each player played the game, as well as how the players compared physically with each other on the field. A player's style was based partially on his noticeable physical attributes, such as his height and weight or the speed with which he ran or threw. The attitude he possessed while playing and the general demeanor he reflected often in verbal exclamations or witticisms also comprised the player's style. Similar to how statistics were contextualized in comparison to other players' numbers, the style of a particular player could be contextualized by seeing him play on the field and comparing that to his teammates and opponents. Much more emotionally driven than statistics, such immediate understanding of the playing style of a player was limited to those who were able to see games in person and see the players competing for either the home or visiting team. Due to the number of times a fan could see the players for the local team, a player's style was obviously much more recognized and accepted in the city for which he played than in the cities his team visited throughout the season.

The baseball persona of a player was thus built from previous accomplishments as well as the player's style in a combination of both the logical and the emotional, and it was imbued with what Cormac Power termed "auratic presence" in his book *Presence in Play*. Power suggests that one way the auratic presence can exist is through the fame or reputation of the present object itself in combination with the knowledge and expectations that an audience possesses at the time of the experience.[17] In the case of the baseball persona created by these players, their reported accomplishments worked to give their on-field style a meaning beyond just what was visible on the field, while at the same time, their physical presence on the field helped to create audience awareness of the extraordinary abilities of the player. Having such an aura made particular players an attraction as they traveled the league circuit, and it helped make those players celebrities within baseball.[18]

Players' celebrity opened up opportunities to use their ready-made, established recognition in other performative arenas that also depended on presence. Once a player reached the level of celebrity to become an attraction within the baseball world, his primary appeal to producers was that he was associated with baseball more than anything that was specific to him as a person. While the player's individual persona still played a role in how he was presented, the most important aspect of his persona was that he was a baseball player. All of his other markers of identity were subsumed by his identification and presence as a baseball player.

With the physical presence of a player on the stage being the primary selling point, the player's aura as an individual took a secondary role. Certainly a player onstage had already achieved enough success for a producer to want to use his celebrity, but the aura of star players was greater than non-stars, and champions held more stature than those who were not. Time and location also played significant roles in perception of stardom. Players may have had appeal and recognition in certain cities more than others, and time passed from a championship—either personal, like in batting or base running, or team-based—diminished the luster of the player as Heywood Broun mockingly lamented.

The risk for theatrical producers seeking to financially benefit from the popularity of baseball was lessened because the audience was not being asked to see the players, who were already-known entertainment entities, differently from how they normally viewed them. Using the players as celebrities gave the producers the opportunity to expand their audience to patrons who may not have attended theaters in large numbers. Many times certain performances would draw the players from the other teams in the league as audience members. When the producers had advanced knowledge of a group of players planning to attend a performance, these baseball-saturated audiences could be promoted as their own special attractions to increase attendance in the theater that night from fans eager to move into at least an approximation of social contact with the players.[19]

The status of a ballplayer as celebrity allowed for other types of identification to occur as well, including identification with larger social roles. In *Heroes, Villains, and Fools*, sociologist Orrin E. Klapp identifies the characteristics of those particular social types in America.[20] Following up Klapp's study, Roger R. Rollin posits that the status of being a hero presupposes the condition of being a celebrity, since acts that have not been perceived by others cannot be deemed to be heroic.[21] In this way, both Rollin and Klapp see the hero as a creation that helps to engender a sense of community. Heroes serve a function for the community in that they are praised and followed, and as they have been established as better than the norms of the community, they are used as models of behavior.[22] Because of that celebrity, baseball players as celebrities had the opportunity to fulfill a societal function as a hero or a villain—or even a fool—beyond just their function within the structure of the game.

These three character types are central to melodrama as well. At the core of melodrama is what Heilman calls the "simple villain-hero structure," with both types identifiable by standards of their time. Any potentially challenging ideas in the melodrama's story are presented in a way to be accepted without resistance by nearly all of its audience. Heilman argues that the characters in melodrama present no internal conflict or insecurity as all of their struggles are external against others. In a world that was presented as a kind of war between good and evil, and us and them, audiences were coaxed into being with "us."[23] In this way melodramas could help expand or contract the larger societal acknowledgment of what heroes and villains could and should be, even if only subtly. Even in a form that reinforced the status quo, these melodramatic stories could shape larger perceptions of what was and wasn't admirable.

After the turn of the century, most players earned around $2,000 a year in salary for their few months on the field. Though it was significantly more than the average American worker made during the whole year, many players pursued other business interests in the offseason. Those who had the opportunity to do stage work found it to be relatively lucrative; top-drawing players had the ability to earn hundreds of dollars a week. Being onstage in the offseason also kept the ballplayer in the public eye, and since baseball contracts generally required yearly negotiation, having a means to display his celebrity with the public gave the player more leverage in negotiating his salary for the next year. Further, producers usually required very little training of a player since he was being asked to essentially play himself and fit the image of a baseball player doing whatever things the act called for. The player did not necessarily have to be good at what he was doing; he just had to be there. A portion of the appeal for audiences was certainly the fish-out-of-water novelty of professionals from one area becoming noticeably amateur in another.

The lack of training for the stage that marked these professional baseball players as clearly amateur actors was put into sharp focus by the increase in training that professional actors had begun to receive in the late nineteenth century. Theatre historian Daniel J. Watermeier notes that the decline in resident stock companies created a need for new training methods. Actors could be trained in techniques that emphasized instinct and feeling instead of the declamatory styles that had been in vogue since before the Civil War. Increasingly, an emphasis on "believable verisimilitude in gesture, vocal delivery, and emotional expression" became commonplace on the American stage.[24] However, these displays of "natural behaviors" were just as dependent on conventions as previous styles had been. The more actors trained in these techniques, the more audiences accepted them as appropriate to real life. As a result, performers who were *not* trained in these conventions were obvious to audiences because of the incongruities in what seemed lifelike, and much more so than in previous eras, they could easily be identified as amateurs.[25] Every round of applause given, cheer expressed, or raspberry blown was done by an audience clear in the context that this was a baseball player before them.

Those audiences in the grandstands and in the orchestra were remarkably similar, as both theatre and baseball offered a suitable distraction from the standard urban lifestyle of the late nineteenth-century American audience. In his book *City People*, exploring the modern city culture of late nineteenth-century America, Gunther Barth includes chapters on both the ballpark and the vaudeville house as sites where these new urbanites could forge their identities in communion with other residents because of the locations' egalitarian natures.[26] Baseball's audience was, as Seymour and Mills state, "a very good cross section of the American public."[27] Access to the park was not restricted on gender or racial lines, and though differences in seat pricing and location may have limited potential mingling of social classes, the ballpark was often filled with a variety of enthusiastic rooters for the home team. Seymour and Mills do speculate that weekday audiences for ballgames were primarily middle-class and professional people, while working class fans filled parks on weekends. Richard L. Miller argues that the ballparks of the 1890s and early 1900s were compact enough that fans saw players' expressions and clearly heard conversations to the extent that fans didn't just passively watch games from afar but participated in them.[28] That participation included engaging and interacting with the players with cheers, jeers, and taunts. It also implied a closeness to the players that allowed easy association and identification with them.

A similarly mixed clientele was described in theaters of the time by Richard Butsch in *The Making of American Audiences*. Theatre performances in the so-called "ten-twenty-thirty houses" (named for the price scale for different seating areas) that specialized in melodrama drew primarily working-class audiences, while farces in the more legitimate theaters drew a slightly higher number of middle-class patrons, though both classes were visible at either location.[29] Just as in baseball, melodrama crowds were persistently vocal in their interactions with the plays. They vociferously cheered, booed, hissed, laughed, applauded, and offered comments throughout the productions, giving themselves the impression of a participatory entertainment where their reactions affected the outcomes—even if they recognized in reality that they didn't.[30]

Robert Ross notes that the American middle class being courted by popular entertainments in the nineteenth century consisted primarily of those who did not make things but instead managed, facilitated, and distributed and/or organized others' projects. Better paid than manual laborers, they fancied themselves above those who worked with their hands and presented themselves as such.[31] These folks had not only the additional income to spend on entertainment but also the time and energy to do so because they did not have to physically exhaust themselves to earn their living. Going out and being in the presence of others was much more possible this way.

By the time baseball became a professional sport, theatre as a whole—and melodrama, in particular—had already attracted middle-class Americans in a variety of ways. Foremost among these was an emphasis on stories that championed, as Ashby notes, "bourgeois values of respectability, status, and self-discipline."[32] Characters appeared onstage singular in their values, morality, and approach, making them easily comprehensible to the middle class without them needing to question their own perspective. The approach encouraged more women in attendance at theaters beginning in the 1850s, which, as Ashby notes, led to a less rambunctious and somewhat passive nightly crowd.[33] Butsch argues that such an atmosphere was due to the society restrictions and expectations placed on women by middle-class society.[34] These restrictions of the Victorian era meant that theater spaces were places where people were permitted to release some of their emotions in an acceptable way. Ballparks provided a similar outlet for emotional release.

As industries, both baseball and theatre benefited by having players representing the game onstage. The players were promoted as celebrities, which could help increase attendance at the ballpark as they served as an advertisement for the local team. Their presence on the stage could bring fans to the theater when baseball was not in season. Further, the industries were also contextualized among other amusements of the day where a set price offered a solid period of entertainment. This positioning helped baseball garner a level of respectability that opened up possibilities for attracting a new audience. The players could promote the wholesomeness of the game, the respectability of its players, and the virtues of sport and competition to an audience that would have been largely repelled by the drinking and gambling which was popularly associated with the game and the predominately male spectators in attendance. The courting of new fans would have been particularly desired in cities that became battleground sites, with teams from separate leagues competing for roughly the same audience.

This book's focus on the beginning through the "deadball" era of professional baseball corresponds to the last era of prominent melodramatic live theatre in the United States. During this time, teams became filled with the best players available rather than players who had roots in their team's locale as had been the practice during the pre-professional era. These new professional players were generally unknown on a personal level by the local fans but were still recognizable since the fans still rooted for the players that made up the local team. Because of this absence of knowledge through the fans' personal connections, the identities the players acquired were done so primarily through their ball playing, thereby creating baseball celebrities.

The end of this timeframe is marked by the ascendancy of Babe Ruth in both baseball and American culture just after the conclusion of the first World War and into the 1920s. A new style of play was reflected in the powerful hitting prowess displayed by Ruth.[35] This new "live ball" era is recognized as a break from the game's previous preference for placement over power. Further, the previously unparalleled popularity attained by Ruth was enhanced by a combination of appearances onstage and in film. For the first time, even though other players had appeared in the medium before him, it was film that played the primary role in promoting Ruth's baseball persona as a celebrity. This book's attention on players who achieved stardom before Ruth is because of the change in the way baseball celebrity culture could be circulated.[36] Thus, the book centers on the time period in the history of baseball when the stage was the primary medium for narrative performance.

The connections between baseball and melodrama extend to today, and understanding their origins can help us understand how contemporary events and players are framed. For baseball historians, this investigation provides insight into how the game developed and grew in association with another popular entertainment industry during this time—and how the way in which crowds engaged with the game and its players remains influential still today. For theatre and performance historians, this investigation illuminates the process of how untrained theatre performers engaged with and were regarded as part of professional productions, what happened when the image/persona of the performer superseded the role they were playing, and how melodrama leeched into the larger popular culture. In both cases, this investigation provides insights into the development and process of using celebrity in the decades surrounding the turn of the twentieth century in a form that depended upon the mutual presence of performers and audience.

This book does not seek to provide a comprehensive account of all professional baseball players on the stage around the turn of the twentieth century. Rather, the focus is on contextualizing the theatrical endeavors of five representative players—Adrian "Cap" Anson, Mike "King" Kelly, Christy Mathewson, Ty Cobb, and Rube Waddell—who illustrate the ways in which a player's persona transferred between two entertainment industries through their participation in multi-act dramas. The players selected as case studies were chosen, in part, due to their on-field excellence marked by their selection to Baseball's Hall of Fame. This was not an arbitrary decision, as the restriction of using only Hall of Fame players was based, in part, on the Hall of Fame's selection criteria. Since a player cannot be elected to the Hall of Fame during his playing career, the player must not only have had a statistical justification of excellence but also have remained identifiable enough in the minds of the electing body to achieve the honor.[37] Furthermore, this is not an attempt to write a biography of each of these players. The events of their lives are relevant in this book only to the extent of their theatrical careers. For Mike Kelly and Cap Anson, they were involved in theatrical endeavors until the end of their lives; for Christy Mathewson, Ty Cobb, and Rube Waddell, their experiences in theatre were much briefer.

To understand how audiences saw these theatrical forays we have to understand how the players onstage were presented by their productions and how they were perceived by their audiences. Then we can see how the perceptions of those players might have complicated their efforts to embody the popular melodramatic character types. Following this introduction, there are five player-focused chapters followed by a concluding chapter that examines the transition from this era. Due, in part, to the overlap in the included players' careers, the chapters are arranged thematically rather than strictly chrono-logically. Chapters one and two concern the stage work of players fitting a model of the public perception of a baseball player and how it was possible in certain circumstances to transcend the player's association with the game. Cap Anson exemplifies the quintessential player appearing onstage and how that presence could be managed to present an image of respectability. Mike Kelly's presentation illustrates how the relationship between celebrity image and reality was complicated by the player's presence. Chapters three, four, and five examine how players who were able to take a more active role in shaping their public image used the stage to suit their own needs, and how players fit recognizable types even when it wasn't necessarily the role they were por-traying in the play. Christy Mathewson's theatrical experience exemplified an idealized middle-class hero who could model how to face challenges in the game. Next, although everyone might want to take on the role of the hero, it doesn't always fit. Ty Cobb showed that villains and heroes might share traits but audience perspective determined which one would dominate the player's persona. Rube Waddell illustrated what happens when the fool is not a character in the story but a performer in the cast. Finally, Babe Ruth demonstrated that the image could effectively and completely obscure the reality to the point that the player's presence became irrelevant.

To provide a balance of interpretive analysis and documentary history, as Thomas Postlewait has suggested should be the goal of cultural histories in theatre, this book makes use of several types of evidence.[38] The recovery of extensive biographical information on players has been one of the hall-marks of modern baseball research, and the biographies used in this study offer valuable factual information regarding the players' lives. In addition, contemporary newspaper accounts of each player's on- and off-field activi-ties also contribute to the understanding of a how players were presented to the audiences of their own time. I analyze dramatic texts in conjunction with the accounts of the stage performances by the players to provide a more complete picture of what was occurring on the stage during the performances themselves.

The personas that each of these players created and utilized in certain ways reflect the tensions evident in American culture and society at the time. In many ways, the persona displayed by each of them both onstage and off conforms to an American white, middle-class, masculine identity that was heavily invested in establishing a prominence in society and maintaining that status once achieved. Further, the alignment of the players' personas with heroic, villainous, or foolish social traits and types helped to establish a narrative within the baseball world that develops along similar lines to the melodramatic theatre in which these players participated. Each season, each series, each game, and even each pitch in baseball was invested with the melodramatic idea that there is a hero and a villain, obstacles to overcome, a few laughs to be had, and something in dire need of being saved.

Cap Anson Plays "Cap Anson"

AMONG THE FIRST professional baseball players to have a supplemental the-atrical career was Adrian C. Anson.[1] Like most of the ballplayers that eventually followed him onto the stage, Anson's theatrical relevance lay in his presence as a recognizable ballplayer. The majority of his time on the stage was in vaudeville houses after the conclusion of his playing career. There he performed baseball-related jokes and songs as well as offered personal recollections from his life in the game. The motto displayed on his personal stationery during this time read, "A Better Actor than Any Ballplayer, a Better Ballplayer than Any Actor."[2] This linguistic juxtaposition, while being primarily an amusing marketing tool, was quite symbolic of the persistent interplay of the two professions that typically occurred when a player appeared onstage. For the typical player, his presence as a ballplayer superseded his theatrical surroundings.

Anson could lay claim to such a bold motto because the 1895 production of *A Runaway Colt* featured him as the first professional player to perform in a starring role in a multi-act play. The appearance traded on the baseball celebrity that Anson had gained on the field through his achievements and style. This chapter focuses on Anson's participation in the play by first examining the persona he had previously established on the ballfield, which prompted his involvement with the 1895 production. Subsequent examination of the production shows that, in many ways, Anson's appearance on the stage in *A Runaway Colt* illustrates how the majority of players who appeared on the stage worked, whether they appeared in multi-act dramas or in vaudeville pieces. In the production, he was playing a scripted, fictionalized version of himself. The play had a theatricalized demonstration of his ballplaying ability as it featured him hitting the game-winning home run. His athletic ability and strength were also displayed in more practical, less baseball-specific ways in the play. The script mined humor from the misunderstanding between baseball slang and everyday conversation.

Anson's performance, however, did more than just show that he was a baseball player; it required the audience to recognize him as a baseball player. His presence as a star in a multi-act drama (rather than a bit part or a vaudeville piece) allowed for more than just one or two of these signifiers that the performer was a ballplayer to be on display. The play had the opportunity to say something about ballplayers, and baseball in general, by emphasizing that the person playing Anson onstage was a player and that what they saw was actually Anson. The portrayal onstage showed Anson fit the model of respectability for white middle-class Americans, and as a representative of ballplayers in general, they could be seen as respectable too. In this way, Anson's performance and the play contributed to the push toward middle-class respectability of the game in the late nineteenth century.

The Iowa native began his professional baseball career when the National Association of Professional Base Ball Players, baseball's first professional organization, was founded in 1871. When the National League of Professional Baseball Clubs succeeded that organization five years later, Anson was among its founding members. As the captain and first baseman of the Chicago team, Anson played in each of the National League's first twenty-two seasons and cultivated a persona that became renowned throughout the game. A player's baseball persona, since it was built, in part, on his achievements over the course of his career, would understandably change over time. This was especially the case in a career as long as Anson's. During Anson's first year in a professional league, the 1871 National Association season, Anson was the fifth youngest player competing that year. In the last seven years of his career before his retirement after the 1897 season, Anson was either the oldest or second oldest player in the National League. Anson's longevity became one of his most considerable and visible career achievements. Many of the nicknames given to him over the years were earned through his longevity, including "Pop," "Uncle," and "Old Man."

By the time he retired, whether it was acknowledged by his contemporaries or not, Anson was the all-time statistical leader in the National League for games played, hits, runs scored, runs batted in, extra base hits, plate appearances, and total bases.[3] Several of these statistical categories did not become officially recognized until well after Anson's playing career ended, so their totals were tallied retroactively. Though not used in his day, these categories are evidence of the dominance of his career. As "counting stats," each of these have been accumulated and tallied, and the sheer numbers of the totals could be easily measured against his contemporaries rather than those statistics that were calculated like an average or percentage.

During individual seasons of his playing career, Anson led the league twice in batting average and placed second an additional five times. Out of his twenty-seven professional seasons, Anson finished in the top ten in yearly batting average twenty times. Player batting averages, a "calculated stat," were printed in newspapers beginning in 1874, and they were in wide use throughout Anson's career.[4] A feared batter, Anson also led the league in hits in 1881 and finished second in that category four other times. Though it may have gone relatively unnoticed (as it was not an officially designated statistical category until 1921), Anson led the league in runs batted in eight times, and he finished in the top ten in the more recognizable category of runs scored ten times over the course of his career. Through these quantifiable achievements, Anson had distinguished himself as one of the premier players in the profession.

One of Anson's most identifiable aspects, reflected in the nickname "Cap" that appears on his Hall of Fame plaque, was his status as the captain of the Chicago National League team for nineteen seasons. Team captains during this time controlled the club on the field, serving many of the same functions as the modern-day manager, and Anson proved himself to be one of the best. Captains were players who controlled the team, but there were also managers who served the same function, only as nonplayers. Clubs would often have either a manager or a captain, with most clubs in the late nineteenth century employing a playing captain such as Anson. The Chicago club under Anson in the decade of the 1880s was league champion five times and finished in second place in three other years. No other team matched that record of success during Anson's career. Anson's clubs had a winning record in the league for fifteen of the nineteen years he led them. As both a player and a captain,

Anson proved through his quantifiable achievements that few, if any, were his superiors on the baseball field.

As much as his statistics stood out against the other players in the league, Anson was easy to visually distinguish through the style of play that helped him achieve those statistics. He could often be recognized as the largest person on the field throughout his career as he stood over six feet tall and weighed approximately 200 pounds. Anson biographer Howard Rosenberg found newspaper accounts of the player demonstrating his size by walking the ninety feet from home plate to first base in only ten strides.[5] Even though a large man, Anson was very devoted to keeping excess weight off and being in shape during the season. He was often found running and using training methods for athletes that were believed to be the most effective at the time. Even as he got older, he was in better physical condition than many of the younger men who played for and against him.[6]

Other visual characteristics made Anson stand out among his contemporaries. The use of gloves by fielders, particularly first basemen, increased throughout Anson's career, and by 1892, Anson was the only player at that position in the National League who was not wearing any type of glove while in the field.[7] With or without a glove, Anson was never considered particularly adept at either fielding or base running because his large frame caused him to be much slower than many of his contemporaries. His principal baseball skill lay in hitting. Even for his time, Anson was unusual in how he stood while at the plate. Keeping both feet together and batting from the right-handed position, he faced the pitcher fully forward with the bat held below his waist. As the ball approached, Anson would raise the bat and swing his left side toward the pitcher to make contact with the ball. This method proved to be deceptive to the defensive players who were unable to guess where Anson would be aiming his hit until he was actually swinging. Anson's size and considerable upper-body strength, combined with the thick-handled bats he swung, allowed him to strike the ball with great force. The balls he hit into play were often hard line drives that were particularly difficult to catch, even by fielders who did wear protective gloves.[8]

Anson's voice, which was considered another notable physical characteristic, was often on display because of the attitude he took toward the games that were being played. In possession of a large voice that carried well in the small ballparks of the day, Anson was well-known for his arguing with the umpire—an act also known at the time as "kicking." Whenever the team perceived any kind of injustice, it was Anson's responsibility as team captain to argue the point. Rosenberg believes that, in addition to any minor out-bursts while not directly confronting an umpire, Anson likely averaged one extended argument with the umpire per game.[9] The traits that made Anson noticeable on the field—his size, obvious physical strength, and voice—were all traits that had been used to great success on the stage by American actors such as Edwin Forrest and John McCullough throughout the nineteenth century. On display for the public in many of the same ways as those actors had been, Anson's prominence on the baseball field reflected an image of masculine identity that actors had popularized onstage for American audi-ences since the 1820s.

Anson held an authority over the Chicago baseball club that was unpar-alleled by any other playing captain of his time. Though a former ballplayer himself, Al Spalding, owner of the club, deferred much of the direct control of the day-to-day operations to Anson so he could devote his energies toward his sporting goods business. Operating under the directives of Spalding, Anson took command of the players both on and off the field, invoking rules of behavior for his players. Fines were levied for drinking or other disorderly conduct. Although the fines were often rescinded later or otherwise proved ineffectual in curtailing the behavior, Anson had the reputation of a strict disciplinarian. Though rare, Anson's authority was occasionally displayed on the field. Biographer Howard Rosenberg noted two such instances. In an event the *Chicago Herald* called "rare" because it occurred on the field, Anson reprimanded a player in full view of the crowd because of the player's apa-thetic play during an 1885 postseason series. Anson also reportedly ordered club owner Spalding off the field when the latter had approached Anson who was in discussion with an umpire.[10] Whether Anson meant the order as a joke or was in earnest, the situation served to display his authority in the baseball world. Anson's performance of authority in these public situa-tions gave further credence to the authority and control ascribed to him by players telling stories about private instances of his maintaining discipline. The culmination of these stories and displays was a perception that Anson was perhaps the most powerful player in all of baseball.

Another important element of Anson's persona was his drive to win that fueled the vast majority of his on-field efforts. He possessed a seemingly unparalleled knowledge of the rules of the game, which he regularly used to his advantage. To that point, much of his frequent arguing developed from his thorough understanding of the rules of the game. With his teams' usu-ally strong base runners, one of his most common points of contention was whether an opposing pitcher was committing a balk while there were runners on base.[11] Though he may have intended to rattle the opposing pitcher, the constant arguing of rules may have also had a similar effect on umpires. As the rules and pure mechanics of the game changed so often throughout his career, these arguments proved that Anson was fully aware of the rules and might receive the benefit in future calls from an umpire. Anson also encouraged his players to take advantage of the rules as they were written to increase the team's chances of winning. These tricks included purposefully dropping fly balls or third strikes in order to record multiple outs instead of just one. Adept at working within the rules, Anson would also break them if he thought it would help them win. Using his size, Anson would at times intentionally and illegally obstruct throws or fielding attempts by players while running the bases, or he would purposefully collide with a baseman to disrupt a play.[12] Through his many arguments and sometimes questionable tactics, he earned the reputation among many of the fans in cities other than Chicago of being a man who did not play in a gentlemanly manner.

Such criticism was not exclusive to Anson as many people felt the professional game could not be reconciled with respectable society. In John Rickards Betts' history of sports in America, *America's Sporting Heritage: 1850-1950,* he points out that a conflict between the concept of fair play and an overemphasis on winning permeated the entirety of sporting culture in the late nineteenth century. At particular issue in baseball at the time was the purity of amateur competition against the corruption of morals evident in the professional mindset. Critics of baseball called attention to obvious instances of rule-breaking as a symptom of the professional mindset that placed winning over sportsmanship due to the financial benefits winning provided. These critics also pointed to aspects of the game, such as kicking, that baseball permitted to occur within its rules. The sanctioning of publicly arguing an official's decision displayed evidence that professional baseball was not suited for decent people. Appeals were made by "lovers of clean sport" to encourage fans to stay away from the game if such unruly behavior was going to persist.[13] The yearly increasing attendance in professional baseball shows, however, that the appeals were regarded more as a wish than a requirement.

Baseball historian David Quentin Voigt explores how professionalization changed the game's social ethic. With money and careers at stake, professional athletes couldn't have been expected to adhere to a previously assumed ethic of generosity, equity, and fun. Since audiences still saw them in terms of collegial players rather than professional workers, the athletes were expected to maintain at least a tempered version of those virtues and to exhibit self-control.[14] This unstated and precarious balance of expectations generated the possibilities of conflict among players and fans due to differences in perception and temperament. Even while striving for the same goals in a game or the season, players had their own methods of doing so according to their understanding of what was appropriate. They had their own personalities that were exhibited through their play and received differently by different fans.

While critics of the game as a whole may have had an issue with how the game was played, fans, sportswriters, and players saw such events in more relative terms. Actions that would be derided when performed by an opposing player would be celebrated if committed by a player on the hometown team. When one of Anson's former players, Mike Kelly, was playing against Chicago for Boston, for example, Kelly repeated an old trick from his Chicago days by running from second base to home plate without approaching third. Though he had never had a problem with it when it happened to his team, Anson's vehement objections to the umpire forced Kelly to return to third base.[15] Expectations that a player should abide by all umpire rulings were further complicated at times by inconsistent interpretations of the constantly changing rulebook.[16] Penalties for overt rule-breaking within the game were slight, even when caught, and the rewards offered by winning were much greater. As such, Anson and many of his players on the Chicago team clearly preferred winning and its benefits to an undue allegiance to a relativistic moral code.

Anson's persistence in arguing minute details (prompted by this emphasis on winning) often led to him being the primary object of derision in cities his team visited. Boston newspapers began calling him a baby in 1875. Though he was one of the youngest players in the professional ranks, the connotation was clearly focused on his frequent "crying" to umpires. The nickname persisted for much of his playing career, and its use was widespread in varying degrees by both writers and fans. For one of Chicago's visits to New York, a local paper tried to draw fans to the ballpark by advertising that a 220-pound baby would be on exhibition at the Polo Grounds.[17] As the most readily recognized player on the field, Anson was the popular target for comments, jeers, and jokes from a crowd spurred on by seeing him at the ballpark. At times, even Chicago's fans directed criticism against and made fun of their team's captain. For a fan to have the chance to ridicule Anson, however, it did have to be done at the ballpark.

Anson understood the value of advertising for a ball club, and the more he made a spectacle of himself while visiting other cities, the more people wanted to come see him be put in his place by the hometown team.[18] While his style of play managed to draw the ire of a number of opposing fans, also helping were the sports writers in the other cities of the league. Anson had no complaints as to whether the reports about him were wholly accurate, and he understood the role the newspapers played in drumming up interest in the game.[19] Just as he rarely complained about anything written about him in the papers, Anson believed a paying fan had every right to complain while at the park, and he took a fair amount of disparagement from the fans both at home and on the road. Anson rarely struck out while at the plate, but pitchers could often get two strikes on him. *New York Herald* writer O. P. Caylor wrote that when that happened, both home and away crowds would begin to chant "strike him out!" After Anson's death, a Chicago newspaper noted his extraordinary ability to disregard the taunts thrown at him while on the field.

For all of his confrontations on the field, Anson kept his focus on the participants of the game and rarely directed any displeasure toward the crowd. His combative stance with the umpires became an expected part of the afternoon at the ballpark. These antics were typically well-received, even in cities the team was visiting, provided that the display did not go on too long.[20] The notoriety Anson received for his battles with umpires made him seem larger than life. After doing advance work to promote an all-star team featuring Anson that was doing a world tour in 1888-89, Leigh Lynch reported that fans in San Francisco were very anxious to see Anson based on his reputation. Lynch said that one fan demanded to know how many umpires Anson had killed, and Lynch believed that unless Anson destroyed the field and committed murder while in the city, the fans would be disappointed.[21]

Anson proved to be a great draw. His Chicago teams consistently led the league in attendance. In the early years of the National League as teams were added and subtracted on a yearly basis, the revenue brought in by the Chicago ball club provided enough financial stability in the early 1880s to keep the league from folding.[22] Teams often received a boost to their attendance whenever the Chicago team was in town, and much of the interest came from the reputation that preceded Anson. By 1891, New York newspapers were reporting that Anson drew more of a crowd to the ballpark than any other star.[23] For theatrical producers looking to use an athlete in a production, a track record as a popular attraction would prove essential, and the persona Anson had built made people want to see him.

However, producers wanting to profit from putting a professional player onstage had to deal with the fact that their appeal was far from universal. While some critics satirically characterized the professional player as a man of leisure, working for only a few months of the year, waking late daily, exercising for a few hours, and receiving an exorbitant amount of money, the majority of the perspectives associated the game with the rougher elements of society. Many fans of the game were fond of gambling and drinking, and newspaper presentations of many of the players often did little to limit the association with these social vices. Accounts of drinking or fights by players were often reported in newspapers, and this rough image became the popular perception of how most ballplayers behaved.[24] The willingness of participants to break blue laws in some cities by playing on Sunday further served to alienate the so-called respectable crowds from associating with the game. Though the National League prohibited Sunday baseball for several years, other baseball leagues permitted the activity—as well as selling alcohol on the grounds on Sunday. This resulted in a mark being against the sport as a whole rather than toward a specific league.[25]

For Anson, and most of the players of the time, the popular perception was not entirely accurate. As Rosenberg has shown, it was true that Anson frequently bet on baseball, but the bets were often made publicly as a boast on his team or as an advertisement for upcoming games and were done within the rules of the National League. The National League allowed betting on one's own team beginning in 1877 so long as the player did not associate with gamblers.[26] As for drinking, though his portrait had appeared in a print advertisement for E. & J. Burke's ale during the 1880s, Anson was famous for his dislike of alcohol and drinking.[27] Along with Chicago club owner Al Spalding, Anson believed that drinking was putting the game in jeopardy and actively sought to correct the vice among the team's players. Anson, with Spalding's support, levied fines on players for drinking during the season, and Spalding went so far as to hire a private investigator to report on the drinking habits of the Chicago players. It was well known by the men throughout the league that Anson could not be corrupted by either gambling or drinking. Unlike many of the players in the league, Spalding felt that Anson "had been above reproach" in his personal life and that "his integrity was unquestioned."[28]

For many, Anson was the face of the National League—recognizable as a player and a captain as well as an owner. When the vast majority of popular and talented players left for John Montgomery Ward's Players' League in 1890, Anson remained with Chicago's National League franchise. The quick dissolution of the Players' League further highlighted Anson as the stalwart face of the National League. He owned stock in the Chicago ball club, and when the New York franchise was on the verge of bankruptcy and the stability of the league was threatened, Anson was among several National League men to invest in that club as well. While he had an obvious financial stake, Anson's support of the National League gave him another opportunity to display his loyalty. Under the national agreement between ball clubs, teams could place a predetermined number of players on a reserve list, thereby preventing other teams from signing them between seasons. Because of Anson's loyalty, his name was noticeably absent from Chicago's list for most of his career, and in the face of occasional overtures by other teams, Anson proudly proclaimed his faithfulness to the Chicago club.[29]

The Chicago team itself reflected Anson's identity in a variety of ways. Following Anson's own character, the team was considered to be the most disciplined in the league. Even for certain players of questionable character, their individual statistical achievements while with the Chicago club often exceeded what they had done or would do elsewhere, due to Anson's diligence.[30] Moreover, the public identification of the team's nickname came directly from Anson. While not formalized at the time, team nicknames were often subject to change and typically were based on some outstanding feature of the club, such as their uniform color, for example. While the Chicago National League club had been known as the White Stockings, in 1887, an influx of new, younger players juxtaposed against the aging Anson prompted a change to the Colts, and at times even to "Anson's Colts" to directly refer to the man who held the reins. When Anson eventually left the club, the team was briefly known as the Orphans until finally becoming the Cubs in 1902—with both nicknames implying an absent parental figure.

Anson was one of the most visible players in the National League who opposed inclusion of Black or other darker-skinned players as part of the league. Weldy Walker directly cited Anson's influence as to why he and his brother, Fleet, as well as other Black players were barred from signing with National League teams. Anson's popularity and sway within the league was a contributing factor in keeping the races separate on the ballfield.[31] Black players would not be integrated into National League baseball until Jackie Robinson's debut with the Brooklyn Dodgers in 1947—twenty-five years and one day after Anson's death. Historian Adrian Burgos, Jr. argues that focusing on Anson as the dominant figure in baseball's segregation serves in many ways to obscure the larger, systemic process that would lead to Jim Crow baseball.[32] That he could be clearly identified as the foremost face of segregation during this time, however, spoke to his prominent place as one of the central figures of professional baseball.

Anson was further involved in keeping Black people on the periphery of the game, often as mascots or oddities on display as part of the game's atmosphere of entertainment. Clarence Duval served that role for Anson's 1888 Chicago team. Burgos argues that the stereotyped presentation of Black men as infantilized mascots (such as how Duval was treated) served to illustrate to those in attendance that Blacks could not be respectable and therefore did not belong in professional baseball.[33] Middle-class respectability would permit acknowledgement of other races but not on equal terms with white people. Making this juxtaposition clear at the ballpark was meant to further highlight the professionalism and respectability of the players who were permitted on the field.

The expectations and privileges of being a gentleman were shifting during this time as well. The ability to be regarded as a gentleman had indeed been democratized and expanded in places it hadn't been before in American society. According to historian Stow Persons in *The Decline of the American Gentility*, membership in what Persons calls "the new gentry elite" that emerged in the late nineteenth century in the wake of the Jacksonian era was available to nearly any white male who patterned his lifestyle after the Emersonian principles of individualism and self-reliance.[34] Away from the field, Anson held certain attributes commonly associated with gentlemen. He had attained wealth through his own physical efforts. He was recognized as a leader and was regarded as a professional.

Merely being a professional baseball player put Anson in a suspect social position, but American society had seen others overcome similar obstacles. Despite the lower social rank normally associated with their profession, actors like Edwin Forrest and John McCullough had been able to achieve gentleman status in their lifetimes through their embodiment onstage of the principles of individualism and self-reliance. Benjamin McArthur points out several factors in his book *Actors and American Culture, 1880-1920* that enabled the rise of actors within the American social hierarchy during this time. McArthur argues that the increasing urbanization of the country in the last two decades of the century resulted in a decline of the role of the church and of polite society as authorities in shaping urban culture. Actors, as part of a larger mass culture that reflected and fulfilled the needs of the urban public, were able to become recognized as respectable members of the society.[35] Vocation was no longer an impenetrable barrier to the higher social status of gentlemen in late-nineteenth-century America. By the mid-1890s, baseball's role as part of that mass culture had increased to the point where it was possible for ballplayers to make a transition to respectability in a manner similar to actors.

Richard Bushman's analysis of American gentility since the Revolution further notes that the category served as a way to maintain an elite culture distinguishable from the common people. Thus gentility did not connote the ideals of democracy as much as those of capitalism. In this way, aligning oneself with the gentility enabled an exercise of power based in cultural superiority and exhibited through a performance of civility and refinement, regardless of one's accumulation of upscale material possessions. Bushman argues that the belief that outward public behavior could raise even the lowly to respectability became prevalent throughout the middle class in the United States in the nineteenth century.[36] Bushman concludes that the middle-class embrace of elements of nineteenth-century gentility helped turn public life into a persisting performance of seeking acceptance and dreading scorn.[37] In general, we can understand enactions of gentility as de facto advocacy of the status quo—inclusion into which baseball still aspired.

The perception persisted both inside and outside of baseball, however, that one could not be both a ballplayer and a gentleman. Prominent former professional player turned lawyer John Montgomery Ward expressed such feelings publicly. He intimated a duality among players, the state of behaving both as a professional player was required to behave and as a gentleman should behave. Players were obligated to kick vehemently against an unfavorable decision as a demonstration to both their owners and fans that they were committed to winning. Of course, the public arguments were not considered to be gentlemanly behavior. Ward believed a vast number of players would have preferred to accept an umpire's erroneous decision and behave in a gentlemanly way if it had not been for the demands of the profession.[38] Though in his personal life Anson possessed all the trappings of a gentleman, most people primarily saw the displays of uncouth behavior on the ballfield and the frequency with which they occurred. The result was that the image of Anson the ballplayer superseded the image of Anson as a gentleman, and the duality could not be effectively reconciled.

This schism did not prevent him from being a celebrity, however, and Anson was indeed a celebrity in the baseball world by 1895. The reputation he had earned through his accomplishments and style on the field preceded him both in league cities and on separate tours. In each of these locations, fans paid to see him, and non-fans came to see the man the newspapers seemed to so often categorize as a menace in person. People were interested in who he was regardless. He appeared in advertisements, and his preferences in presidential elections were reported in the newspapers.[39] Those newspaper writers—as well as the advertisers of E. & J. Burke brewery—borrowed from Anson's baseball fame and, by taking him out of his baseball context, attributed a level of credibility to him regarding his apparent choice of beverage or politician. These agents performed the role of the cultural mediator by promoting Anson's expertise as a leader as a justification for the relevancy of his perspective. When theatrical producer and playwright Charles Hale Hoyt attempted in 1895 to capitalize on Anson's achieved celebrity from the ballfield in the theater, the basis for it was in his ability to draw people to see him in person. Celebrity provided him his greatest potential as a theatrical star.

During the same time period Anson's persona in professional baseball was being developed, the American theatre was changing in ways that made it possible for athletes to appear as theatrical stars. In the 1870s, the established production model of a star actor traveling to different stock companies and performing in several plays in repertory was eclipsed by a new, more cost-efficient model. The new combination companies formed in one city and then toured an entire production of one play with a complete cast and required scenic elements to different cities. Still based around a star performer, these new performance packages changed not only touring practices but also the existence of stock companies in New York which had specialized in repertory performances.

One effect of the change was on the quality of set pieces used in productions, as John Frick points out in the essay "A Changing Theatre: New York and Beyond" in *The Cambridge History of the American Theatre*. Longer runs of a play permitted more money to be invested in the spectacular elements for a particular production rather than for multiple plays.[40] As a result of the increased investments, the aesthetic quality of the scenic elements was greater and could better reflect a producer's desire for spectacle. The productions by Henry Irving in 1883, for example, included more three-dimensional set pieces than had been seen before on American stages. Accompanying the increase in scenic realism was an increased desire for verisimilitude in the presentation of roles. English actor E. S. Willard scheduled a special matinee for local potters when he performed in New York portraying a potter in an 1890 production of *The Middleman* in order to lend credence to his ability to perform the tasks of the profession correctly.[41] Representational settings and verisimilitude were marks of a push in the commercial theatre toward authenticity in productions.

Even more authentic was the use of professionals to portray people from that profession onstage. For athletes onstage, it began with professional boxers John L. Sullivan and James J. Corbett, who had both starred in different plays as boxers in the early 1890s.[42] Under the star-system that preceded the era, a star performer would have to know several roles and be able to play them in repertory. That was no longer the case. While neither boxer could be considered a gifted actor in comparison to other theatrical performers, the nominal star of a production did not necessarily have to be a competent actor in the wake of the change to this combination company model of theatre. Both men were indeed stars of their profession, having earned recognition as champions in the sport before they appeared onstage in starring roles.

Previous to his starring role in *A Runaway Colt*, Anson had appeared onstage once before. On October 5, 1888, both the Chicago and New York teams went to see Charles Hoyt's *A Parlour Match* at the Theatre Comique in Harlem after the conclusion of the second game of their three-game series. Comedians Charles E. Evans and William F. Hoey starred in the production, and before the performance, they met with their friend Anson. According to the *Chicago Daily News*, Anson confided to Hoey at the meeting "that he believed he was cut out for an actor, although cruel fate had decreed it otherwise." Hoey convinced him to give it a chance that night and, as the *Chicago Daily Tribune* wrote, "they hurried him behind the scenes and drilled him for about fifteen minutes in the lines written for the boss of a gang of laborers." His costume of long grey whiskers, a wig, and blue overalls mostly obscured him, but Anson delivered two lines and appeared in a dance number alongside the rest of the cast.[43]

The reactions of the players from both the Chicago and New York teams to Anson's appearance in the play drew special attention to him. According to the *Chicago Daily Tribune*, Anson kept step during the dance by intently watching the man next to him, and he nearly fell down a trap door after trying to avoid a bucket of water being thrown at another character. The *New York Times* reported Anson did not have much to do in the part, but "what he did was done rather awkwardly."[44] Anson maintained to the *Chicago Daily News* that he thought he could develop into a fine actor, noting, "With a little training, I think I would be all right."[45]

The *Chicago Daily Tribune* reported that Evans and Hoey offered Anson an engagement for the winter, but he refused because of his impending tour of Australia with other baseball stars. In a brief interview in the *Chicago Daily News*, Anson said that Hoyt had offered him $500 a week to play "Monk" in one of the playwright's new pieces, but Anson doubted the sincerity of the offer since Hoyt knew about the Australia trip as well.[46] Rumors again appeared in 1891, suggesting that Hoyt was writing a play about Anson, but the player would not actually work for the playwright until four years later.[47]

Even though Anson was not necessarily an adept performer on the stage, he was also not merely a prop for the production. Anson's inability to perform to the conventional standards of a realistic part actually helped foreground his presence in the theater as a baseball player. Hoyt wrote *A Runaway Colt* specifically for Anson in an attempt to capitalize on Anson's celebrity and draw people to see in him person. The play called more for Anson's presence than for his limited acting ability. His presence onstage required audiences to see him as a baseball player and as a representative of all baseball players. Hoyt's careful creation of a gentlemanly image for Anson's character conformed to a white American middle-class masculine ideal as a ballplayer and had the additional benefit of furthering baseball's courtship of late-nineteenth-century middle-class respectability.

When *A Runaway Colt* was produced in 1895, it was Hoyt's thirteenth play to debut in New York City and the fourth at his own theater. As Douglas L. Hunt points out, after beginning with several purely farcical plays, Hoyt started to write more satirical comedies concerned with social themes such as women's suffrage and Prohibition.[48] Along this vein, *A Runaway Colt* deals with gambling and baseball's place in society in a melodramatic way, but it also contains some of the same broad humor that made Hoyt's earlier plays popular. Hoyt had written characters enamored with sports in previous plays, but this was his first play focused around a sport and an athlete.

The story of the play begins with a young man, Manley Manners, who has contracted to play baseball for the Chicago team without the knowledge of his well-respected family. As the play opens, he has left the team without permission. At his family's home, he awaits a visit from Chicago Captain Adrian Anson, whom he hopes can convince his father to let him rejoin the team. After Reverend Manners eventually grants his permission, the family follows the team south to St. Augustine, Florida, and then back to Chicago. Meanwhile, a scheming bank cashier has convinced Manley's younger brother to bet bank money on Chicago winning a game, so that he (the bank cashier) can blackmail the family—after Chicago loses the game—into letting him marry the young woman they have been raising. The expected happy ending comes as Anson saves the day in the bottom of the ninth inning with a two-run home run, thereby not only winning the game but saving the entire Manners family in the process...pretty typical late-nineteenth-century popular melodramatic theatre fare.

The image of Anson presented in the play is managed to an almost impeccable degree. The play's presentation of Anson addresses the man's reputation in the first act. To keep his family from suffering embarrassment as a result of small-town gossip, Manley has persuaded Anson to register at the hotel using his first name as his surname. When Anson arrives at the house early to speak to Manley before his scheduled arrival for dinner at six, the family hears Anson announced as Mr. Adrian. In contrast to the descriptions of Anson given by some of the Manners family, calling him "awful" and a "brutal creature," the servant reports this Mr. Adrian looks "very respectable."[49] The duality created in the play between Anson's preceding reputation and his physical presence as Mr. Adrian allows for some humorous moments when he is described to himself to be a "terrible man" and, based on misconstrued newspaper reports, a pugilist and a thief. While the horrible Anson is said to "drink terribly," the gentlemanly Mr. Adrian refuses the offer of wine, stating simply that he "doesn't indulge." Established as a family man with a wife and two daughters, a businessman who can offer Manley a well-paying job, and as a very polite teetotaler, one member of the family remarks that Mr. Adrian is "so different from Anson."[50]

Even though the split is played for comic effect, this duality of Anson reflected the public's perception of him. As a ballplayer, he was a terrible force on the field, but Anson held all the bearing of a gentleman when he was away from it. Hoyt used the juxtaposition of the mythic tales and terrible image of Anson the ballplayer against the physical presence of the real Anson onstage to humanize him, and the emphasis on his gentlemanly conduct distanced him from the negative associations his name carried. By the end of the first act, when Anson and Adrian are revealed to be the same person, the audience, like the Manners family, has been guided to see Anson not only as the ballplayer but also as the person—one who is a ballplayer and also respectable enough to pass in a reputable household.

As the play continues and moves from the domestic setting of the Manners' home to the ballfields of St. Augustine, Florida, and, in the final two acts, Chicago, the idea of Anson as a baseball player is reintegrated into this gentlemanly mien. The skills that make Anson a fierce competitor on the ballfield prove useful in his ability to save the family from ruin. His physical strength, honed over the years through his playing, allows him to lower Dolton Manners down through a window to retrieve the betting ticket that would guarantee his family's ruin if lost. During this rescue, Anson also displays his cunning by convincing Babe Manners that she cannot let go of the rope or her brother will fall. The situation forces her to stand and listen to a young man, Tennyson Greenfield, who has been trying to clear up a misunderstanding with her.[51] The strength and intelligence for which Anson was known on the field are recontextualized into the performance of noble acts of saving a family and helping a young couple in love get back together.

After the first act, the play does not ignore the unruly aspects of Anson's baseball persona; rather, it redirects them somewhat to make him seem much less contemptible. Deserved or not, the overriding perception of Anson had him as a public user of profanity.[52] In the play, Tennyson, who has never uttered a profane word in his life, claims that to do so is one of the treasures in life and should be saved for a special occasion. Anson jokes that Tennyson has obviously never had to deal with an umpire. When the young man is set to eventually let loose a string of profanities at the end of the act, Anson clasps his hand over the man's mouth and warns the women present to run because he will not be able to hold him for long.[53] By using another character to offer up a defense of profanity, Hoyt is able to justify Anson's association with swearing and use it to comic effect without actually putting the words in Anson's mouth. Further, Anson's joke gives an extremely limited context for when he believes such action is permissible for him—only within the boundaries of a ballgame, and then still only in confrontation with an umpire. Anson's attempt to prevent the cursing by Tennyson by physical means reinforces the implied limit between what is allowed by Anson the ballplayer and what by Anson the gentleman.

In a similar fashion, Hoyt addresses the most notorious element of Anson's persona—his proclivity for arguing with the umpire. During the final act, as characters are describing the ballgame being played offstage, a character enters to say that the umpire has beaten the Chicago team by calling a player out who shouldn't have been, and as a result Anson was kicking. The event occurs offstage and the stage directions state that the "quarrel at back gradually subsides" before the curtains are drawn back by a character and the final inning is played in full view of the audience.[54] The description by the characters frames Anson's protest as a justified cause, putting the audience in sympathy with not only Anson but also the family whose salvation depends on a win by his team. Further, by placing the argument offstage, Hoyt effectively deemphasizes that aspect of Anson's persona and implies that his other qualities are much more representative of his true self.

Throughout the rest of the play, Anson's virtues are on display as much as his vices are softened. While in Florida, Tennyson counters Anson with "I know you *won't* have a drink, but *will* you?"[55] Anson's continued refusal reinforces his actual teetotaler position by accentuating the difference between doing it for maintaining a public image versus doing it for his own personal reasons. Anson's honesty is emphasized when the play's villains approach him about throwing the game. With the intention of a $2,000 bribe, which is approximately the yearly salary to be paid to Manley Manners, and the reasoning that one game does not decide a championship, the villainous Will Haight approaches Anson in his office offstage. After several crashes are heard, Will staggers back to the stage "a total wreck" just before the act ends. In the act's final tableau, Anson asks him threateningly if he has anything more to say. Will replies, "Not a word." Later, as the two Haight brothers arrive at the ballpark to witness the decisive game, they recall the thrashing Will had received from Anson earlier in the play.[56] Despite Anson's reputation for fighting and aggression, the play again puts strict parameters on when Anson would actually resort to violence and makes it clear that fighting would only commence in the cause of doing what is right.

In a minor plot point, Anson discloses later in the play that the one thing that could cause him to take a drink would be Rosie Hope, the eccentric New York socialite and celebrity-chaser who has set her sights on Anson in Florida. The situation is presented as one of the penalties of greatness and celebrity. Anson fears the possible scandal that could begin in the gossip section of the New York papers if she is spotted with him because each is known in their own way. Anson goes out of his way to avoid contact with her. In one of the play's funnier moments, after tearing off his overcoat in response to hearing the sounds of someone possibly drowning, Anson deliberately puts his coat and hat back on and hastily exits the stage when the victim is announced to be Rosie. He declares, "I'm a married man with a family of girls. I don't want any woman, young or old, running after me." His aversion to even the appearance of marital impropriety is repeated in the play after he has pulled

Dolton back in through the window. The young Babe Manners hugs him as he uncomfortably exclaims, "What would Mrs. Anson say!"[57]

When each notorious vice of baseball players is touched upon—drinking, gambling, and carousing with women—they are all addressed specifically as things in which Anson does not take part. As if to reinforce the idea of his overwhelming virtue in relation to the popular perception of a baseball player, Anson's dissociation from each negative aspect is shown at least twice in the play. Hoyt has effectively styled Anson's character into a popularly acceptable representation of a ballplayer by acknowledging yet minimizing Anson-the-character's ungentlemanly conduct while also highlighting all of his honorable points as a man. Hoyt's play illustrates that a baseball player can be a gentleman while also exhibiting the game itself as a virtuous endeavor. Hoyt conveys that the game could involve men of physical ability who fulfilled the American male ideal of self-sufficiency and personal fortitude.

In his time as a theatre professional, Hoyt had seen the actors who had embodied that ideal gain a level of respectability that he was effectively proposing was within reach for ballplayers. The play makes it clear, however, that respectability is not going to be available to all. Listed among the characters in the play is a mascot named Sleigh Bells. The character does not have any lines in the play but is the target of what would otherwise seem to be a small throwaway bit of business. As the Black character passes by to leave the clubhouse, the attendant makes his feelings about the character clear to Anson and states that he has no use for having him around. Anson defers by responding that the character amuses the boys and they must have a mascot. Turning the focus toward a joke about Anson's age, the attendant tells Anson that he'll one day outgrow this nonsense.[58] Without this bit in place, the presence of a Black man among the many other nonspeaking characters filling the clubhouse and assumed to be ballplayers would seem to be a conspicuous advocacy for an integrated game. Instead, the play avoids this possibility by providing a justification for such separations. Positioned to defend the character's presence against the views of someone even older than he is, Anson is shown to be up to date with what was acceptable in the contemporary society.

In the play, the most impassioned defense of the game occurs at the end of the first act and comes from the character of the bishop visiting the Manners' home. First shocking the family by expressing his personal admiration for Anson, the bishop explains his own past with the game as the way he paid his way through college. He cites the myriad of professions in the stands—from clergy and physicians to merchants and college professors—as proof of the game's respectability. When asked by a member of the family whether the game exists only for gambling, the bishop replies that people already gamble on everything from yacht races to national elections, and he maintains that both drinking and gambling can be avoided at the ballpark.[59] His argument for the game is successful with the family, and it serves as a blueprint for how Hoyt constructs the play itself to bring the game toward respectability by showing the benefits to its players, the decency of the fans it draws, and the negation of its association with gambling.

While the promotion of Anson as the ideal baseball player takes central focus in the play and proves the reputability of players, other players are shown to be further examples of admiration. Manley Manners is a noble, upstanding young man whose guilt at the breech of familial trust forces him to reconcile both his family and his desired profession. Hoyt's use of names throughout his play to connote each character's internal moral standing reinforces the fusion of masculine propriety. All of the ballplayers seen onstage are presented as respectful young men. Even though they poke fun at the former ballplayer, Sager, who is now the clubhouse attendant, they all respectfully shake his hand when they discover that he was responsible for getting Anson to play professional baseball. The game is presented as good, honest work requiring intelligence and physical strength built through training. Those who have played the game profit from it—and not solely financially. As the bishop says, "the boys who win the battles on the ball field grow to be the men who win the battles of life."[60] Moreover, the bishop himself serves as a visible example that the money that can be made from the game can elevate the poor into positions of respect.

In the final act, as the fans are arriving for the game at the ballpark, Hoyt subtly appropriates an element of well-respected contemporary homes by having guests announced as they arrive. Not every fan in attendance is so honored, but the scorecard vendor and an offstage orchestra announce several high-profile baseball fans who all happen to be actors. Among the fans announced are DeWolf Hopper, Digby Bell, H. C. Barnabee, Nat Roth and Della, Nat Goodwin, and George W. Floyd. As each arrives, their identities are reinforced with either musical accompaniment, such as the song "Baby" from Hopper's starring turn in *Wang*, or a spoken reference to a well-known role, such as Barnabee's Sherriff of Nottingham from the Kovan and Smith operetta *Robin Hood*.[61] Like the bishop's focus on those from the professional ranks as fans in his appeal to the Manners family, Hoyt uses several well-respected people as attending fans who would be known by his target audience of theater-goers. Each actor mentioned was a well-known fan of the game, and though the characters who appeared onstage were not the actors themselves, the inclusion of them in the play as a procession serves as a visual reinforcement of the decency of baseball crowds and, by extension, the game itself.

Hoyt shows that baseball is something that has both a history and a future and should, therefore, be respected by having the old-timer Sager talk to the players in the clubhouse. It is clear in the world of the play that the future of the game does not involve gambling. Though a wager is a key element to the plot, there are no players involved in it beyond Will Haight's futile attempt to bribe Anson to throw the game. Indeed, the characters who are involved in the bet are shown throughout to be either villains like the Haights or fools like Dolton Manners. Hoyt further distances them from the idea of professional gamblers, whose impetus for placing a wager is to solely make money, by establishing for both Rankin Haight and Dolton Manners a larger motivation for their actions—to be wed to women who would not normally have them.

The production debuted on November 12, 1895, and had three performances at the Weitling Opera House in Syracuse. Initial reviews conveyed that the play showed promise and that Hoyt's writing suited Anson well.[62] The show toured through upper New York stages, stopping in Auburn, Oswego, Troy, Buffalo, and eventually Brooklyn, before its scheduled opening in New York City. Before opening in the city on December 2 for its three-week run, Hoyt changed the final act to put more baseball action onstage, including the entire final inning between Anson's Colts and the Baltimore team—complete with audible cracks of the bat and decisions of the umpire.[63] When possible, Hoyt employed other actual players to participate in the final inning. The presence of other professional players on the stage, like Arlie Latham and umpire Tim Hurst, increased the authenticity of the play's climactic ballgame. The intended effect was that when Anson hit the ball tossed to him from offstage for the game-winning home run, it would seem like a moment that could have actually happened rather than purely a scripted one.

The production traveled to Chicago where it spent the week of Christmas at the Grand Opera House before moving to Milwaukee and eventually closing its run in Minneapolis on January 11. It was not successful financially, and its tour, which was scheduled to proceed to Cleveland and Pittsburgh, was much shorter than anticipated. Anson claimed later that Hoyt closed the production because he was having difficulties with another of his shows running at the time and decided to cut the run short. Anson boasted that the production came within $23 of breaking a record at the Grand Opera House in Chicago—with $2,000 coming on Christmas night alone—and that it had the most successful week by a show in Chicago since the 1893 World's Fair.[64] The report from Chicago in the *New York Clipper* notes that the production did have a successful week. However, the same piece implies that the show was intended to run another week at the same location but a change of bill had recently been made.[65]

The play certainly had neither the longevity nor the financial success of Hoyt's previous pieces. The critics directly blamed Anson as a performer. From the beginning of the production reviews commented on vocal quality that was monotonous and line delivery that varied neither for situation nor staging.[66] With his legs and hands in constant motion, he was visibly uncomfortable onstage until the final act when he was required only to play baseball, and he appeared to one reviewer that he was desperate to be sitting whenever he was standing and just as anxious to be standing when he was sitting.[67] This description stood in stark contrast to the imposing and dynamic figure he presented on the ballfield, where he always seemed to be in control. Though he claimed that for his debut in Syracuse that he was simply waiting for his cue, reviews from several different locations noted that whatever scene he was playing would grind to a halt when he forgot his lines. The rest of the cast did not fare much better in many of the reviews, with the most scathing notice coming from Anson's hometown *Chicago Times*, which called the entire production a "spectacle of incompetence for three long hours."[68]

The problem, some believed, was that in seeking Anson to play Anson, Hoyt received precisely that. The same *Chicago Times* review believed that Anson "defied every canon of histrionic art." President of the National League Nick Young told the *Washington Post* a month after the play's closure that he was not surprised it failed and that the public did not take to Anson as an actor. He added, "He has a stern, cold demeanor on and off the ball field, and an audience in the theater wouldn't warm to him despite his great reputation as a ball player."[69] In a satirical article calling Anson a disciple of the Eleanor Duse style of realistic acting that eschews exaggerated nature while onstage, the *New York Sun* declared that Anson's triumph was "as a realistic portrayal of a man who cannot act, and doesn't propose to try."[70] While both Young and the writer for the *Sun* were judging the artistic merit of Anson's performance, Anson's failure as an actor in fact served to strengthen his authenticity and presence as a ballplayer on the stage. His inability to effectively play the role in a convention-conforming, aesthetically pleasing way served to reinforce the idea that he was, in fact, only a baseball player, and it helped to increase the authenticity Hoyt hoped would mark baseball as a respectable profession.

The alterations Hoyt made to the play between its opening in Syracuse and its debut on the New York stage were done to give the production more authenticity. The review of the opening performance by the *Syracuse Standard* began with a lament that the ball-playing of the final inning near the end was not visible to the audience. It was merely described by the characters in the grandstand and supplemented by the very impressive sounds of the bat striking the ball. The same paper reported that Hoyt had already made changes before the play left town for a one-night performance in Auburn, New York.[71] The changes centered on putting at least some of the described action from the ballgame onto the stage so it could be seen by the audience. As the spectacle of the final act grew, so did the cast, until it swelled to more than forty members, most of whom were employed solely for the staged ballgame.

As mentioned above, real-life players were engaged (when available) to play the roles of the Baltimore club. Early in the New York run, several actual members of the champion Baltimore team greeted Anson backstage and were enlisted to play themselves in the staged game, much like Anson had been years earlier by his comedian friends.[72] Other professionals like Arlie Latham and Tim Hurst joined the production piecemeal during the run to work alongside the actors cast to play real-life ballplayers. The incorporation of other actual ballplayers in the game did make the playing of the final inning more credible as well as increasing the spectacle of the show's end, but more conspicuous was the inclusion of actors filling the roles of other well-known people.

With the addition of a realistic baseball scene into the play, hiring only professional players to fulfill those additional roles would not have been cost effective, so the roles were filled by actors instead. The *Brooklyn Eagle*'s review noted, supported with a quote from Anson, that the actors cast to play several of the ballplayers were much too overweight to be believable in their roles and that one of the actual Chicago players in the audience was quite amused to see his portrayer onstage.[73] Also, Hoyt had included the above-mentioned parade of famous actors into the grandstand just before the game was set to start. Along with actors portraying Colt players such as Bill Lange and Bill Everitt, as well as players for the Baltimore team, stand-ins were also required to fill the roles of recognizable theatrical actors such as Digby Bell, DeWolf Hopper, and Nat Goodwin. The absences of these real-life actors, who were identified both by name and by a distinguishable role they had played, as well as the presence of noticeably unfit ballplayers, worked to enhance Anson's presence as the only person onstage who was not being impersonated by another. Just as his inability to conform to the conventions of stage acting emphasized Anson's authenticity in his role, Hoyt's specific calling of attention to Anson's presence through the absence of others reinforced the perception that Anson was exactly who he appeared to be onstage.

In the preview for the play's first performance, the *Syracuse Herald* wrote that Hoyt was not treating his subject for the play satirically for a change because he "admires the game and the sturdy, honest athletes engaged in it." [74] The preview went on to say that the play showed "how honestly, incorruptibly, and how far beyond the reach of the influence of the gambling fraternity our national game is." Hoyt used Anson as baseball's standard bearer in a play he hoped would show the world that the game was honest, incorruptible, and an asset to society. Crucial to Hoyt's case was Anson's presence in the role portraying himself. Though considered an aesthetic and financial failure primarily because of his performance, Anson's inability to be seen as anything other than a ballplayer bolstered Hoyt's implied argument. By foregrounding the authenticity of the man who was the popular representation of professional baseball players in the last decades of the nineteenth century, Hoyt's play asserted that baseball and its players were worthy of respectability. Hoyt's writing made Anson and the game seem respectable, but Anson's performance made the content seem believable. Following the play's run in Chicago the *New York Clipper* noted that "baseball cranks consider Anson a great actor. The people of the dramatic profession consider him a great ball player." [75] That he was both was what made him so effective for Hoyt. Anson's presence in the theater gave a body and voice to a baseball player whose profession had not been seen in a favorable light before the turn of the century.

Still, Anson's reputation would carry the mark of his failed stage performance back to the ballfields for the final two seasons of his career. The crowds that enjoyed seeing him fail on the field had a fresh wound at which to pick. He was teased by fans, players, and writers both on the field and in the papers. Opposing teams asked him why the rest of the cast had not used coaching signals to tell him when to act. [76] To make a living as he grew older, while occasionally playing exhibition or semi-professional games, Anson turned to vaudeville. More than ten years after his final year in the league, beginning in the fall of 1910, his acts centered on his career and legacy in the game like most ballplayers on the stage. He offered his opinions on current ballplayers and told stories of his playing days when, by his account, players were uniformly better. He recited a baseball poem by Grantland Rice and eventually included skits written by Billy Jerome, Ring Lardner, and George M. Cohan. In addition to vaudeville houses, where he would perform up to four times a day, Anson also sought bookings to perform his act at league parks. His acts became popular enough to be included on the Orpheum circuit of vaudeville theaters. Refusing or denied financial assistance from the league in which he was once the most prominent figure, Anson's theatrical career eventually provided him with a steady income following his retirement from the game. It also gave many people the opportunity to see him who had never seen him in person on the baseball field. Before his death in 1922, Anson's occupation listed in the Chicago census records of the 1910s was marked as "actor," but all of his performances featured him appearing only as himself.

Mike "King" Kelly Performs Success and Experiences Failure

THE 1888 BOOK *Play Ball: Stories of the Diamond Field* recounted Mike Kelly's first theatrical endeavor.[1] As a boy in Paterson, New Jersey, he produced a play for the other neighborhood boys alongside childhood friend and fellow future professional baseball player Jim McCormick. At the end of their play, the eighteenth-century English thief Jack Sheppard was hanged for his crimes.[2] Except for the quick reaction of his father, McCormick (who was playing Sheppard) nearly perished at the same time as his character. Until that point, Kelly explains, he and his friend were convinced that the best professions they could have as future careers would be as railroad engineers, baseball players, or actors. While the incident seemed to have cured McCormick of the acting bug, Kelly ended the tale with, "I still have hopes, however."[3]

Earlier in 1888, Kelly made his Boston stage debut as Dusty Bob in Charles Hale Hoyt's *A Rag Baby* at the Park Theatre. Though he had briefly appeared in a one-time benefit sketch in Detroit earlier in the decade, the Park Theatre appearance was his first time portraying a character in a full-length play. Despite poor weather and a play that was nearing four years old, the Park was full to overflowing. At Kelly's first appearance late in the third and final act, the show was stopped for several minutes due to the large and loud reception he received for stepping onstage.[4] The headlines featured Kelly's name prominently in the newspaper reports afterward, and he was mentioned in the stories well before the production's star, Charley Reed. The Hoyt & Thomas Company enjoyed packed houses throughout Kelly's limited engagement during the production's Boston run. Such attention hardly seemed fitting for a novice actor with only ten lines in the play, but the acclaim surrounding Kelly was due less to his acting ability—or even his being a baseball player—than it was to his status as Boston's newest celebrity figure.

Like the other ballplayers of the time who appeared on the stage, Kelly's participation was clearly a gimmick used to bring patrons to the theater. However, none of his contemporaries had fame on a scale comparable to Kelly. As it was with other players, his persona was built initially through his achievements on the field and the style with which he accomplished them, but after his sale to Boston, Kelly's persona became inseparable from the ideas of wealth and success. This chapter examines Kelly's persona before and after the sale and the interplay between his work on the field and on the stage until his death in 1894. By the time of his Park Theatre debut, Kelly's stage presence became about more than just being a professional baseball player. I argue that Kelly's conscious performance and embodiment of what became his baseball persona while onstage were complicated by his changing status as a celebrity over the years. By first describing how his persona was constructed (both before and after his leap to celebrity), I examine how those ideas transferred with Kelly to the stage. Playing larger venues in multi-act dramas and eventually turning to less-prestigious vaudeville stages, Kelly embodied the success and affluence of his persona; but as his baseball career began to fade, his embodiment of that persona reflected the decline. Performing in more intimate surroundings, removed from the social distance required by celebrity, Kelly's performance failed to embody those same ideas, thus spotlighting the human instead of the image.

Kelly played professional baseball at the major league level for thirteen years. His career spanned three leagues and four cities, but most of his statistical success came as a player for Cap Anson's Chicago National League team. During the seven seasons he spent in Chicago (from 1880 to 1886), Kelly led the league twice in batting average and three times in runs scored. He consistently appeared in the top ten players in the league in those two categories as well as in hits, doubles, and home runs. As a key member of

Anson's team, Kelly helped Chicago finish in first place in the league in five of the seven years he played there and in second place during one other year. Following Kelly's departure, Chicago would not win another league championship under Anson. While Kelly's statistics and on-field accomplishments placed him among the elite players in the game, it was his style of play that distinguished him from many of his contemporaries.

Highly regarded by other players for his intelligence, Kelly was believed to be either an innovator or contributor to the development of several tactics that are still used in the game today. Marty Appel, one of Kelly's biographers, notes that Kelly was credited along with Anson as possibly originating the hit-and-run before it was popularized and put into consistent use by the Baltimore Orioles of the 1890s.[5] In his own book, Kelly suggests himself as the first catcher to start using signs to the pitcher, which became standard practice within two years.[6] Perhaps his most recognizable innovation in the game was what would come to be known as the "Kelly Slide." The typical technique as a base runner approached a base was that he would extend himself forward and slide directly toward the base. Kelly's technique required the runner to slide his body behind the base and beyond the reach of the fielder. The runner would then use only one foot to touch the base. The fielder is given less of an opportunity to tag the runner with the ball, thereby increasing the possibility of the runner's success.[7] The maneuver was copied very quickly by other ballplayers and became one of the standard plays of the game.

Kelly excelled as a base runner. He would slow down while running between bases so that he might coax a throw from one of the fielders to the base he was heading to in an attempt to get him out. Through his delay, another runner might have time to score, and Kelly's speed was such that he could often retreat or advance safely.[8] In addition, a key element of his base running prowess came from his ability to deceive the pitcher and catcher regarding his intentions to steal a base. Kelly would initially feign indifference toward stealing. Standing motionless on first base until the pitcher began to deliver the ball, Kelly would then take off for second base and often have such an advantage that the catcher would find it useless to attempt to throw him out. This technique was deemed so effective that it was included in a chapter on base running in an instructional book from 1884 on how to play the game.[9] Biographer Howard Rosenberg found articles describing how Kelly made his deceit even more effective. He would also periodically bluff stealing in order to draw a throw from the catcher while he returned to first base.[10] While this fooling of the opposition had a strategic use, it also had an entertainment value to crowds since it appeared that Kelly was toying with the other team. For all his technical skill, Kelly was perhaps an even better showman.

His actions on the field routinely ended up in the newspapers. He noted that the names of his teammates didn't show up as often as his own and suggested that they should "break a window" and get themselves talked about. As he remarked, as far as the newspapers were concerned, he did sometimes seem to be "the only player."[11] For the portion of his career when foul balls were not counted as strikes against the batter, Kelly would often purposefully foul off pitches with either full swings or bunts in order to extend his at-bat indefinitely. The practice had the dual benefit of annoying the pitcher while simultaneously entertaining the crowd. Each foul ball and subsequent bit of laughter from Kelly would delight the crowd and enrage the pitcher until Kelly eventually drew a walk or found a pitch to his liking.[12] In this way (and others), Kelly was an opportunist who took advantage of situations as they arose.

One story from an opponent in 1887 tells of Kelly scoring from second. Looking back to the field, he saw that the batted ball had gone through a gate in right field and the fielder was giving chase. Immediately Kelly ran to shut the gate, allowing the other runners to score as well.[13] In another instance, to prevent an appeal by the defense that a runner had not touched a base— which would have continued the game rather than allowing his team to have scored the winning run—Kelly threw the ball into the crowd and the umpire was forced to let the play stand.[14] Without any rules prohibiting it, Kelly supposedly inserted himself in a game during the middle of a play as a foul ball came near the bench. Announcing "Kelly now catching for Chicago," he caught the ball and argued the batter must be called out since no rule specified when one player may be substituted for another. Kelly reportedly lost the argument, but the league enacted a rule the next day prohibiting such substitutions.[15] Kelly's actions in these situations were technically within the rules, or exploited the lack thereof, that had been established in the league, and they served to create for him an aura of playfulness and excitement that made him a player whom people wanted to see.

Kelly also flagrantly broke the rules when he thought he would not get caught. For instance, he became noted for his penchant for disregarding third base on his trip around the bases. At the time, games were officiated by only one umpire who typically stood in the middle of the diamond and had to keep watch of the ball during a play. When a ball was hit to the right side, the umpire's back would be turned to third base, where a runner could take an unseen shortcut. Appeals by a team against the runner were often unsuccessful as the umpire could not say that he saw anything at all and was only allowed to rule on what he saw. Rosenberg's research notes at least four attempts by Kelly in 1881 alone, the first year the practice was reported in the newspapers.[16] The play became less successful for Kelly later in his career as his reputation grew and umpires, opponents, and crowds were increasingly aware of the possibility. While playing in Providence, an attempt by Kelly was thwarted as the groaning of the crowd alerted the umpire, and Kelly was forced to return to third base.[17] In *Play Ball*, Kelly tells of pulling the trick later in his career against Chicago and Cap Anson. He was called out after Anson argued with the umpire—but after the game, Anson admitted that he had been partly cheering for Kelly as he cut the base.[18] This conflicted reaction was likely what fans of other teams felt as well when Kelly performed the trick.

His frequent challenging of the rules gave Kelly repeated opportunities to "kick," or complain, to the umpire. In fact, even before he joined the Chicago team, Kelly had gained a reputation as a "kicker."[19] In his book, he mentions several times that he believed kicking against the umpire was one of the main attractions of baseball, despite the protestations seen in the newspapers. He argues that a good player could only be seen as great in a fan's eyes through their ability to kick.[20] In addition, he used talking as a tactic during the game, with a steady stream of chatter from either the bench or a coaching position just off the field. He often attempted to disrupt his opponents by trying to make them laugh with his constant talking.[21] Several stories exist of Kelly's ability to affect the game itself through only speaking. For example, Boston writer Tim Murnane recalled that when Kelly was catching he would shift his body so the umpire could not see the location of the ball. He would then yell "strike" before the umpire could rule on the pitch.[22] In 1886, after a runner had advanced to second on a passed ball, the player asked Kelly if it had been a foul ball. Kelly responded that it had and the player started back toward first. After he was tagged with the ball and called out, the player and his captain protested that Kelly had lied. The umpire replied that he had never said it was foul and the player had instead asked Kelly.[23] Once while coaching at third base, Kelly called out to the pitcher to see the ball. When the opposing pitcher tossed the ball to Kelly, he stepped out of the way and let it roll away from the field so Kelly's teammate could advance from first base.[24]

Kelly's relationship with the fans was also dependent, in part, on his constant chatter. To him, talking was an opportunity—like his kicking—to make the game more entertaining. He often teased the fans in the stands by boasting about his own skill or taunting the other team, and, in turn, fans made Kelly a target when he made a mistake or his team was behind. In 1887 at a game in Indianapolis, after being thrown out at the plate, Kelly was taunted with the phrase "razzle-dazzle," which he had yelled at the fans earlier in the day. Kelly responded to the crowd with a bow.[25] Actor Digby Bell, Kelly's friend and a big baseball fan, believed the effect the crowd could have on a player was similar to that of applause for an actor—and that a player would play better to gain the support or sympathy of the home fans.[26] Kelly, however, was a draw even when on the road, particularly among the Irish population of a city. In St. Louis, he played up to a group of fans in the bleachers known as the "Kerry Patch."[27] For Kelly, interactions with the crowd (whether supportive or not) had an integral role in not only how he played on the field but also how he performed.

Through all of these actions and achievements, Kelly acquired a good amount of fame in baseball: players knew they had to be aware of his tricks, sportswriters regularly reported his exploits, and fans came to the games to see him. Kelly's fame was localized, however, and it stayed almost exclusively within the game at that point. In the classifications of fame offered by Chris Rojek in his study on celebrity culture, Kelly's fame while playing for Chicago would be considered renown but not full celebrity. For Rojek, the distinguishing characteristic is the proximity of the famous to those who are paying attention. The renowned individual maintains a social or para-social level of contact with the audience much the same as Kelly did through his interactions with fans. The crowd sees themselves on the same level socially as the renowned. The leap to celebrity requires more distance between the famous person and the audience, which serves to separate the two from each other.[28] For Kelly, the agent that distanced him from his audience and put him at the celebrity level was his sale to Boston and the resulting image of wealth.

Within baseball, Kelly's value to a team existed on multiple levels. The abilities of proficient batsmen like Kelly often played a significant role in putting their teams in positions to win. Winning teams, of course, generated more revenue than did losing teams, through increased attendance during regular season games within the league, larger gate receipts from exhibition games played against non-league members, and postseason contests between the leagues that were often winner-takes-all series. Kelly's playing helped propel

Chicago to multiple league championships, and he was called by one team-mate the "life and soul of the Chicagos."[29] Between his first and second years with the Chicago team, the average per-game attendance jumped by 400, and as the team moved into a new park for the 1882 season, attendance averaged 3,000 per game.[30] With a fan-focused player like Kelly also contributing to a winning team, Chicago was a very popular and profitable ball club.

On the field, catching was the most physically demanding position on a baseball team before protective equipment such as masks or even gloves came into use. Players who were willing to play the position had much greater value to their teams, and they could often demand higher compensation than other positions on the field.[31] Kelly appeared as a catcher for more than a quarter of the games he played for Chicago. Though he was mostly used as a relief catcher, filling in for the regular catcher earlier in his career, Kelly had evenly split the catching duty with Silver Flint in 1886. As a player, his all-around play was matched only by one contemporary catcher, Buck Ewing, but as a trickster and as an attraction, he was unrivaled by any of his contemporaries. After the 1886 season, Kelly's last with Chicago, team owner Al Spalding felt Kelly had a value to the team that was hard to measure beyond his statistical achievements. Spalding believed Kelly's trickery on the field, his ability to steady young players, and his general amusement of spectators all increased his actual value.[32]

Kelly understood this multi-faceted value he had to a team, and he expected to be compensated appropriately. Announced as an effort to keep costs under control, the National League had set a cap at $2,000 for a player's salary in 1885.[33] However, these salaries could change throughout the season with bonuses paid or fines levied. Spalding, a well-known temperance supporter, used such fines and withholdings of payment in an effort to keep his players from drinking, and he hired a private investigator to report on his players' off-field habits—particularly Kelly's, who was famously a frequent bar patron. A detective reported to Spalding that he had seen Kelly in a Clark Street saloon at three in the morning. While the papers sanitized the story by saying that he had been drinking lemonade, Kelly corrected the report by stating publicly, "I never drank a lemonade at that hour in my life. It was straight whiskey!"[34] Rosenberg's research shows that in 1886 alone, Kelly lost $325 from his contract as a result of his drinking.[35] Making less than what he had been signed for and much less than his actual worth, Kelly made public his refusal to play for Spalding's team again after that season.

Due to an implied clause in the contract of every professional baseball player, Kelly was bound to the Chicago team until they decided what to do with him. The reserve clause was not formally written into player contracts until the 1887 season; however, a clause in the standard contract required the player to abide by the written laws of the league. The implication of signing the contract was that the player was subject to the agreement between the National League and the American Association from 1883 that had explicitly stated the reserve clause.[36] An attempt by the New York team to buy Kelly's rights for $7,750 was rebuffed because Spalding refused to let Kelly play for that city.[37] Boston, which had traditionally seen larger than average crowds whenever Kelly's Chicago team visited, offered $5,000 at first, then $9,000, and eventually met Spalding's asking price of $10,000.[38] The sale was conditioned on the Boston team reaching a contract with Kelly, who wanted more than the standard $2,000. The agreement they reached called for Kelly to receive the maximum salary per league rules, but the Boston owners also agreed to pay Kelly $3,000 more to use his picture for advertising purposes— a right they already owned in the standard player contract.[39]

The amount paid for Kelly was unprecedented in the game and in American society. Players had been sold before, but none for so high a price—nor had the player himself benefitted from the transaction. The previous records for selling a player had actually come from entire teams being sold to another club and the new club choosing which players it would like to keep. On October 30, 1864, for example, the Columbus Buckeyes were sold to the Pittsburgh Alleghenys for $8,000, with ten players retained by the purchasing club. On September 16, 1885, the Buffalo Bisons were sold to the Detroit Wolverines for $7,000, with four players remaining on the new team. Seymour and Mills note in *Baseball: The Early Years* that the selling of players' rights capitalized on their increased value versus their relatively low salary.[40]

Though the high amount of money being associated with Kelly was unique among baseball players, it seemed even larger in comparison to what his fans were familiar with in their own lives. American industrial workers averaged approximately $480 in annual earnings in 1890, which meant that Kelly's annual salary was ten times what the workers in the crowd were making on the average.[41] Kelly was earning as much per year as United States senators, and the sale price with which he was associated topped the annual salaries of the U.S. vice president and the Cabinet secretaries.[42]

In 1881, circus owner Adam Forepaugh had held a contest for the most beautiful woman in America. The winner was promised $10,000 and the lead in his parade and spectacle entertainment titled *Lalla Rookh's Departure from*

Dehli. When actress Louise Montague was declared the winner, she was promoted as the "$10,000 beauty," and the phrase entered the American popular
culture lexicon.[43] The corresponding dollar figure of Kelly's sale price made a
transference of the nickname inevitable, and he began to be referred to as the
"$10,000 beauty" as well. The monetary figure became ubiquitously linked
with Kelly as Boston club owner Arthur Soden often put a photograph of
the certified check on public display.[44] Within a month of the purchase, the
Boston club publicized a $10,000 life insurance policy they had taken out on
Kelly to protect their investment.[45] Very soon, Kelly not only became associated with that dollar amount but also became a shorthand unit to measure
a player's worth. After it was publicized that the Pittsburgh club wanted to
purchase Cap Anson from Chicago, owner Spalding said that Anson was
worth three Kellys.[46]

The monetary price on Kelly quantified his success achieved through his
work on the field, and he was quickly whisked into the higher social circles
of Boston. Prompted by his friend Nat Goodwin, the actor, Kelly transferred
his Elks membership from the Newark (New Jersey) lodge to Boston as the
newspapers jokingly questioned if Newark had received the going rate.[47]
Though closely aligned with men in the theatrical profession, the Boston
Elks lodge also included the mayor as well as many of the city's prominent
businessmen. The social status Kelly gained within the Boston sphere radiated
beyond the baseball world. At a party held by actor and fellow Elk George W.
Floyd in August 1887, Kelly was mobbed by women and men, all hoping to
"squeeze the hand of the $10,000 beauty."[48]

For many of his Irish fans in Boston and beyond, Kelly's wealth took
on further meaning. As numerous immigrants received less in wages than
native-born workers, particularly as unskilled laborers, Kelly's visible ascent
from his poor origins personified for them the American dream of success.
Furthermore, rather than sublimating his ethnicity in his social and economic rise, he remained identifiably Irish through his public behavior. In
many ways, Kelly was following a path that had been laid down by boxer
John L. Sullivan. Historian Michael Isenberg argues that Sullivan was the
first significant mass culture hero in America after the Civil War. Sullivan's
flaws were as visible as his boxing feats, and he came to be seen as a public
symbol available both to celebrate and vilify American Irish in the nineteenth
century. The Boston Irish who celebrated Sullivan and Kelly were an amalgam of the middle and working classes and held no unified perspective on
morality. As Isenberg points out, they created heroes who mattered to them

in the moment and who often offered images of social mobility, economic affluence, and increased prestige amongst their peers.[49]

In many ways, Kelly had become a celebrated personification of the popular Stage Irish type that was seen on stages throughout the United States.[50] At work, he was as industrious as he was indifferent to rules. He played the game with swagger and boisterousness. He was visibly impetuous and profane, with a penchant for arguments with umpires. Isenberg notes how the Irish were perceived in stereotyped terms—with public displays of all of their emotions, from happiness to anger to sadness. Focusing more on their positive traits, the Irish embraced the stereotypes to some extent.[51] Kelly became an idealized Irishman: celebrated, uncompromising, and far from the abject poverty many of his fans or their families had personally known.

As sociologist Judy Scully argues in her study of immigrant Irish bar owners, the enacting of a Stage Irish identity was both empowering and an admission of powerlessness, as the historical conditions that have come to identify the Irishman as a drunkard and the pub/barroom as his natural habitat embody an unresolvable contradiction.[52] The pub itself supplied an important gathering place for Irish working men. It was a center for local politics as well as union meetings, and information flowed easily to and from the barroom. It was an important location in which to be seen and recognized, and it provided opportunities to be measured against peers. In these rooms, among a city's local Irish population, the humanity eclipsed the stereotypes.

The ebullient Boston press dubbed Kelly baseball royalty.[53] After the sale, any mention of Kelly in the papers referred to him alliteratively as "King Kelly" or featured some association with his sale price. Most commonly both were used. Associated primarily with these two signifiers, the $10,000 beauty and the king, Kelly's identity—built through his loquacious personality and innovative play—was repackaged into a new statistic that held much more weight with those who did not follow baseball: money. What this rebranding effectively did for Kelly was to elevate him beyond a valuable baseball player into a star attraction. He was an instant celebrity.

Whether a celebrity or not, once a public persona is established, associated ideas must be perpetuated to become aspects of that persona, and a key component of sustaining Kelly's identification with wealth was his embodiment of affluence, which was seen at the ballpark, around the city, and in the newspapers. Baseball capitalized on Kelly's star appeal by making him the key element of their advertisements for games. At his very first appearance as a member of the Boston team at an exhibition game in Baltimore, posters were plastered all over town touting the appearance of the Boston team and the "$15,000 Kelly" (combining his 1887 salary with his sale price).[54] Similar billboards were seen in Pittsburgh later in the year bearing the more common "$10,000 beauty" moniker.[55] The treasurer for the Boston club, James B. Billings, was right when he remarked after acquiring Kelly that he would be "the greatest kind of an advertising card and his engagement will make the present season one of the most prosperous the club has ever enjoyed."[56] Average game attendance for Boston in 1887 was nearly double that of the previous season, while the total attendance for the entire league increased by more than 55,000 from the previous year.[57]

Around Boston, other industries adopted Kelly's name to help sell their products. He was asked to serve as master of ceremonies and referee for several unnamed sporting events in Salem and Haverhill, Massachusetts, during his first few months in the city.[58] Later that year, a cigar appeared around the city called "The Only Kell."[59] In the offseason between his first and second years in Boston, Kelly also was asked to write a book about his life and his experiences in baseball. The book, *Play Ball: Stories of the Diamond Field,* was the first baseball autobiography produced in the United States and had a first printing of 25,000 copies.[60]

Kelly's raised profile also heightened expectations for his on-field performance, as many Boston fans expected that having him on the team guaranteed them the league championship for 1887. Fans expected Kelly to get a hit every time at bat and to score a run every time he was on base. In the 1887 season, he did not lead the league in any statistical category as he had in three areas the previous year. The closest he came to the top was second place in doubles and third in stolen bases. Aware of all his tricks, crowds around the league were vocal about Kelly's play and were equally vocal that umpires should not let him get away with anything.[61] The newspapers speculated that the additional attention took a toll on Kelly's performance on the field since it was impossible to fulfill the role the public expected of him.[62]

After arriving in Boston and following his transfer to the local Elks club, Kelly had been approached by actors Nat Goodwin and Charley Reed to appear onstage with them. A local minstrel company had also reportedly approached him to appear as their interlocutor. Kelly had managed to gain some additional theatrical experience since his childhood. He told a crowd in Boston that as a young man he had played in a nonspeaking role in a Paterson, New Jersey, theater that required only that he be thrown through a window. In July 1884, while a member of the Chicago team, Kelly appeared in a small role alongside umpire-turned-actor Frank Lane in a three-man farce called "He Would Be an Actor; Or, the Ball Player's Revenge." The single performance was at a benefit for an attendant at White's Theatre in Detroit. His fellow Chicago players were in attendance, and as Kelly's character was being hit with a clapboard to end the show, Cap Anson started shouting for them to keep hitting him.[63]

In early 1888 while he was stranded in New York for four days following a blizzard, Kelly reached a deal with Boston theatre producer Charles Thomas of the Hoyt & Thomas Company. In a week-long special engagement in March, Kelly would appear as Dusty Bob alongside Charley Reed's Old Sport in a remounted production of Charles Hale Hoyt's *A Rag Baby*. For appearing in two scenes as well as the all-cast dance number finale, Kelly was to receive $250.[64]

The play, one of Hoyt's earliest, had debuted in New York in 1884 and had become a favorite in New York and throughout the northeast. The melodramatic farce begins as a man named Christian Burial has hidden his child at a boarding house in order to get back at his wife for threatening divorce. His brother-in-law, Tony Jay, buys the drugstore next door to the boarding house as he waits to steal the baby back. Because he knows nothing about dispensing medicine, Jay hires Old Sport to help him run the shop, which includes fighting rats in the cellar and running off tramps looking for free alcohol. Old Sport, who repeatedly calls himself a sporting man, is in training for a fight with Dusty Bob, who has been brought into town specifically to fight him. Jay and Old Sport break into the boarding house after starting a bonfire in the street as a distraction, but come away with a rag baby instead of the child. Fearing that their child has been kidnapped, Burial and his wife make up just before the real child is brought out by one of the girls of the boarding school who has fallen in love with Jay and was afraid he would fail in his attempt to get the baby.

The role of Dusty Bob required Kelly to storm the stage looking for Old Sport. After finding him, Bob is quickly defeated as he is thrown into the cellar with the door shut behind him. He emerges from the cellar alone on the stage with a bear trap attached to the back of his trousers, providing a sight gag as he exits. He returns to the stage at the end carrying Old Sport, who has fallen from the second story window. As a commotion occurs outside, Bob speculates that it is the boxer John L. Sullivan passing by, which revives Old Sport immediately. The happy ending leads into the final chorus number and dance by the entire cast.

The play was written before Kelly's ascent to stardom both on and off the field, but his addition to the cast served to highlight portions of the play. Throughout the story, Old Sport professes his love for all types of sports, from pedestrianism to boxing to baseball. His idolization of boxer Sullivan leads him to repeatedly shake Jay's hand since it was "the hand that shook Sullivan's." Jay eventually uses this idea to make Old Sport fall for the woman who has been trying to get his attention—Jay tells Old Sport that she once kissed Sullivan. Used for humor, Sport's obsession with all things sporting speaks to the image at the time of the typical "crank" or sports fan. Obsessed with his hero, Old Sport tries to do everything to look like, act like, and be associated with Sullivan. In much the same way, Kelly was an idol to many of the people in those Boston audiences who had lined up to shake his hand and who were aware of what fashion he was wearing, what cigar he was smoking, and what equipment he was using.

Kelly's appearance was expected to bring in large houses throughout his run during Holy Week in Boston.[65] The Park Theatre was packed at the opening on March 26, 1888, and the applause on his opening line lasted nearly a minute, forcing Kelly to acknowledge his friends and fans.[66] Most of the reviews were ostensibly favorable but acknowledged that Kelly's performance could stand a little work.[67] The production closed on March 31 and was then slated to tour the northeast for two weeks. Kelly, who was in training for the upcoming season, did not accompany the tour but did reprise his role in Lynn, Massachusetts, on Saturday, April 8.[68]

Recounting his involvement with the play in his book, Kelly tells a story about attending his first rehearsal. Arriving at the theater fifteen minutes early and finding the curtain drawn, he sat in the orchestra seating and fell asleep while waiting for the rest of the company. He believed he saw the footlights come on and the curtain rise on a parade of stars who were all dead, including Junius Booth Sr., John McCollough, Charlie Thorne, E. A. Sothern, John T. Raymond, Charles Fechter, Harry Montague, Charlotte Cushman, and Adelaide Neilson. The parade stopped as they all bowed to the arrival of William Shakespeare, who placed a laurel on Neilson's head. The scene vanished in mist with a clashing of music as the curtain came down—and Kelly awoke. Leaving the theater, he met Charley Reed outside, who told him they had waited for him onstage for a half an hour but eventually cancelled rehearsal because he had not shown up.[69] In the book, the story precedes Kelly's account of his opening night of the show. By presenting a company of greats emerging before him, the fanciful story serves to contextualize his stage abilities in that he acknowledges a significant distance between himself and the finest actors in history.

Though the part of Dusty Bob was not written for Kelly, audiences had several ways to identify him with the character. Such alignment of a fictional character and Kelly's persona contributed to the play's success. A character announces Dusty Bob's arrival before the audience sees him. This was similar to how Kelly's arrival in Boston was announced in the papers, which began to generate interest in him even before he appeared. In both cases, the person's arrival is managed so it creates anticipation in the audience. Dusty Bob is essentially a hired gun brought in to beat Old Sport, and he is intent on doing the job that his employers have paid him to do. Kelly's auratic presence in the role was already imbued with the remunerative fame he had gained upon coming to the city. After he left the production, the sporting section of the *New York Clipper* claimed that Kelly could have remained with the company "at a very large salary."[70]

Kelly returned to captain the Boston National League team for the 1888 season, but neither his statistics or the team's standings improved dramatically from the previous season. Even his record sale price had been matched early in the season when his Boston team purchased the rights to his old Chicago teammate John Clarkson for another $10,000. Yet Clarkson's purchase had little if any negative impact on the association of wealth with Kelly's persona, which he actively maintained. Part of Kelly's display of wealth was through his dressing the part. After the sale, newspapers often remarked on how he was dressed in the most current fashion of the day, from a Prince Albert frock coat, vest, and fancy shirt to a multicolored sash that was a half yard wide. In addition, Kelly was often found sporting diamonds on a charm, as cuff links, or worn on his shirt, and he carried a gold-topped cane with him as he traveled. He would accessorize himself with several lap dogs, including a small poodle called Nellie. Kelly also had a parrot named Paul that he believed was a luck-bringing mascot.[71]

The performance of wealth requires not only visible evidence of having it but also exhibitions of its fluidity—coming in and going out—so that it seems endless. Kelly received several of these accessories in public ceremonies. At various times while on the field Kelly was given gifts or other tokens of admiration, like a box of cigars and a statuette of himself batting, as well as a satin jockey's hat and an arrangement of flowers spelling "Kel."[72] Once, Kelly came to bat at the top of the fourth inning of a game in Chicago as Cap Anson, after having just argued with the umpire, created an awkward situation when he walked out with a rifle to present to Kelly on behalf of an admirer.[73] The Boston Elks gave him a gold watch with rubies and a large "K" set in diamonds that was valued at $500 in May 1887.[74]

In addition to receiving these valuable gifts, Kelly illustrated that he had multiple sources of income beyond his baseball salary. Even before his sale—perhaps used as a negotiating ploy in his standoff against the Chicago ownership—a newspaper reported that Kelly might not continue his baseball career because he had apparently made more than $100,000 from speculating on wheat after the 1886 season.[75] The sale of his book within just a few months in 1888 brought him $1,500.[76] Kelly also partnered with a former umpire named John Kelly to open a bar in New York following the 1888 season. He reported that he had to go back on his promise to accompany an all-star team to Australia because the bar, called "The Two Kels," was making so much money that he could not afford to leave it.[77] He often relied on his association with wealth as a source of humor. Approached in the clubhouse by club treasurer James B. Billings before a game in Boston, Kelly declared loud enough for everyone to hear, "You can't do it, Billings. I haven't got a cent; you can't borrow anything off me."[78] His expenses were often aligned with the traits of the Stage Irishman as well: he was exceedingly generous to people and charities, sometimes borrowing from one person to help out another. Capitalizing on the cultural link of wealth to success, Kelly became proficient in presenting himself as an embodiment of the success of his work rather than remaining tied to the image of the work he did as a ballplayer. He was still identified as a ballplayer, but, by presenting himself as of a higher, nonworking class, he was identifying with the fruits of the labor rather than the labor itself.

At the end of the 1888 baseball season, Kelly agreed to return to the stage to participate in another remounting of a Hoyt production, beginning a two-week run on December 24 as the tough Rob Graves in *A Tin Soldier* at the Fourteenth St. Theatre in New York. Now, with two full baseball seasons behind him as a national star, Kelly's public persona was played up in the advance publicity for the production. It was reported that Kelly originally asked the Hoyt & Thomas Company for $2,000 to appear in the small role but was negotiated down to $1,000 and a new overcoat. The *New York World* reported that the fee Kelly received was the largest given to a nonactor. Hoyt stated in the piece that he believed that Kelly would draw in more than enough money to make up his salary.[79]

The production was advertised as one of Hoyt's great comedy-farce successes and "a seasonable satire on the plumbers' trade."[80] Its story revolves around a character named Rats who has just become a plumber's apprentice and is now enjoying fleecing his former employer, Brooklyn Bridge, alongside his new boss, Vilas Canby. As the curtain rises, Rats is returning a costume he took without Bridge's knowledge—a costume he used to crash a party where he insulted a woman. While Bridge tries to keep his wife from finding out about the blame that is being placed on *him*, his two housemaids are working in union with the two plumbers to overcharge, under work, and otherwise swindle the Bridges. At the same time, Victoria Bridge is hounded by the neighbor's servant, who borrows things and relays messages from her employer that the Bridges must not be as wealthy as they let on. In the end, Bridge finds out it was Rats who got him into trouble, and Canby, through a case of mistaken identity, is being ridden off on a rail.

As in *A Rag Baby*, Kelly's role as Rob Graves in *A Tin Soldier* required him to fight. After having brought in Victoria's mother's trunk, Graves re-enters just as Bridge's business associate says that he would pay $10 to have Rats beaten up. Graves demands $15, and once Bridge says that he would make it $25 if the job was done well, Graves replies, "Young feller, I'll blot him off the earth."[81] Though he loses the offstage fight that closes the first act, Graves returns in the third act when Canby wants two scheming colonels tarred and feathered. Graves asks for $50 but eventually agrees to $5 and admits that he will have to postpone his grave-robbing plans for that night. After his gang has already grabbed Canby and Rats in place of the two soldiers, Graves delivers the final line of the play when he demands his $5.

The play had received runs in each theatrical season since it had debuted in New York in May 1886, well before Kelly's connection with it. Kelly got second billing, behind Eugene Canfield, who played Rats, in the early advertisements for the two-week run.[82] Upon appearing onstage with the trunk, Kelly was greeted with "round after round of applause" and caught a large floral baseball with his name on it in red when it was thrown to him by admirers before he delivered his first line.[83] The *New York World* indicated that in his New York debut Kelly had "latent histrionic talent" that could be developed.[84] Still, Kelly was not hired for his acting ability. The Christmas Eve opening audience was filled with baseball fans, and the attendance for the run was reportedly good.[85]

Unlike his previous stage appearance in *A Rag Baby*, Kelly's participation in the role played more off of his fame for being well paid than for any of his on-field accomplishments. In Hoyt's interview with the *World* before the opening of the play, the discussion of Kelly's involvement revolved around his exorbitant salary demands for his participation; and Hoyt noted that even though Kelly's demands were not met, he still became the highest paid non-actor to appear in a play. Seeing Kelly in the role of Rob Graves, the audience was presented with two separate onstage negotiations for more money, and the final line reinforced this association as Graves demanded payment for a job that (in the play) was not particularly well done. In the transfer of his baseball persona to the stage, Kelly was no longer dependent on being a baseball player as much as he was being recognized for being a well-paid baseball player.

In the 1889 season, both Kelly and his Boston team rebounded in the National League. The team finished in second place, just one game behind the champion New York club. Kelly had led the league in doubles, was second in stolen bases, and won a poll conducted by the *Sporting News* on who was the league's most popular player. He received a medal with a gold mask and diamonds for bases.[86] It was also during this year that performer John W. Kelly (no relation to either the ballplayer or his bar-owning partner) wrote a song for vaudeville performer Miss Maggie Cline called "Slide, Kelly, Slide." The title phrase had begun as a call to the ballplayer while he still with Chicago but had entered American slang as something to yell at someone who was attempting or should be attempting to avoid danger. The lyrics are based on the ballplayer and mention his catching and playing the outfield as well as the plans to "take you to Australia" should he have continued success.[87] The song became incredibly popular and was eventually recorded on Edison's wax cylinders in 1891 by George J. Gaskin. According to Kelly's biographer Marty Appel, the recording became the first popular recording to be considered a hit that could not be classified as opera, religious, patriotic, or classical music.[88]

Kelly's financial success was obviously the exception to the rule among professional players. Upset over what they considered to be unfair working conditions, players organized into a collective called the Brotherhood of Professional Base Ball Players in the late 1880s. Seeking firm salary commitments to be explicitly stated and honored in contracts, as well as more specificity in the reserve agreement, the players were continually rebuffed in their attempts to negotiate with National League owners. In an effort to withhold their labor from the owners, the Brotherhood formed their own league after the 1889 season (not abiding by the National Agreement between the two established leagues, the National League and the American Association). Forming teams in the same cities as direct competition with the other leagues, most players switched allegiances to the new league by staying in the same city. Kelly was one of the Brotherhood's biggest supporters, which further endeared him to his working-class fans.[89]

Kelly briefly stopped doing stage work in full-length shows after the 1889 season during the war between the National League and the Brotherhood; however, he still used the stage for publicity during this time. At Hooley's Theatre in Chicago on Thanksgiving Day in 1889, Kelly was conspicuous in one of the stage boxes in the theater as a guest alongside Hoyt for another of his plays called *A Brass Monkey*. At the beginning of the second act, Kelly and Hoyt came onstage and interrupted the play, asking the actor playing the auctioneer in the scene for his pen and ink. Hoyt introduced Kelly to the audience and, after a brief discussion of acquiring other players, had him sign his Brotherhood contract in view of the audience. The pair then allowed the play to resume, with Hoyt telling Kelly, "now come outside and I'll pay you what advance money you need."[90] Kelly was the biggest star in baseball, and his willingness to stand with his fellow players borrowed from that. This bit of public advertising for the new league played on Kelly's image of wealth and success as a means to promote an association with success for the new league. Such advertisement was particularly needed in Chicago since the most notable player who had *not* switched allegiances to the new league was that city's Cap Anson.

The Players' League put a good product on the field but ultimately could not compete with the two more-established leagues. As the most visible player in the league, Kelly was often called on to comment on the battles between the leagues—particularly as the National League began to use its wealth to convince players to return throughout the season. Kelly refused an offer of $10,000 from Al Spalding to return to the National League, though he did accept a $1,000 loan from the Chicago owner.[91] Kelly's steadfastness with the Brotherhood gave him his first public association with failure. On the field, his Boston team won the Players' League championship under his leadership, but he played in only eighty-nine of the 129 games. Though his batting average remained high, he appeared among the league's top ten in only one offensive category. During the year Kelly was twice publicly given high-profile gifts. He received a gold-topped cane from admirers in Chicago when his team visited the city.[92] Drawing more attention, however, was the gift of a cottage, stable, and property in South Hingham, Massachusetts, valued at $10,000 and given by a collection of his friends and admirers in Boston, including boxer John L. Sullivan.[93]

The collapse of the Players' League after the 1890 season left Kelly scrambling for baseball work after having publicly burned several bridges with the National League. In the next season, 1891, Kelly took over the Cincinnati team in the American Association, which came to be known as Kelly's Killers. After only eighty-six games, Kelly was released to join the Boston team in that same league to help salvage their dwindling gate receipts; however, he quickly jumped back to the National League team in the same city after appearing in only four games. Kelly remained with the Boston team in the National League for the 1892 season but played very poorly through his seventy-eight games. His batting average sunk to a career low of .189 when it had consistently been over .300 in previous years. Despite his waning ability, he remained a draw for fans. Still interacting with the crowds, Kelly began using the opportunity to verbally respond to the stories that appeared in the newspapers about his increasing failures in the game.[94]

During this time, Kelly's theatrical work nearly halted completely. He would appear for only one night in Hoyt's *A Temperance Town* at a Boston Elks benefit in December 1892 at the Park Theatre.[95] In 1893, he began to take more advantage of the opportunities provided by the vaudeville stage. For most performers in the late nineteenth century, the move from multi-act full-length plays to working in a vaudeville house was a clear step down. While there certainly was a loss of prestige associated with such a move, an actor's salary usually suffered as well (from a combination of reduced pay and an irregular work schedule). For these performers, the transition from standard playhouses to vaudeville houses was often one done out of desperation. Kelly, whose performances in multi-act dramas were not his sole means of support, had little to lose by playing in vaudeville. The change was a permanent one for Kelly, however, as he never played in a multi-act drama again once he began playing in vaudeville. Still a draw, however, his presence in the vaudeville houses served as a de facto declaration or assertion of continued celebrity—almost a reminder of the past to the audience—and it depended on the juxtaposition of Kelly's long-standing aura with his physical form that was now on display in front of them. He had experienced a similar decline on the ballfield, too, where the contrast between his celebrity and his reality was much more visible.

In January 1893, Kelly appeared in blackface for a few days in Wood and Sheppard's minstrel act called "Winning Cards," performing an olio of songs, dances, and funny stories which closed on the seventh of the month to a good house.[96] Beginning on January 16, Kelly partnered with Billy Jerome, who had appeared with him in "Winning Cards," for a vaudeville act at the Imperial Music Hall as part of the Henry Burlesque Company. Kelly and Jerome paired to sing songs, and Kelly recited "Casey at the Bat."[97] Starting on March 26, Kelly performed as a "special engagement" doing a similar act with the Lilly Clay Company run by Sam T. Jack in Chicago and drew good audiences for two weeks.[98]

Jerome formed his own company with Kelly at the center for a tour of the Midwest after Kelly ended his engagement with Jack's Lilly Clay Co. The William Jerome Vaudeville Club began its run in Chicago on April 10 at the People's Theatre, ending on the 15th before moving to St. Louis to the Standard Theatre from the 16th through the 22nd. The tour continued on to Louisville and Indianapolis before reaching Cincinnati for a run from May 7 through 13 at the People's Theatre. Throughout the tour, Kelly was in negotiations to join the New York National League club for the 1893 season, which had already begun. After receiving a silk umbrella and a gold-headed cane from admirers after one show at the People's Theatre, Kelly said, "I began my ball playing in Cincinnati, and I think I'll wind up my acting right here."[99] While the rest of the company continued on to Columbus and Detroit to finish out what was originally intended to be a ten-week schedule, Kelly appeared in his first game with the New York Giants on May 25.

Unlike his previous ventures in Hoyt's plays that has each been written well before Kelly became involved, the vaudeville act could be tailored specifically to him. Thus, it is no surprise that his act capitalized on the quick wit that crowds had seen him display on the ballfield. In addition to comic banter between the two partners, Kelly's act with Jerome featured several comic songs, including one called "Papa Wouldn't Buy Me a Bow Wow," and a duet that had them shaking hands at the end of every line, with Kelly exasperatedly asking, "Now will you be good?" After reciting "Casey at the Bat," Kelly would sing a short comic verse about being forced to continue to play in the Bowery if New York did not want him and if Boston refused to pay him his salary. In an interview with the *Chicago Record*, Kelly and Jerome discussed how Kelly could make more money on the stage since Boston would not pay him his demand of $3,000 for the year. Jerome was quoted as saying, "You see, 'Kell' has been drawing the biggest salary of 'em all and he can't afford to accept a cut like that. When he once accepts a cut he will never get up again." At the time, Kelly was earning about $150 a week with the Jerome Vaudeville

Club.[100] Clearly, the persona he displayed did not venture far from the theme of wealth and success that had by now become synonymous with his name. His image now also incorporated his financial successes from the publicity surrounding his appearances in Hoyt's plays.

Recitations of "Casey at the Bat" had become a staple of Kelly's performing career when he resumed stage work in early 1893. Ernest Lawrence Thayer's poem, which was subtitled "A Ballad of the Republic, Sung in the Year 1888," had first been printed in the *San Francisco Examiner* on June 3, 1888. The poem became popular after actor DeWolf Hopper, a big baseball fan, had it given to him to recite as a between-act entertainment at a performance of *Prince Methusalem* in front of mostly baseball players and fans at Wallack's Theater in New York in May 1889. Hopper would integrate the poem into his repertoire in 1892 and could perform it on command.[101]

The popularity of the poem sparked a controversy over who might have been the real author—as several people had stepped forward to claim credit— as well as who the true subject of the poem was supposed to be. Several theories were offered for the real-life inspiration for the fictional slugger, ranging from a player named John Cahill, who was playing in the California League during 1888, to a left-handed pitcher named Dan Casey, who played in the National League during that time.[102] In July 1888, a month after the poem's release, *The Sporting Times* published the last eight verses of the original poem in New York, substituting Kelly for Casey. Shortly after its publication in the East, a story arose that Mike Kelly had written the poem, citing his recent publication of *Play Ball* and the supposed influence of Boston's cultured atmosphere inspiring a newfound love of poetry. Fond of a good story, however preposterous, Kelly did nothing to dismiss these rumors and perpetuated the idea that the poem was at least based on him.[103] Like that of the poem's title character, Kelly was a recognizably Irish name. He was flamboyant and dramatic, perceived to be the best player on many of his teams, and likely would have represented the best chance to win the game in the poem's climactic situation. The interaction with and admiration from the crowds that mark Casey's demeanor had already become part of the real ballplayer Kelly's image.

Kelly delivered the poem in January 1893 after his performance in blackface in "Winning Cards" and continued to use it over his next two years of performing in various vaudeville venues. Not a trained actor like Hopper, Kelly's delivery of the poem apparently ranged wildly. One review derided his "sing-song, school-boy" recitation,[104] while another noted his soft voice, nervous manner, and unorthodox gestures, describing his delivery of the moment of Casey quieting the crowd "as though it were a poem on the death of a child."[105] One article reflecting on Kelly's entire career well after his death noted that reviews for his performances featured "a lot less applause when he finished than when he entered."[106] His recitations consistently drew unfavorable comparisons to the much more experienced Hopper. At a performance in 1893 in front of several teams (including Kelly's New York team), Kelly was reported to have left "in wild disorder" after Hopper was called on to deliver the poem.[107] The advantage that Kelly's recitation had over Hopper's—and what made it a hit with audiences—was the possibility that the story was autobiographical for him.

For Kelly, whose theatrical career had been marked by treating his success in a comic fashion, the failure of Casey/Kelly at the end of the poem would have served him in the same mold. However, Kelly began reciting the poem after his baseball talents had begun to erode and found himself more frequently acquainted with failure than he ever had been while playing baseball. In the 1893 season, although he was still reserved by the Boston National League team, the team owners were unwilling to meet a salary demand that they felt was no longer equal to his ability, so they loaned him to a New York club. Kelly appeared in only twenty games for the New York Giants in 1893 and was reportedly out of shape the entire season, which likely prevented him from playing in the major leagues again.

Kelly's inability to perform the poem in an acceptably pleasing way added to the perception of decline by allowing the audience to see past the aura and to the physical reality of the moment. Kelly's decline made his physique nearly incompatible with the playing persona from his early career. Unable to take off extra weight during the season, he was slow on the field, and the yearly published sporting guides noted his arm had become steadily weaker throughout the last decade.[108] Fans who had once attended games to see Kelly now saw a body that was incongruous to his aura. The achievements that had been the first element of his budding celebrity were no longer likely, and the only remaining aspect of his celebrity was the distance from social contact with the crowd that performances in vaudeville actually provided. Though he remained witty and verbose, fans no longer had to go to the ballpark to hear him. They could go to a vaudeville house.

Anson later wrote that Kelly's fondness for whiskey allowed money to slip through his fingers like "water slips through the meshes of a fisherman's net."[109] Kelly remained well-dressed and splendidly accessorized, and he was also a frequent gambler at cards, billiards, and horse races. He told the *New York World* in May 1893 that spending much of what you earned was one of the requirements of being a star.[110] He was also noted as donating to every charitable case that asked him.[111] A man who had written Kelly for a loan of $5 to start him along the path to success received $1 as a gift from the ballplayer.[112] As a friend of many theatre people, Kelly had reportedly paid for a stranded troupe to return to New York without promise of repayment after their production disbanded on the road.[113] However, as Kelly lost his association with success, his streams of revenue dried up. It was revealed that he did not actually have an ownership stake in the bar in New York. Instead, he had been paid to let them use his name.[114] Furthermore, he had mortgaged the house that was given to him. In 1893 it was put up for sale for unpaid taxes, and there was $2,000 left on the mortgage at five percent interest.[115]

Kelly liked to be the center of attention, but it is clear that he had trouble being put on the spot while performing. For all his theatrical activity, he maintained a consistent case of stage fright even in front of the friendliest audiences. During the run of *A Tin Soldier*, Kelly remarked that he lost fifteen pounds on opening night and never would have gotten through it at all without another actor feeding him his lines.[116] He believed he was better at singing and dancing than he was at delivering lines and speeches on demand—at least he claimed he was more comfortable doing the former than the latter. [117] Yet before he partnered with Billy Jerome, he had said once that he would gladly rather let champion fighters John L. Sullivan or Jim Corbett hit him with a cleaver than have to sing onstage.[118]

To make money after the 1893 baseball season, Kelly became part of Mark Murphy's farce company performing in *O'Dowd's Neighbors*. He claimed that he was getting $50 per week and twenty-five percent of the gate receipts.[119] It was reported that beginning in the fall of 1894, he would star in a new play to be titled *The Irish Adonis*, about a hero who runs away from home in Ireland to the United States, where he becomes the king of the baseball players and is later found by his father.[120] However, Kelly left the company in April 1894 to manage and captain the Allentown team of the minor Pennsylvania League.

Unable to reach an agreement with any major league team, Kelly's agreement to run a minor league team was similar to being relegated to vaudeville stages after being popular in more prestigious playhouses. The move was seen as a final effort by Kelly to stay in the game of baseball while trying to make some money from his fame.[121] Near the end of his career, he was using his theatrical connections to enhance his on-field image. The way he played the game was always supplemented by the latest gags and popular songs that were given to him by his friends in the theatre, and it became one of the ways in which Kelly could attempt to drum up interest in his team.[122] While playing in a game for Allentown, he traded humorous comments in a running dialogue with an Irish comedian who was in the reporters' box.[123] While on the field, he would occasionally deliver the laugh he had used in *A Rag Baby*. When approaching the plate, he would strike a pose that his character had taken in *O'Dowd's Neighbors*. Throughout the games, he would whistle the tune to "Papa Wouldn't Buy Me a Bow Wow." Even as his playing skills eroded, Kelly remained an attraction because of the show he put on while on the field.

Unlike Anson or the typical ballplayer who took to the stage in the late nineteenth century, Kelly's appeal never depended solely on him being a professional baseball player. The persona Kelly created moved fluidly back and forth from the field to the stage. At the time of his death from pneumonia in November 1894, it was reported that he was preparing to go on the road again for another vaudeville tour. With all of his gimmicks, tricks, and abilities as a showman, he was capable of being both success and failure, an idolized star and an everyday fellow.

Kelly apparently seemed much more comfortable when he felt he was surrounded by friends rather than put on display. He performed "Casey" in barrooms and for his Elks brethren, likely in situations where it was requested but the pressure was much less for him.[124] Performing the poem on command surrounded by his fans and fellow Elks brethren added a further layer to his persona as well. His presence in the pub—a place of recognized comradeship and community—also further subjugated him to the culturally constructed stereotype he enacted. Alongside the working class Irish in the pub, Kelly re-entered the realm of the renowned while simultaneously enacting the conditions that made him a celebrity. These recitations of "Casey at the Bat" were infused with an auratic presence that was now more closely associated with failure than with success, and Kelly's substandard performance of the poem added to this perception by uniting failure and authenticity. It wasn't an actor performing; it was a baseball player. It fused the image and the man.

Kelly serves as a good example of the capricious nature of transferring achieved celebrity based on physicality to another arena where the body is also put on display. As the aura becomes incongruous with the body that it is attached to, humanity begins to eclipse celebrity. As such, Kelly's embodiment of "Casey" was imbued with the auratic amalgam of his images: he was at once the "$10,000 beauty," the admired ballplayer, imaginative and unmatched on the field, while at the same time he was an aging icon and a less-than-talented performer who had been on a theatrical descent from full-length plays to vaudeville and beyond from the moment he began to appear onstage. Present in these smaller rooms, Kelly could be more human than star, and the tale of Casey's failure to hit the ball was delivered by both the legendary image of great hope who was approaching the plate and, simultaneously, by the body that seemed to have just swung and missed for the third time.

Christy Mathewson and the Creation
of a Melodramatic Stage Hero

IN EARLY APRIL 1913, an article in the society section of the *New York Times* reported that Christy Mathewson was going to make his debut as a playwright.[1] The celebrated New York Giants pitcher was collaborating with established playwright and lyricist Rida Johnson Young. Young had accompanied Mathewson and the Giants as they toured through southern states as part of their recent spring training. The article's location in the paper next to the notable marriages and deaths in New York City—rather than in the sports or theatre section—spoke to how this professional baseball player was seen in the city. The respectable mien that Mathewson had accrued from his playing had already been accepted into New York society . . . and it was about to transfer to the stage.

According to the article, the play was going to "dramatize the human interest side of baseball with several exciting incidents from Mathewson's actual experience."[2] Though he never appeared onstage, Mathewson's persona was crucial to the play's fictionalized portrayal of contemporary events. This chapter examines the persona Mathewson built as well as the transfer and utilization of that persona by Mathewson and Young into the melodramatic world of *The Girl and the Pennant*. The elements of Mathewson's persona that were embodied onstage in the character of Copley Reeves reflected traits that many Americans believed constituted the ideal hero—which aligned with the heroes expected in melodrama. The playwrights employed that hero to address the continued negotiations of American middle-class respectability.

Following the work done by Erving Goffman in *The Presentation of Self in Everyday Life* (1959), Orrin E. Klapp conducted a type analysis of popular American social types in *Heroes, Villains, and Fools: The Changing American Character* (1962), with the focus on his titular types. From Klapp's perspective, a person belongs to a particular social type "when his appearance and behavior approximate it so closely that he is widely recognized as an example of it—whether or not he is willing to declare himself as such."[3] In Klapp's estimation, the hero as a social type is recognized by being better than the norm and serves as an ideal to others in the hero's ability to rise above the ordinary. Noting an identifying theme and multiple subcategories that fit the overall type, Klapp distinguishes five categories for heroes. "Winners" are determined by their status as champions or through the defeat of others in competition. "Splendid performers" are recognized by audiences to be exemplary in their field. The third category, "heroes of social acceptability," requires the person to be attractive, well-liked, and embraced or accepted by various groups. "Independent spirits" are identified by standing alone or by their willingness to forge a unique path. The final category of "group servants" is seen through their helping of others, their cooperation, and their self-sacrifice.[4] Mathewson's celebrity in baseball fit well into each of Klapp's five categories due to his baseball accomplishments and the style that created his baseball persona.

When on the field, Mathewson clearly displayed the traits of the first two of Klapp's categories. Through both his team and personal achievements, Mathewson was identified as a "winner." Teammate Larry Doyle famously declared that it was "great to be young and to be a Giant," and during Mathewson's seventeen years with the club, the statement was quite apt. The team finished first in the National League five times and finished second an additional five. The Giants represented the National League in the World Series against the American League champions four times, including three consecutive years in 1911, 1912, and 1913, and they were champions in 1905.[5] Mathewson was widely acknowledged as the team's best player. He was the team's most recognizable player as well, standing six feet and one inch tall and appearing to rise even taller above his peers when on the pitching mound. The team's success made them a popular attraction in the city. Their games at home were seen as events in the largest existing market in professional baseball, and they consistently attracted notable names and faces from the local political, business, and entertainment worlds, such as George M. Cohan, Will Rogers, and Lillian Russell.[6]

Beyond New York, Mathewson had been recognized nationally as a star on the field since his performance in the 1905 World Series. In that series versus the American League Champion Philadelphia Athletics, Mathewson won three of the Giants' four victories, with each one being a complete game shutout. During the regular season that year, Mathewson led the National League for the first time in both wins and Earned Run Average. Before the end of his career in 1916, he would lead the league in wins four times and finish second another five times. He was first in the league in both ERA and strikeouts five times apiece. When he retired from playing, Mathewson's statistical achievements placed him second in baseball history in wins and third in strikeouts.[7]

Amber Roessner identified the 1905 World Series as the beginning of Mathewson's widespread glorification by the press as sportswriters began the process of describing him as a saint and savior. From that point forward, Mathewson's name regularly appeared in newspapers across the country. This process of hero-crafting by sportswriters allowed for some exaggeration to fit the narrative they offered to readers because it illustrated greater cultural truths.[8] While statistics offered a quantifiable measure of Mathewson's achievements, the writers provided a larger, emotional context to help shape the public's perception.

Mathewson earned a reputation as a "splendid performer" in part because of how well he played in high-pressure situations. On the field, Mathewson was atypical for a pitcher at the time because he changed his pitching approach depending on the situation. Most pitchers, particularly young ones, put their maximum effort into each pitch, generally becoming less effective through the course of the game as they physically wore down. Mathewson, however, would conserve energy by reducing the effort on pitches in situations where the team was ahead and where a hit or even a single run would not necessarily jeopardize the outcome of the game. In his 1912 book on what it was like to be a pitcher in the major leagues, *Pitching in a Pinch*, he explained that the pitcher must remember that he has eight other men in the field who can help him to record an out. While exhaustion was one reason why a pitcher should not continually put forth maximum effort, Mathewson believed that the act of deceiving the batter by keeping more effective pitches in reserve was even more important.[9] By doing so, he felt he had a better chance for victory in situations where the game was on the line. For Mathewson, success in these situations where the team was "in a pinch" was the point of separation between being a "Big Leaguer" and not. In those moments, the pitcher "must have something besides curves then. He needs a head, and he has to use it."[10] While the rest of the book's chapter gives examples of instances when such a strategy both worked and failed, the explanation of how Mathewson was able to consistently find success shows that his status as a "splendid performer" was not attained by chance.

Mathewson was both attractive and universally well-liked, as "heroes of social acceptability" should be. At a time when people in baseball did not often fraternize with players from another team, let alone players from the rival league, Mathewson was liked and respected by nearly everyone in baseball. Even Ty Cobb (the subject of chapter four), the notorious American League player who rarely even got along with his own teammates, considered Mathewson to be a friend. In the forming of a new players association called the Fraternity of Baseball Players of America, the Giants pitcher was offered the position of president. Though he declined the presidency, he did agree to serve as a vice president alongside Cobb.[11]

When combined with his prominence in New York and throughout baseball, these qualities of attractiveness and likability made businesses and corporations seek Mathewson out to endorse their products. The items he chose to endorse and the way he recommended them contributed to the image of him as a wholesome and decent man. Beginning in 1910, his name appeared as author of a series of books for boys which were ghostwritten by other authors. The young protagonists of these books were all made in Mathewson's image in that they were upstanding and industrious young men who were courteous, polite, and above all, went about their lives and their playing the right way, with sportsmanship and respect. Mathewson's endorsement of a safety razor was contingent on having tried it before deciding. He also appeared in advertisements for cigarettes, believing they had done him no harm, but he expressed reservations that there might be a danger to young people who smoked to excess. Because of the negative connotations associated with alcohol, he steadfastly refused to lend his name to a bar on Broadway despite considerable financial return.[12] Even after his playing career ended, Mathewson's name and nickname, "Big Six," were used on an indoor baseball game that promised "all the thrills of the diamond." Acknowledging his appeal to the general public, Piroxloid Products Corporation placed an advertisement in *Playthings* magazine promoting the game to potential retailers, asserting that "Matty's name on this game means profit to you" because fans associated his name with quality.[13]

Strengthening Mathewson's endorsements and furthering his social acceptability in early twentieth-century America was the public manner in which he followed his conscience—particularly in religious terms. Upon entering professional baseball, Mathewson reportedly promised his mother that he would not play on Sunday. Biographer Michael Hartley traces Mathewson's religious devotion, which grounded much of his behavior, back to his mother, Minerva. Raised in a Baptist family, Mathewson attended the Baptist preparatory school Keystone Academy in Factoryville, Pennsylvania, which had been built on land purchased from his maternal grandfather. Christianity remained a big part of his life as an adult, even as part of the marriage agreement between him and his future wife, Jane Stoughton, in which she agreed to become a Republican, like her future husband, if he agreed to become a Presbyterian.[14] Large segments of the Christian community embraced Mathewson regardless of their Protestant denomination.

Standing firmly with Mathewson on the issue of refusing to play baseball on Sunday was evangelist preacher Billy Sunday, who had been a professional baseball player alongside Cap Anson and Mike Kelly in Chicago during the 1880s. While other evangelists denigrated baseball as an unworthy pursuit, Sunday promoted the game as an illustration of the American character, and he championed Mathewson as the prime example of the game's wholesomeness. Other Christian worshippers viewed the Giants pitcher similarly. Just before the beginning of the 1911 World Series, a service was held at the Grace Methodist Episcopal Church in New York with some of the Giants players present. Though Mathewson was not in attendance, the mention of his name caused such a cheer by the congregation that the Reverend C. F. Reisner had to remind everyone that they were in a house of worship rather than a ballpark.[15]

Mathewson's absence from the playing field on Sundays was widely conspicuous. Giants' owner Andrew Freedman was legally prohibited from having his team play at home on Sundays but, spurred by the profit to be had, did so on occasion. Mathewson was not expected by his owner to play in those games.[16] Other teams frequently took advantage of the situation when hosting the Giants, particularly in cities where no Sunday blue laws existed, and scheduled doubleheaders with the knowledge that they had a better chance to win if they were safe from facing Mathewson on the pitching mound.[17] This public display of his piety, framing his actions in a religious context—particularly against the "win at all costs" ethic seen throughout professional baseball—helped to reinforce Mathewson's middle-class respectability nationwide.

Few popular figures of the time were accepted by both the baseball community and the religious community as Mathewson was. Making his wholesomeness even more prominent was the juxtaposition with his manager, John McGraw. A man of little formal education, McGraw held baseball as the center of his life. He had been a player for St. Louis and Baltimore in the late 1890s and early 1900s and had gained a reputation for his rough, fiery style of play that began to characterize the upstart American League. He brought that same spirit to the National League when he was hired to manage the Giants beginning in the 1902 season. McGraw demanded strict discipline for his players as he directed them in what to do in every baseball situation as though they were automatons. Stiff fines were levied against players who did not comply with his commands. He argued vociferously with umpires and, like he had done with other players during his playing career, would intentionally put his spikes through the tops of an umpire's shoes when he was particularly displeased.[18] Off the field, the behavior of McGraw, who was the public face of the Giants, personified the perception of the typical baseball player. He could frequently be found at racetracks and pool halls in the company of gamblers like Arnold Rothstein, who was eventually part of the 1919 conspiracy to fix the World Series.[19] McGraw and Mathewson were great friends, however, despite their differences, and the constant presence of one made the other's behavior stand in sharp relief. At the beginning of their careers with the Giants, they and their wives shared a seven-room apartment in a very respectable section of New York near Central Park beginning in 1903.[20] It is likely that without the Mathewsons, the McGraws would not have been welcome in such a respectable neighborhood.

Part of what made Mathewson so widely acceptable as a baseball player was what also categorized him as an "independent spirit": his college background. The idea of college men playing baseball professionally was often seen to be incongruous, at least socially. College attendees were meant to be educated, well-bred, and refined, while ballplayers were typically believed to be well short of those virtues. At the turn of the century, many hotels and restaurants separated ballplayers from the rest of the more respectable clientele, and others refused service to ballplayers altogether.[21] Mathewson was able to show that the idea of collegiate respectability could be maintained even as a professional athlete.

While the number of players with a high school education more than doubled between 1900 and 1914, Mathewson biographer Philip Seib reports that only twenty-two percent of professionals playing between 1900 and 1910 had attended college, and the number rises only slightly for the following decade.[22] However, college ballplayers were often sought out by teams for various reasons. As was the case with Mathewson, more fans were willing to come watch them play since they brought perceived respectability to the club. The college ballplayer also brought value to the playing side of the roster. Two of the most successful managers of the time, Philadelphia's Connie Mack and the Giants' McGraw, both believed that if physical ability and temperament were equal, college players had an advantage over other players because of their ability to think through situations.

At the heart of Mathewson's likability and acceptance was the general integrity he possessed, befitting the idea of the intelligent and honorable college man. This was one of the primary aspects of his baseball persona. On the field, Mathewson was believed to be completely honest and above reproach, even to the detriment of his own team. When a single umpire worked the game and could not get a clear look at a particular play, Mathewson was occasionally consulted for help on a decision.[23] One story maintains that upon sliding into home plate, Mathewson had stirred up enough dust obscuring everyone's view that the umpire waited until Mathewson volunteered that he was out before making the call official.[24]

Mathewson's honesty also played a role in one of the most notorious mistakes in baseball history, committed in September 1908. Running from first base, Giants player Fred Merkle failed to touch second base in the bottom of the ninth after the presumed winning hit had been made. Upon Chicago's appeal, Merkle was called out and the game was declared a tie due to darkness. A win in the game would have given the Giants the pennant outright. Instead the team had to play a tie-breaker game for the right to go on to face the American League's Detroit Tigers in the World Series. At the conclusion of the season, just before the additional game was played, the league's board of directors considered whether the tie game should have counted in the Giants' favor, and they sought affidavits from the players involved in the game. They made their decision based on Mathewson's affidavit, given voluntarily, who saw from the first base coaching position that Merkle had not touched second. As George Dovey, one of the directors, declared, "We took all the other affidavits and threw them out. Matty's word was good enough for us." Dovey also pointed out that Mathewson's honesty cost him the significant amount of money he would have made from playing in that year's World Series, as the Giants ended up losing the additional game to Chicago.[25]

Befitting the image of a well-rounded college man, Mathewson displayed interests outside of baseball. Like several other players during the era, he wrote pieces for newspapers periodically in which he gave advice for youngsters on how to play the game correctly or explained current events or big games in baseball. For most players, the articles would include input from the player but be ghostwritten by a sportswriter with whom the player was friendly. During his career, Mathewson followed this pattern, but after his retirement he informed his ghostwriter, John N. "Jack" Wheeler, that he would be doing his own writing going forward.[26] His 1912 book, *Pitching in a Pinch*, was another collaboration with Wheeler, and Wheeler's foreword to the book emphasizes the uniqueness of Mathewson's education, asserting that "as a college man, [Mathewson] is able to put his impressions of the Big Leagues on paper graphically."[27]

Though nearly all of his course grades were in the 90s, Mathewson left Bucknell University after his junior year and never actually completed his degree.[28] Later in his life, in a brief autobiographical piece titled "How I Became a Big League Pitcher," Mathewson advised all young players not to follow his path but to finish college first before entering professional baseball.[29] Still, Mathewson's attendance at college became permanently linked to his persona, and he stood as the most positive representation of how respectable college-educated men could make baseball.

Even Mathewson's offseason work was unusual in how it aligned with middle-class respectability. While other players often had jobs that were more strenuous physically than mentally, usually involving manual labor in their hometowns, Mathewson was known to work as an insurance agent in New York.[30] A flipbook produced by the James Perry Agency showing Mathewson's delivery declared him to be a "Premier Pitcher of the World and Special Agent of the Prudential Insurance Company of America."[31] Upon seeing Mathewson in his office, author Homer Croy wrote that "it is hard to remember he is a baseball player" and that Mathewson was impressive as a businessman and a gentleman.[32] Mathewson served as more than just window dressing as he was quite active in the business. Before the 1913 season, under the letterhead of "Christy Mathewson, Insurance," he suggested an insurance plan for Cincinnati Reds owner August Herrmann which would reimburse him up to $10,000 for each of his players if they should die, and he did not need their signatures for the policy to be valid. Mathewson specified that there was no limit of liability, and should the special locomotive car carrying the twenty-five insured men derail and everyone be killed, Herrmann could recoup $250,000.[33] The public at large began to trust Mathewson as a businessman over the course of his career. During the beginning of the First World War, when the American stock exchange was closed to avert panic, newspapers printed Mathewson's assertion that he was going to continue with his market investments and intended to buy as soon as the exchange reopened; it was cited as something that helped to assuage public fears about the economy.[34]

While there may be the expectation that a professional ballplayer would be a "group servant" to his team while on the field, Mathewson exhibited an amount of self-sacrifice that was remarked upon by his teammates. A significant portion of Mathewson's success as a pitcher came from his use of a pitch he called the "fadeaway." The pitch quickly became associated only with Mathewson throughout baseball, and young players would send letters asking him how to throw it. Thrown by a right-handed pitcher, the fadeaway traveled toward the plate like the mirror image of a typical curveball. Instead of the ball moving away from a right-handed batter as it approached, the ball would move in toward the batter. For left-handed batters, the pitch would move away from them. The pitch put unusual stress on the thrower's arm, however. The typical delivery of a pitch ended with the palm faced toward the body (in the case of a curveball) or toward the ground (in the case of a fastball). The fadeaway acquired its reverse action as a result of the palm of the hand being turned away from the body and finishing facing toward the sky on release of the ball. Mathewson claimed that to throw it was "killing on the arm." The delivery of the pitch, which later came to be known as a "screwball," was reported to have permanently altered famed 1930s pitcher Carl Hubbell's arm to hanging from his side with the palm facing away from the body.[35] Because of the pain associated with it, as well as its effectiveness, Mathewson would save the pitch until he was "in a pinch" and needed it for a potentially game-deciding situation. Teammates like Red Murray knew about the discomfort Mathewson felt in throwing the pitch but also knew that Mathewson would use it if he felt it was needed. His teammates would know when he was throwing it because left-handed batters would jump out of the way since the pitch looked like it was coming straight for them when it was being thrown in the strike zone.[36] Mathewson's persistence in throwing the pitch throughout his career was based on his desire to continue to help his team despite whatever pain he experienced. Doing so earned the pitcher a respect and devotion that was unparalleled on the team.

More public, however, were Mathewson's instances of forgiveness of teammates who had made mistakes in crucial games. In these moments, Mathewson prioritized the solidarity of the team over personal feelings or achievements. In the wake of Merkle's mistake of not touching second base in the game against Chicago, Mathewson declared that "it could happen to anyone" rather than join the chorus of blame toward his teammate. A similar situation occurred in the deciding game of the 1912 World Series against the Boston Red Sox. With Mathewson on the mound, Giants outfielder Fred Snodgrass dropped a fly ball that ultimately led to the loss of the game, the series, and nearly $1,500 apiece for each Giants player. In the clubhouse after the game, Mathewson put his arm around the outfielder and assured him that "any man is likely to make an error." On the train back to New York, a similar refrain was repeated as Mathewson went up and down the aisles trying to console upset teammates, reminding them that they "can't blame a man for a physical error."[37] The Giants already knew about Mathewson's feelings on the occurrence of physical errors in baseball. During June 1901 while the team was in St. Louis, Mathewson was in the eighth inning of what could have been only the third perfect game in the history of baseball when Giants centerfielder George Van Haltren dropped a fly ball for the only error of the game.[38] In between innings, while in the dugout in front of his teammates, Mathewson made a point to go to Van Haltren and pat him on the back reassuringly before going back out to the mound and completing the no-hitter.[39]

Mathewson's appearance and behavior in the eyes of the public marked him as a hero. Roessner argues that Mathewson was presented to fit the lingering Victorian sensibilities among the middle class. He was shown as a moral and clean-living Christian gentleman.[40] Klapp's analysis of types does not require that a person qualify in each category in order to be seen as a hero. Most heroes would show qualities in one or two of these categories. Mathewson, however, could be solidly identified in all five categories. The purpose of a society creating heroes and the other social types is a functional one. They create a sense of community through different methods. Heroes like Mathewson are praised and followed and can be used as models of appropriate behavior since they are better than the norm.[41] According to Klapp, among the major services social types perform for a community is an assistance with professionalization. A hero in this position can serve as a person to be emulated with regard to work performance as well as in the role of instilling pride in the workers of the profession.[42] When faced with new or unusual circumstances, a hero can provide a model for the right course of action.

In baseball at the beginning of the second decade of the twentieth century, the influence of gambling and other shady dealings among its participants had become increasingly more of a concern since it threatened the sport's burgeoning respectability and increased acceptance among the American middle class. LeRoy Ashby noted that baseball's attendance had doubled between 1903 and 1909, and the influence of the middle class was visible throughout the ballpark.[43] Perhaps most conspicuous was the increase in the number of women attending the ballgames as compared to the era of Anson and Kelly. The changing role of women in American society posed a dilemma to the baseball establishment. How could baseball profit economically and socially from women's interest in the game but also keep them from having too much influence on the profession? Using his heroic persona as the basis for the main character in *The Girl and the Pennant*, Mathewson's play set forth a model illustrating how baseball could deal with these pressing issues.

In contrast to Anson and the typical use of the stage by professional ball-players, Mathewson did not physically portray the role that utilized his persona. As in Anson's case, the player's inability to act well or otherwise conform to an aesthetically pleasing portrayal onstage reinforced the reality of the player's status as a ballplayer rather than an actor. By not having Mathewson physically embody the role and allowing a trained actor to portray the character, the audience's focus was redirected away from the physical presence of the actor and back toward the content of the performance, as was more typical of theatrical pieces. In this way, Mathewson's physical absence allowed the auratic presence of his persona onstage to better reflect the content of the play. The play's association with Mathewson would remain quite apparent to those watching.

As *The Girl and the Pennant* opens, the various members of the Eagles professional baseball team are gathered at their Sligo, Texas, spring training site preparing for a season in which they and the Hornets are expected to battle for the league championship pennant. Among the players in attendance are Skeets Marvin, a third baseman who fancies himself a comedian; Pitman, an older left-handed pitcher who is at the end of his career; Chief Wayne, a Native American catcher; and the two Reeves brothers, Punch and Copley. Punch is the twenty-five-year-old left-handed pitching star of the team, while his older brother, Copley, who was a star in college at Yale, mostly sits on the bench and is charged with trying to keep his brother away from the alcohol that has been affecting his performance. A stipulation in their deceased father's will prevents Punch from receiving his share of the sizable inheritance until he goes six full months without Copley seeing him inebriated.

The new Eagles owner, Miss Mona Fitzgerald, has just inherited the team from her father. She has requested that her father's favorite player, Pitman, remain on the team. As word arrives that Miss Fitzgerald will be visiting the field, the news upsets manager John Bohannan because he had expected her to sell the team to an investor who was going to give him (Bohannan) half ownership of the franchise. Bohannan, put in financial debt after his wife ran off with another man, conspires with the rival Hornets owner Henry Welland to help the Hornets beat out the Eagles for the pennant. Meanwhile, before the end of the first act, Miss Fitzgerald—despite several suggestions that she should rethink the decision—reaffirms her trust in Bohannan as manager because her father had been able to trust him.

Listed among the names of the supernumerary baseball players in the cast of characters are Fred Terkle, Hans Flagner, and Cy Dobb. These burlesques of the names of several well-known contemporary players give the first tangible clue that astute viewers should try to identify the other elements of the actual profession in the premise of the play. Player drunkenness was perceived as a fairly common problem of the day, and rumors were whispered of occasional dishonesty among players. Neither of these required a specific case to be recognized as a problem. However, the presence of women in professional baseball was a unique situation. Two and a half years before the play's debut, the first woman had gained control of a major league baseball team as Helene Hathaway Robison Britton assumed full ownership of the St. Louis Cardinals on the passing of her uncle, M. Stanley Robison, in March 1911. This unusual situation became more prominent in the newspaper due to the events that occurred over the next few years before the play's debut in 1913.

Britton's father, Frank De Hass Robison, had owned the Cleveland Spiders with his brother before acquiring the Cardinals and bequeathing the team to Stanley's control in September 1908.[44] Once ownership passed to Britton, the other owners in the National League expected her to sell quickly. She, however, refused initial purchase offers in April 1911 from Chicago businessman Charles Weeghman, since he wanted only ownership of the franchise and its players and not the ballpark or anything that tied the club to the city of St. Louis.[45] Holding on to the team, she ceded the presidency of the club during that month to an executor of her uncle's will, E. A. Steininger. Shortly thereafter, her own lawyer, James C. Jones, became president, and she held a vice president position until her husband, Schuyler Britton, assumed the club's presidency in January 1913. Upon their divorce in February 1917, Helene Britton became the first female president of a major league club. Despite not occupying the top executive position in the six years between gaining ownership and becoming president, she was very active in the club's management throughout this period. She gained a temporary restraining order in April 1912 against Steininger shortly before his dismissal that June when he tried to replace the Cardinals' secretary with someone more favorable to him. The suit brought by Britton and her mother against Steininger stated that she did not believe he was voting their 995 shares in their best interest.[46]

During her first season in control, Britton deferred on the field to manager Roger Bresnahan, whom her uncle had brought in and had respected greatly. Bresnahan, a former catcher for the New York Giants and teammate of Mathewson, had been acquired by the Cardinals in December 1908 for a steep price and was installed as a playing manager. Under his leadership, the Cardinals had improved modestly from their previous season in both 1909 and 1910. Bresnahan justified Britton's continued belief in him during 1911 by guiding the team to its first winning season since 1901. Following the season, Bresnahan accepted a five-year contract for $10,000 per year and ten percent of the club's profits for the duration. In June 1912, Britton declared that Bresnahan had complete control over all on-field decisions. Bresnahan was noted for his fiery personality and style of play similar to his previous manager in New York, John McGraw, and Britton asserted that Bresnahan was at his best when he was fighting.[47]

The partnership between the two was precarious, however. During the 1912 season, after a loss to Chicago, Bresnahan and Britton had differing opinions over some of the decisions in the game. Bresnahan declared afterward that "no woman is going to tell me how to run a ball game!" and the two reportedly did not speak again during the season. A public glimpse of acrimony between them came in August when reporters revealed that Britton was responsible for blocking a trade advocated by Bresnahan that would have sent Miller Huggins to Cincinnati, where he would have become their manager. Framing her veto of the deal in economic terms, Britton believed that if Cincinnati wanted Huggins as a manager, they should pay to acquire a manager instead of only a ballplayer, as the Cardinals had when acquiring Bresnahan. Complicating the relationship further was the fact that Bresnahan was involved in a local business group that had proposed an offer to buy the club from Britton with the intention of installing Bresnahan as president.[48]

The 1912 team failed to live up to competitive expectations, finishing sixth out of eight National League teams and once again with a losing record. The regression of the team brought about questions of whether Bresnahan was actively trying to alter the pennant race between Chicago and his former club, the Giants, by not playing his best players in key series.[49]

In what seemed at the time to be a bizarre move, the Cardinals released their player/manager at the end of the 1912 season, placing him on waivers, while remaining publicly adamant that they would not seek to improve their club through his trade or sale, nor would they bring him back under any conditions. Here again, club economics were presented as the driving point since not only had Ivy Wingo replaced Bresnahan as the club's primary catcher, but the aforementioned Huggins could replace Bresnahan as manager, providing a net savings of $4,000.[50] Britton refused to go into the details of the dismissal publicly. However, she was quoted in *The Sporting Life* during November as saying she "had placed confidence in Mr. Bresnahan for a time, but his actions forced me to get a man in his place."[51] That same month, *The New York Times* reported that she had told him before his dismissal that she believed that he had not "tried hard" during the past year.[52] Bresnahan, only one year into his new five-year contract, demanded his remaining $40,000 rather than the $2,500 buyout offered by club president Jones. The ordeal was reported in newspapers nationwide for a few months until an agreement was reached in early January 1913 that gave Bresnahan half of the money he was seeking and allowed him to become a free agent.[53]

These events occurred during the offseason before *The Girl and the Pennant* was announced and were likely fresh on the minds of the playwrights. Audience members who would have understood the parodied names of real-life players Fred Merkle, Honus "Hans" Wagner, and Ty Cobb in the cast list also would have recognized Miss Mona Fitzgerald as a version of Helene Hathaway Britton, and her nefarious manager, John Bohannon, as Roger Bresnahan. For those who might still have been unaware, the connection is made more explicit during the first act when Fitzgerald and her friends first meet the ballplayers shortly after Bohannan's conspiracy with Welland is divulged to the audience. Fitzgerald's coquettish friend, Alice Tilford, greets the Eagles manager with "how do you do, Mr. Bresnahan?"[54] Bohannan immediately corrects her on his proper name, but that does not prevent Alice from repeating the mistake again in the second act.

Other ballplayer characters also seem to have real-life counterparts who had played on the Giants team with Mathewson. The shared position between

Giants catcher John "Chief" Meyers and Eagles catcher Chief Wayne implies an equivalence between the two, even as most Native American ballplayers during the era were laden with the nickname "Chief" whether they liked it or not. The jocularity of the Skeets Marvin character as well as his position on the field suggest former third baseman and occasional vaudeville performer Arlie Latham, who, despite having a career mostly in the 1880s and 1890s, played a couple of games with the Giants in 1909 at age forty-nine. Pitman, the old left-handed pitcher, can similarly be linked to left-hander Hooks Wiltse, who had been the oldest player on the Giants teams during both the 1911 and 1912 seasons. The younger left-handed pitcher in the play, Punch Reeves, shared not only an age and position similarity with Giants pitcher Richard "Rube" Marquard, but also a reputation for enjoying the nightlife of New York City to the point that it would affect his performance on the field.[55]

Audience members looking for an onstage representation of Mathewson needed go no further than Copley Reeves. Though he was neither a pitcher nor a star on the Eagles team, Copley did share several of the markers of Mathewson's baseball persona. The audience learns that Copley, like Mathewson, had gone to college and has had ample success in the business world. His personal sacrifice for the sake of his brother becomes apparent in the first act as he deftly defers his own romantic feelings for Miss Fitzgerald so that Punch can court her.[56] Overall, Copley is shown to be a hard-working, respectable man and a paragon of virtue and fair play in baseball—qualities that might have been recognizable as a version of Mathewson even if his name had not appeared as a co-author of the play.

Under the definition given in David Grimsted's study of the melodramatic form, *Melodrama Unveiled*, Copley fits the mold of the melodramatic hero who is "simply perfect." The typical melodramatic hero was pious and virtuous, sentimental and faithful, and would often function as the force for redemption in the play. Though he might have faults that were addressed through the course of the action, the melodramatic hero was representative of what was supposed to be good in the world.[57] When the melodramatic hero was based on a historical person, the character could be easily shaped by the playwright to address the notable faults, or they could be ignored completely with little notice by an audience. The task was more difficult in a play featuring a melodramatic hero based on a contemporaneously living person whose faults—whatever they were perceived to be—might strain the credibility of the necessary perfection of the melodramatic hero. Mathewson, or his heroic persona, could be an appropriate melodramatic hero because, as his qualification in all five of Klapp's categories shows, he could be widely appreciated in a heroic manner. His persona was already perceived to be as perfect as a melodramatic hero needed to be. Further, by not having Mathewson himself play the role, the illusion wasn't broken by any lack of acting ability.

The many allusions to recognizable players helped to establish a connection to the real world of professional baseball while maintaining a detachment of fantasy. In spite of the apparent frivolity of the script, it did address concerns that were central to both ballplayers and men in general. Copley, as the melodramatic hero and onstage proxy for Mathewson's persona, could deal with the fears held by professional baseball. Though they seemed overwhelming in the real world, the concerns regarding cheating and manipulation of the game as well as the encroachment of women into the organized structure of baseball could be manageable in the fantasy world of the play.

The play uses the star pitcher and Copley's younger brother, Punch, to examine one of baseball's ills. Ballplayers had a reputation for debauchery. The behavior was not confined only to just drinking; it frequently involved socially illicit connection with the opposite sex. The problem was often softened for the public by newspaper writers who would write off such behavior as an expression of the players' boyishness. Both role players and star players alike were noted for their dalliances and their carousing, which would, on occasion, affect their performances on the field.[58] In the world of the play, Punch Reeves exhibits these tendencies.[59]

Punch's drinking is a known secret throughout the game of baseball, though the players are unaware of the stipulation in his father's will. Welland relies upon Punch's reputation to help him secure the pennant for the Hornets over the Eagles. With Punch's drinking leading him down a morally troubling path, he is lured to go out on the night before he is set to pitch the deciding game for the pennant. Welland arranges a meeting between Punch and a chorus girl of whom Punch is fond. The chorus girl is to invite him out for the evening with the intention of getting him so intoxicated that he would be unable to face the Hornets the next day. Concerned about Punch—as well as their chances in the game—several teammates scour the city looking for him when he had not returned to the Reeves' shared apartment by late the next morning.

As the players tell Copley that they have found his brother, he makes them wait until he has left the room before they bring him in. Once Punch is deposited in his own room, Copley leaves for the game, locking Punch in the apartment as he goes to prevent Punch from arriving at the ballpark in a stupor. Copley asserts that the public must be led to think that Punch's absence is due to an injury or that he has gotten into a fight with Bohannan. The private matter is made public after the game when Welland feeds the story of Punch's confinement to the newspapers. In defending himself to his brother, Copley explains that locking him in kept him out of sight, and since he didn't see Punch drunk, they will divide their father's estate in one week when Punch has put in his full six months. In detailing his own battles with temptation and his following Punch around for the last two years, Copley invokes the sense of family as a guiding force that has kept him both sober and devoted. Punch leaves with a renewed effort to change his boyish ways and to become "a man" like his brother.

Though in a fantasy world, the play alludes to the misbehavior of players as more than just a degradation of social conduct but as being financially irresponsible as well. Faced with fines and scandal because of their actions, players wishing to remain in professional baseball are given a model to follow. By emphasizing self-sacrifice and supplication to a larger group (i.e., family) in the afterglow of having won the pennant through his direct efforts, Copley as a melodramatic hero relies on identifiable traits of the "group servant" category of the heroic social type. By showing how this problem could be corrected in this fictional world, the model for correction in the real world is established. The close association between Copley's melodramatic hero and Mathewson's social hero implies that what one can do, the other is capable of doing. These same traits, notable in Mathewson's persona, extended to him the same status as a model of correction for real players who drank.

Beyond just personal respectability, such behavior placed the player in a position where he might be forced into corruption which put the whole structure of professional baseball at risk. Though it was not dealt with on the scale as it was with the Chicago White Sox of the 1919 World Series, the specter of fixed baseball games was prevalent through much of the pre-World War I era.[60] A frequent method of influencing a ball game was through a player "laying down" by not trying his best, whether on the mound, in the field, or at the plate. Given the frequent nature of failure in baseball, such behavior could be hard to prove as intentional. Managers, too, could affect the outcome of a game simply by not playing certain players, as was alleged at Cardinals manager Roger Bresnahan.[61]

This is precisely what Eagles manager Bohannan receives a voucher for $25,000 and a promise for more from Welland to do in *The Girl and the Pennant*. Knowing that the Hornets were weak against left-handed pitching, Bohannan chose to start a younger, more inexperienced left-handed pitcher named McCracken over his star left-hander Punch in the last meeting between the two teams. As a result of his cumulative managerial decisions, the Eagles lost two games to the Hornets. When questioned about it by Copley, Bohannan defends himself by saying he was saving Punch for the tie-breaking game, which, as Copley points out, would likely not have been needed if Punch would have been pitched initially. Bohannan remains at the mercy of Welland throughout the play because the tip to buy into United Realty that he was given proved to be worthless. He is now dependent on Welland's promised World Series money.

Again, Copley acts heroically to save the situation. Suspicious of dishonesty on the part of his manager, Copley confirms his suspicions the day before the game by tricking Welland into acknowledging that he has known Bohannan for years after the manager has said that Welland was the one owner in the league he did not know. During the game, after an umpire had already ejected two Eagles players for yelling from the bench, an offstage argument between Copley and Bohannan gets the manager ejected by the same umpire. Without Bohannan running the game for the Eagles, Copley is able to be put into the game and the Eagles come back to win in the bottom of the ninth inning after being down to their final out. The following day at Miss Fitzgerald's house, Copley confronts Welland with the documents proving his conspiracy with Bohannan. Among the proof is the deed to the land Bohannan bought as well as the endorsed purchasing check made out by Welland, which had never gone through because, as a director of United Realty, Copley has had the check in his personal safe all summer in case proof of this illicit association was needed.

Having essentially freed his dishonest but desperate manager from Welland's debt, Copley offers a deal to the owner before he takes the evidence to the authorities. As Welland reaches for his money, Copley orders him in the language of an economic transaction to leave the house, the town, the game, and the country immediately and to "put it all to the credit of American sport in general."[62] The banishment of Welland from the country echoes an earlier speech in the play by couching willful dishonesty as something un-American. Again relying on indicators of Mathewson's persona, namely his intelligence evident through his high position in the business world and a personal sacrifice that comes financially this time, Copley invokes the larger group of honest Americans to establish his place as a melodramatic hero. The presence of this type of player in baseball shows that the game can rid itself of its dishonest elements by emphasizing the fundamentals of the American character that all players, regardless of ethnicity, should strive to embrace.

While debauchery and corruption were known problems in the baseball world, the advance of women into the territory presented a new and acute menace. The underlying tensions of the play's premise reflect fears that penetrated the era's hegemonic masculine psyche. As Michael S. Kimmel shows in his essay "Baseball and the Reconstitution of American Masculinity, 1880-1920," the concept of masculinity—particularly that of the white middle-class male—was believed to be under duress at the turn of the century due to men's decreasing economic autonomy, the influx of immigrants into cities, and the burgeoning women's movement. Baseball represented a way of reclaiming that lost masculinity. By participating in the game, or even just by watching it, men would realize the values of hard work and fair play and would profit from baseball's unique combination of solo and team play, thus allowing them to recapture a sense of autonomy that had been lost during their indoctrination into the team mindset of new industrialism. If the world was a feminizing space, the baseball field offered an oasis of masculinity that strengthened the body and soul.[63] First treated as a novelty in the newspapers, then as a joke, Helene Britton's presence in baseball at the time developed into a direct threat to the masculinity of the game, one of the last sanctuaries available to the American male psyche.

The play examines part of these fears by suggesting that women in baseball would have a feminizing influence upon the players. The first act presents the introduction of women into the masculine work world of the ballfield. To begin the second act, at the end of the season, the players are placed more firmly within the more cultured and apparently feminine world of high society as they attend a tea party at Miss Fitzgerald's estate. Upon his arrival, Bohannan states that the day's newspapers are ridiculing the team for attending the gathering. This is the latest symptom of a larger affliction. Since the beginning of the year, the stands at the ballpark have been "packed with screeching females." Further, the "disease" has spread to the players as Chief Wayne has taken up playing bridge and Pitman was in the clubhouse practicing the tango. All of this has turned his team into a national joke.[64]

If, Kimmel reasons, baseball crowds are dominated by women, the effect is to emasculate the ballplayers. Yet the feminization of the Eagles has apparently not affected their abilities on the field since the team remains at the top of the standings with the tie-breaking game looming. What does threaten their abilities are the ever-present temptations that women represent. Punch is lured out the night before the game by the chorus girl arranged through Welland. Although, like the screeching female fans, the chorus girl is absent from the stage during the play, she is represented by a violet-perfumed note that is presented to the pitcher while he is at Miss Fitzgerald's gathering. In this way, Punch's lapse—which threatens the pennant, his inheritance, and his potential relationship with Miss Fitzgerald—is never embodied on the stage. Instead, elusive and ethereal, it is a female temptation that is idealized and made more threatening through its absence.

The three women who do appear onstage embody both the nascent and the active fears about the new woman that extend beyond mere titillation. The first woman to appear onstage, the prim and precise forty-year-old Miss Elvira Squibbs, maintains a manner and relationship to Miss Fitzgerald that suggests the typical role of a woman in authority. In the schoolmarm mold, she insists on strict discipline and rigid decorum. She also is an enthusiast of "mental science" or, at the least, the power of positive thought. Squibbs reflects the masculine fears of the independently minded woman who can and has survived without the attachment to a husband or other male figure.

The character of Alice Tilford reflects another fear of the early-twentieth-century male. As a souvenir-seeking coquette, Tilford's frequent exclamations of "I love base-ball" are mocked by the players. However, her acquisition of souvenirs distinguishes her through the course of the play. Tilford's acquisitions are used as comic devices and allude to humiliations and defeats suffered by the ballplayers. Saying it was "so clever of him" to strike out on such a little ball with such a big bat, Tilford asks Chief Wayne to put his initials on the ball that struck him out. By the end of the play, among the things she has taken include a player's mackinaw coat, a catcher's mask, a full uniform taken piecemeal from various players, and one of the team's equipment trunks in which to take all of her souvenirs home. The men eventually accept that what Tilford wants, she will get, and they offer little resistance. Her new possessions frequently are recontextualized in stereotypically feminine terms. Though she says she will tell all the girls that the catcher's mask is "the great John Bohannan's muzzle," she first declares that the mask would be "just lovely filled with ferns."[65] More directly, she notices Copley's collegiate fob in the shape of a baseball mitt. Earned by him for his achievements on the field while at Yale, the item is quickly secured by Tilford. After its capture and having attached it to her own necklace, Tilford rechristens the item by telling the player that she does not like to see men wear "jewelry."[66]

The independent-minded matron represented by Elvira Squibbs and the childish usurper of property, Alice Tilford, serve as separate poles of the conflicting perception of the contemporary new woman. Just as Squibbs shows the feminist desire to develop autonomously, Tilford is presented as an equivalent desire to remain protected and provided for. Additionally, by using her "mental science" all season, Squibbs, like the corrupt interests around the game, has been actively trying to alter the outcomes of games, while Tilford is shown to be as childish as the players who succumb to drinking and temptation. This dichotomy briefly touches upon a tension at the central premise of the play. Believing the matronly Squibbs to be the new owner, the player Skeets exclaims, "owned body and soul and by that!"[67] While the quote expresses the perpetual disquiet between owners and players, the situation presented in the play is now complicated by issues of gender. Until now, the labor concerns of ballplayers had been primarily defined along relatively benign employer-employee lines in times of general agreement and categorized as a master-chattel relationship during periods of unrest. As Tilford later states after Bohannan has temporarily convinced Miss Fitzgerald to sell Copley to the Hornets, "My goodness, she can buy and sell 'em just like slaves, can't she?"[68] The insertion of gender into the mix puts the players in the traditionally feminine role of property—an option not presented as particularly palatable to the ballplayers. Squibbs is presented to be relatively physically unattractive to the ballplayers while Tilford's pleasing looks are offset by her attitude toward accumulating property. The acceptable balance between the two poles represented by these characters is suggested to be in Miss Fitzgerald.

Though she has come to own the team through inheritance rather than through her own personal hard work, Miss Fitzgerald is presented as the right kind of woman to have in baseball. First, she thinks of herself in masculine terms. In her introductory speech to the team, she briefly refers to herself as a boy before rephrasing. Miss Fitzgerald says that since her father didn't have any male heirs, she took the role and had been learning the game since she was very young.[69] Later, she takes Copley's advice to "square her shoulders like a man" to prevent his sale to the Hornets.[70] Described at her first appearance as "very feminine—not the managing type at all," Miss Fitzgerald displays a male mindset that contradicts the appearance of feminine frailty.[71]

Yet, for some in the play, certain traits that are seen to be strengths in men are characterized as feminine weaknesses as Miss Fitzgerald is compared to her father. In her speech, Miss Fitzgerald describes how Old Fitz owned the team as the sport grew around him and as the team moved up from the bottom rungs of the minor leagues to the major leagues where it now stands. His love was not for money but for the game itself and for the players with whom he worked.[72] These were seen as admirable traits in a man, even to Bohannan, who had a very good working relationship with the Eagles owner; however, the manager characterizes the same traits in Mona as symptoms of feminine "sentiment." Upset that Miss Fitzgerald requires that Pitman, who had been with the team and her father since their beginnings, remain on the team, Bohannan bristles that she is passing up an opportunity to make money from selling the team because of this implied feminine sentiment.[73] To try to defend her similarity to her father, Miss Fitzgerald acquiesces to Bohannan's demand at the end of the first act that he remain the boss of the team. In so doing, she places herself under the protection of a more experienced male figure whom she believes has her best interests at heart. After all, her father had told her that she would never have any trouble with Bohannan as the manager. However, the audience is aware that Bohannan has already begun his double-crossing, and the implication is that Miss Fitzgerald's success will come only when the right kind of man is protecting her.

David Grimsted argues that the essential difference between the hero's goodness and the villain's evilness in melodramas was evident in how they treated women who were considered defenseless.[74] Because women were considered to be in constant need of protection, actions taken against them by men who were presumed to be in protective roles were always considered the most heinous. Often heroes were content to remain complacent in a situation until provoked by the possibility of harm coming to a woman. Despite her position of ownership in the play, Miss Fitzgerald remains in a precarious position throughout. The estate left to her by her father consisted of little more than the ball club, which becomes her primary means of support. Bohannan's encouragement for her to sell is done under the guise of assisting her financial state because she's a woman. He explains that if he made mistakes that cost the team money, he would feel bad because he would be putting a woman in jeopardy.[75] Of course, his willingness to continue with his deception following that exchange shows his true character. Given the same information, Copley challenges Bohannan directly in the second act but only because he feels that he must. Copley states that if a man owned the team, he would prefer to let that man fight his own battles, but Copley is not content to "stand by and see a woman double-crossed."[76]

Key to Bohannan's role as a villain toward Miss Fitzgerald is that their encounters leave her feeling as though she's "nothing but a female."[77] The

connotation here is that Bohannan focuses only on the traditional feminin-
ity as weak and powerless. In the second act as he tries to sell Copley to the
Hornets, Bohannan steamrolls Miss Fitzgerald into agreement. As he leaves,
she finds herself again placed within the confines of the traditional female
position, and, as the stage directions note, she "turns mechanically to tea
table and begins serving tea."[78] Once her strength is bolstered by Copley's
advice to present herself as more masculine, she declares that the sale is off
since she is exercising her "woman's prerogative."[79]

Miss Fitzgerald does not solely exist in the play as a defenseless female.
She takes over management of the team during the final inning of the deciding game once Bohannan is thrown out. Asking one of the ejected players to
relay the signals to the bench for her, she chooses to insert Copley as a pinch
hitter. In a display of her baseball acumen, Miss Fitzgerald orders a surprise
double steal with two of the team's slowest runners on base. As the steals and
Copley's hit give the Eagles the win, Miss Fitzgerald's actions are presented
to show that a woman can be a benefit to the game of baseball—provided
it is the right woman. Once again, though, her success is made possible in
large part by Copley's efforts.

Copley's ability to make Miss Fitzgerald break the mold of the defenseless
woman, even temporarily, marks him not only as a melodramatic hero but
also as a model of masculine treatment of the new woman. To convince her
to resist Bohannan's requests that she sell immediately, Copley tries to anger
her into keeping the team by emphasizing the weaknesses and foolishness
inherent in females.[80] His success shows that even independent women are
still able to be manipulated by the right man as long as it is one who has
good and honorable intentions. His willingness to allow her to be in control
exists until the end of the play as the two inevitably become a couple. She
asks if she would have to propose to him. After a brief misunderstanding,
he asserts his control in the relationship by assuring her that he would do
it—though he does ask how he should.

For all the fears that women evoke for the game, the typical light comedy
ending reinforces the place of the man in the world of the early twentieth
century. Elvira Squibbs relinquishes her independence in order to accompany
Pitman to his Kentucky horse farm. Alice Tilford ends up with the ultimate
baseball souvenir—a ballplayer husband. Ending the play with the implied
marriage between Miss Fitzgerald and Copley shows the world set right again.
Copley has removed drinking and debauchery from the clubhouse. He has
expelled a corrupt owner not only from the game but from the country. Most

importantly, he has essentially saved the Eagles both from having to be sold (because of his wealth from his business interests) and also from continued ownership by a single woman. His goal of trying to keep her family name in baseball ironically ends with the promise that Miss Fitzgerald will soon become Mrs. Reeves.

For the content of the play to affect any change in baseball, it would have had to have been seen. For it to have been seen, it would have had to have been a hit. Mathewson had reason to believe that the play could be a hit based on Young's track record. The playwright had had two popular hits with the plays *Brown of Harvard* in 1906 and *The Boys of Company B* in 1907 as well as the 1910 operetta *Naughty Marietta* for which she wrote the libretto.

The play's initial production by the Arch Selwyn & Co. production company did not last very long in New York. A series of delays reportedly brought on because of Mathewson's absence from the theater while he was playing for the Giants in the World Series caused the production to open a week later than originally scheduled. The same newspaper item stated that the play "needed some additional baseball atmosphere."[81] It finally opened at the Lyric Theatre on October 23, 1913—less than two weeks after Mathewson was charged with the loss against the Philadelphia Athletics in the Series' decisive fifth game. Despite his apparent availability, Mathewson did not attend the play's opening night, and it was not reported whether he attended any subsequent performances either.

Several reviews were relatively lukewarm and noted the lackluster performance but seemed optimistic about the long-term chances for the play. The review appearing in the *New York Clipper* purported that the play was destined to be a "great big popular success."[82] The *New Rochelle Pioneer* wrote that the play was "destined to have a long career on Broadway."[83] The *New York Times* review asserted it was an "invigorating entertainment" and found the last act to be particularly well-written.[84] The *New York Herald* suggested that the play might help fans to bridge the long winter before the beginning of the next baseball season.[85] That, however, was not to be the case. Audiences seemed to have agreed more with the review in the *Auburn Citizen* that called the production a "picturesque fiasco," and called Mathewson "wise enough to keep away from the scene of the disaster."[86] One of the production's major failings, according to the *New York Tribune*, was keeping the climactic baseball game offstage and relayed to the audience as though a horse race was being announced. The *Tribune* review summarized what they believed to be the appeal to the "unusually exotic audience" in attendance at the first night as well as who was likely to blame for the production:

> Leaving aside the sporting—if Mr. Mathewson will pardon the word—interest of last evening's event, an interest is always felt wheneve the man of action ventures into the more subjective world, when Colonel Roosevelt discusses futurist art or the Emperor William composes a song—setting this apart, and coming down to the purely artistic merits of the play, one may only surmise, of course, where Mr. Mathewson leaves off and Mrs. Rida Johnson Young begins. It is to be hoped that he doesn't go very far, for Mr. Mathewson is a great and serious athlete, and, from any serious point of view, the piece is very horrible indeed. Almost as, or perhaps even more, terrible than "Brown of Harvard," which Mrs. Young also wrote, and thousands of people appeared to like immediately, as, indeed, they may like this.[87]

Variety reported on November 7, 1913, during the play's second week, that the production had lost an estimated $5,000 between the show's expenses and the disappointing house receipts. It closed in its third week after a total of only twenty performances. The play was briefly revived for a one-week run about two months later in the first week of January 1914. A completely different company featured a new cast to showcase the stock company's new leading man in the Harlem Opera House managed by Benjamin Franklin Keith.[88]

Whatever Mathewson and Young sought to do, it does not appear to have been successful. Financially, the play lost money. Critically, the production received several very negative reviews. Practically, both baseball-related issues the play addressed lingered as Britton eventually acquiesced to leaving ownership of league teams to men and players continued to fix games. By the time the play was published in 1917 with some minor changes, Mathewson's name had been removed as an author for an undetermined reason, and Young considered it her only failure.[89] For Mathewson, it was his last foray into theatre.

The competitive nature of the game guaranteed that baseball would always have star players who topped the statistical leaderboards year after year. What it needed to create were heroes who transcended on-field achievement into larger cultural relevance, and the heroes of melodrama offered a model to follow. Though other players had been admired before him, in Mathewson, all idealized aspects of the American middle-class hero could be found. Like those melodramatic heroes who offered uncomplicated virtue, an understandable and socially acceptable morality, and the promise of a hard-fought and honest attempt at victory, Mathewson provided baseball enough of a template that audiences could affix their own hopes and desires. Assisted by the hero-crafting sportswriters of the time, Mathewson's heroic presence was powerful enough that it operated sufficiently even in his absence. He served as a model of the middle-class gentleman hero against whom all others could be measured. As the needs of society and American culture have changed over time, the particular aspects of the hero have embraced the changes and changed right alongside; the hero as a type, however, remained central to baseball's narratives.

CAP ANSON, CHICAGO WHITE STOCKINGS,
BASEBALL CARD PORTRAIT, 1888.

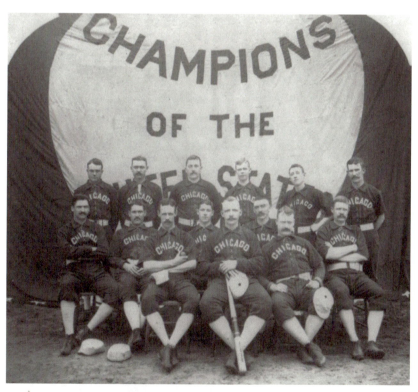

CHICAGO NATIONAL LEAGUE BASEBALL TEAM, 1885–86. ANSON, THE CAPTAIN
AND FIRST BASEMAN, IS SEATED FRONT AND CENTER WITH THE BASEBALL BAT.

CHARLES HALE HOYT,
THE MAN WHO HAS
MADE THE WHOLE
WORLD LAUGH.

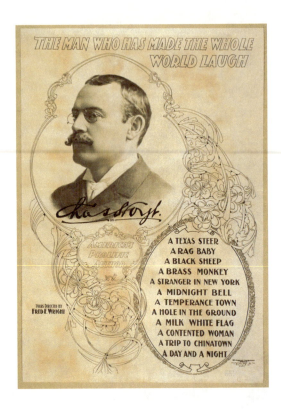

KING KELLY, BOSTON BEANEATERS,
BASEBALL CARD PORTRAIT, 1888.

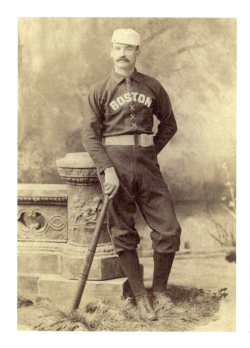

MICHAEL J. "KING" KELLY, FULL-
LENGTH STUDIO PORTRAIT,
STANDING, WEARING A BOSTON
BEANEATER BASEBALL UNIFORM
AND HOLDING A BAT, 1887.

THEATRICAL POSTER FOR HOYT'S *A STRANGER IN NEW YORK*, 1897.

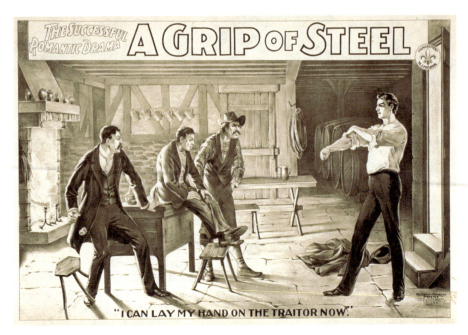

THEATRICAL POSTER FOR *A GRIP OF STEEL*, 1899.

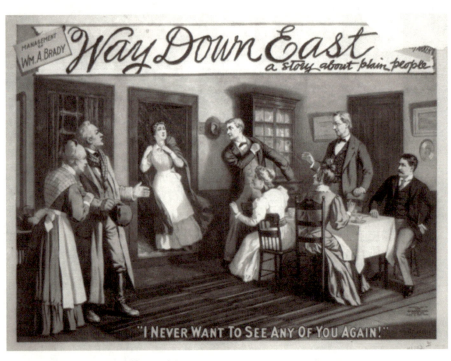

THEATRICAL POSTER FOR *WAY DOWN EAST*, 1897.

HEAD-AND-SHOULDERS PORTRAIT OF CHRISTY MATHEWSON,
PITCHER FOR THE NEW YORK GIANTS, 1910.

CHRISTY MATHEWSON, NEW YORK GIANTS,
BASEBALL CARD PORTRAIT, 1909.

TY COBB AND CHRISTY MATHEWSON IN NEW YORK DURING WORLD SERIES, 1911.

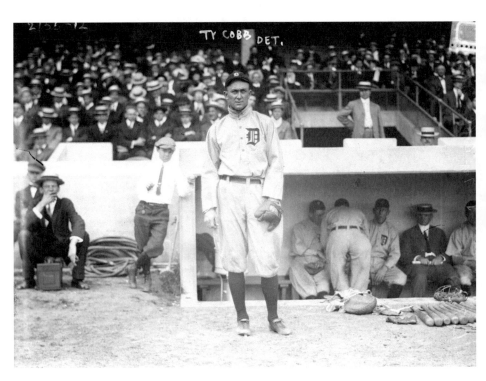

TY COBB, DETROIT, AMERICAN LEAGUE, 1913.

RUBE WADDELL'S
BASEBALL CARD, 1911.

BABE RUTH, FULL-
LENGTH PORTRAIT.

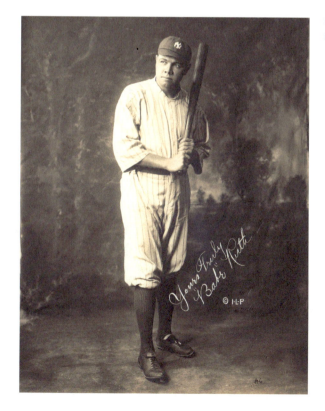

BABE RUTH SELLING TUBERCULAR CHRISTMANS SEALS IN
THE LOBBY OF KEITH'S THEATER, WASHINGTON, D.C., 1921.

BABE RUTH AND ANNA Q. NILSSON FILMING THEIR MOVIE "BABE COMES HOME."
NILSSON IS ON THE BED LOOKING AT RUTH WHILE RUTH IS UNDERNEATH THE BED
AND HAS A MOUSE TRAP STUCK ON HIS FINGER. BASED ON THE RELEASE DATE,
THIS WAS MOST LIKELY TAKEN IN 1927.

Ty Cobb Performing a Hero, Playing the Villain

WHILE OUT DRIVING in New York's Central Park just after the 1911 season, Ty Cobb was stopped by a policeman. In Cobb's autobiography, *My Life in Baseball: The True Record*, he states that he was told to get down from the car. Cobb maintained that he was not speeding and refused to get out of the car. When the officer attempted to drag Cobb from the vehicle, Cobb "made a little pugilistic history" and punched the man in the face. The officer stumbled away from the vehicle and disappeared into the park. Cobb, who was no stranger to being in trouble with the law, was sure that he would shortly be set upon by a legion of police ready to exact revenge and he "would get 99 years for this." It was then that Cobb noticed a man with a camera hiding in the bushes nearby. Cobb reported that the entire incident was meant to be an attempt to "grab off some Page One space" by the producers of the play that Cobb was rehearsing.[1] Rather than let Cobb know what was going to happen, which would have required some acting on Cobb's part to get the desired result, the producers instead chose to let Cobb be himself in the moment, which is what they got.

The incident illustrated some of the issues that Vaughn Glaser faced in having Ty Cobb as the star of his production of George Ade's *The College*

Widow. Scheduled to tour the country for sixteen weeks, from just after the conclusion of the 1911 World Series through mid-March of the next year, Cobb was given a large guaranteed salary of at least $10,000 to appear in the play.[2] For Cobb, the tour was clearly a money-making opportunity since his theatrical salary was larger than what he had yet received for any one season of playing for the Detroit Tigers in the American League. Glaser, however, was tasked with managing which version of Ty Cobb audiences would see when he walked onstage: the exceptionally skilled ballplayer and Southern hero—or the outsider with a reputation for violence. This chapter examines how the transfer of a player's baseball persona onto the stage became complicated when a player's persona sharply contrasted with what he was supposed to play, since the persona would supersede the character played regardless. In this case, the issue was making a player fit the role of the melodramatic hero when he had the reputation of a villain. One review of the play said of Cobb's acting that "he never, for a moment, seems to forget that he is Ty Cobb 'playing' at hero."[3] In fact, he had become so adept at "playing Ty Cobb" that audiences had a hard time seeing him as anything else.

Even before he reached the major leagues, Cobb was active in creating an image of who Ty Cobb was. In 1904, after receiving only limited playing time and being released from an Augusta, Georgia, team in the Class C professional South Atlantic League, the seventeen-year-old Cobb agreed to play for Anniston, Alabama, in the semi-professional Tennessee and Alabama league. Such a small league below the fully professional ranks was normally outside the scope of newspaper sportswriters in the cities, but Grantland Rice of the *Atlanta Journal* inserted into the newspaper a note stating that "rumors had reached Atlanta from numerous sources that over in Alabama there's a young fellow who seems to be showing an unusual lot of talent." Many years later, while sharing the stage with Cobb at a banquet, Rice explained that he had received a great number of letters detailing the young man's play and promoting him as someone who would eventually be a major league player. Due to the pressure, Rice felt obliged to acknowledge the player with notice in the paper. After hearing the story, Cobb confessed to the crowd and to Rice that he had written all of the letters himself using a variety of handwriting styles and assumed names like Jackson, Jones, Smith, Brown, Kelly, and McIntyre. As motivation for the deceit, Cobb explained, "I was in a hurry."[4] Though he had grown up playing a style of baseball that was, as he described it, "as gentlemanly as a kick in the crotch," he felt he could do well in the professional game if given a chance.[5]

Cobb not only proved himself to be a major leaguer, but what he accomplished on the field put him in the category of one of the greatest baseball players of all time. He was elected to the Baseball Hall of Fame in the first class of 1936 after appearing on 222 of 226 ballots—more than any other player in the inaugural induction class—and, as such, he is considered the first player enshrined in the Hall of Fame. He led the American League in batting average twelve times over his twenty-four-year career. From 1907 to 1919, he failed to win the batting championship only once (he came in second that year). His nine consecutive seasons leading the league in batting average still stands as a Major League record, as does his career total of twelve. He hit at least .320 in all but two of his twenty-four seasons, and in three seasons, he held an average over .400. His career batting average of .366 remains the highest of all time.

When he retired after the 1928 season, Cobb held more than forty-three records in batting, base running, and durability.[6] Among the most notable records he held were in the categories of base hits and runs scored. The eight times he led the league in hits remains a record, and he became the overall career leader in base hits in 1923. His career total of 4,189 stood as the record for more than sixty years until Pete Rose broke it in September 1985.[7] Cobb was the all-time leader even longer in runs scored, from the 1925 season until October 2001, when his career total of 2,246 was eclipsed by Rickey Henderson. Cobb still ranks in the statistical top five of all time for at bats, singles, doubles, triples, outfield assists, and stolen bases, and he remains in the top ten for games played, total bases, and runs batted in. His record fifty-four credited steals of home plate remains as one of the virtually unbreakable records in baseball.

Standing just above six feet tall, Cobb was physically talented with both great speed and extraordinary coordination; however, the overall playing style he developed when he was younger was the most consistently visible aspect of his created playing persona. That style was shaped in large part by how he mentally conceived of the game. Part of Cobb's psychological strategy on the field was to do unusual things that had a very low chance of success so that he could keep the other players off-balance. Usually, but not always, when the Tigers were already well ahead, Cobb would attempt plays that did not appear logical or had a very low chance for success, such as trying to steal a base even before the pitcher began his wind-up, or trying to advance another base while an infielder held the ball. He strove in many ways to be unpredictable while on the field. In Cobb's estimation, establishing himself as a threat for something unusual had more value toward his long-term goals than the potential run he represented on the base paths.

Cobb made himself into a threat within the bounds of the game. When at the plate with his split-handed grip, he was a threat to bunt or to make contact to place the ball with precision, while also being a threat to make more powerful contact with the ball. As a result, defenders were caught in between. On the bases, he was always a threat to steal a base, so pitchers were uneasy. In the field, his speed and accurate arm made him a threat to make plays that others could not, so runners advanced at their own peril. As such, Cobb's autobiography explains that the opposition might be forced into making a mistake with "that Crazy Cobb" on the field.[8] Quickly, his "Crazy Cobb" persona became known to fans as just "Ty Cobb." The acknowledged construction of this persona was a cornerstone of Cobb's on-field behavior and shaped how all of the players and fans at the ballpark understood him.

Cobb publicly championed what he called the "scientific approach" to baseball, which required the hitter to use his intelligence to prioritize placement of a base hit between fielders rather than always swinging full strength with reduced precision.[9] By "playing the percentages," Cobb greatly increased his likelihood of getting on base. Not content to just follow Wee Willie Keeler's famous dictum to "hit 'em where they ain't," Cobb capitalized on opportunities that presented themselves during a game. More often, however, he created his own opportunities.

One way he felt he could put himself at an advantage on the field was through physical conditioning. Cobb frequently swung three bats while he was on deck waiting for his turn at the plate. The increased weight of three 40-ounce bats in his hands allowed a single bat to feel much lighter while at the plate, and it could be wielded with more combined force and precision. The practice was unusual for the time, and Cobb felt he needed to defend the action in his 1914 book *Busting 'Em* as being more than just mere superstition.[10] He used the same principle one spring when the team was training in Louisiana. Newspaper reporters remarked on how much slower he appeared and speculated that Cobb was not going to be as quick on the field in the upcoming season. After spring training was over, Cobb revealed that he had asked a cobbler to install lead weights into the shoes he wore all spring in order to increase the strength and endurance in his legs.[11] Cobb's opinions and methods of conditioning subsequently became widely publicized during the First World War. His reply to an Air Service trainee's request for conditioning advice was distributed to all trainees of the Service under the Chief of Aircraft Operation's endorsement.[12]

Another method that Cobb used to work the percentages in his favor was his constant study of the men he played against; he would then adapt his own approach to take away whatever advantage they had in the field or exploit any weaknesses they exhibited. Recognizing his inability to hit the curveball thrown by left-handed pitcher Doc White, he repositioned himself in the back of the batter's box so he could judge the breaking pitch more accurately. Against right-handed pitchers, since he had a better view of the ball, Cobb moved up to the front of the batter's box to swing at a curveball before it began to break.[13] By watching the timing of how a particular outfielder raised his arm to return the ball to the infield or identifying other idiosyncrasies of the players on the field, Cobb knew he would be able to advance a base when the opposition was not expecting it.

Cobb was also adept at manipulating players to help him achieve his goals. Like many hitters, he would feign a bunt attempt on one pitch so the infielders would play in closer to him on later pitches and not be able to cover as much ground defensively when he was swinging away fully.[14] But he used more unusual methods of manipulation as well. Having had little luck facing Eddie Cicotte in his career, Cobb designed a tactic meant to rattle the pitcher. In his autobiography he describes leading off the ninth inning in a tight game against Cicotte. Cobb took his place in the batter's box and began talking to the hitter on deck while ignoring the pitcher completely. With his back toward the pitcher and his bat held by his side through the entire at bat, Cobb took four straight pitches for balls, and Cicotte became so enraged that he had to be taken out of the game.[15] While Cobb's apparent recklessness on the bases and adjustments on the field might have seemed at times ill-conceived or haphazard, he had carefully considered and evaluated the short- and long-term benefits of doing them. Through his physical conditioning, attentiveness to situations, and knowledge of other players' behavior, Ty Cobb could be easily identified as the most prepared player on the field in his era, if not also the most intelligent.

Cobb approached the game mentally with the "idea that you have something over the other fellow," which he considered to be a primary component in achieving victory.[16] For him, that often meant showing the opposition that there was nothing they could do that would intimidate him. Frequently finding himself the target of beanballs from opposing pitchers because of his style of play, Cobb explained that his preferred course of action was to immediately taunt the pitcher on his wildness and move closer to the plate to tempt the pitcher to throw at him again.[17] In his opinion, a ballplayer should not show any fear or allude to any personal weakness lest it be used against him.

Included among the things that Cobb believed showed weakness was kindness, and he was ready to take advantage of players whom he thought were too nice. Cobb saw this as his particular advantage over future Hall of Fame pitcher Walter Johnson. Johnson, who was renowned for his pitching speed and accuracy, had accidentally hit one of Cobb's teammates in the head with a pitch and immediately ran in to try to help the motionless player. Seeing that Johnson was afraid of hurting anyone, Cobb began to routinely stand almost on top of the plate when facing the pitcher until the strike count was in his favor. Then he would return to his normal position in the batter's box and wait to hit the next pitch which Johnson inevitably threw in the strike zone. Cobb felt that Johnson's politeness permitted him (Cobb) to hit well over .300 against the pitcher over the course of their careers.[18]

Cobb also took advantage of the friendship that fellow southerner and great hitter "Shoeless" Joe Jackson offered him throughout their careers by manipulating the uneducated hitter for Cobb's own personal gain. At the end of the 1911 season, Jackson led Cobb in the batting race by nine points as their two teams met for a six-game series. Though the two had always shared a friendly relationship, Cobb refused to acknowledge Jackson's greeting as the two passed on the field during the first game and stared at a point six inches above Jackson's head. Cobb continued to ignore Jackson's attempts at conversation throughout each of the games. The confused and dismayed Jackson slumped at the plate through the series while Cobb concentrated only on making hits until he had surpassed Jackson in batting average. As soon as the last out was made in the final game, Cobb ran over to Jackson, greeted him warmly, and congratulated him on a fine season. Cobb finished with a .420 average while Jackson had fallen to .408. Cobb summed up the incident in his autobiography published just after his death by writing, "it helps if you can help them beat themselves."[19]

Though Cobb ostensibly liked both of the players mentioned above, his attitude toward the game required that he make enemies. Every member of the other team was Cobb's "blood enemy," no matter what previous experiences he had in playing against them. This was the only way, Cobb believed, that a ballplayer could gain any prominence.[20] While on deck, he would watch the pitcher and construct a personal hatred toward his opponent, gritting his teeth while swinging his three bats, so that he would be in the right frame of mind to defeat the pitcher. When he became the manager of the Tigers, Cobb insisted that his men not fraternize on the field with the opposing team so that they could maintain a state of mind ready for combat. For Cobb, the game was a continuous battle. In fact, he frequently likened it to warfare, and he was always on the attack. Obsessed with victory, whether team-based or personal, he felt that if he could demoralize or humiliate his opponents at any point during the game, it put him in a better position to win not only in the present but also in the future.[21]

The Ty Cobb persona based on the Crazy Cobb that crowds saw on the field displayed both physical strength and sly intelligence. It preyed on both the physical and mental weaknesses of other players. It put the other players off-balance by presenting a constant threat to do something that was unexpected and not typical. Within the game, this persona put Cobb in an advantageous position: he knew why he did the things he did even when it was not clear to others. Outside of the game, the Ty Cobb playing persona was neither predictable nor readily understandable, and that made him intriguing to watch.

The persona also displayed several of the traits identified by Orrin Klapp as qualities of a villain in American culture. The villain is not necessarily diametrically opposed to the idea of the hero; instead, Klapp describes the villain's role as that of often being the preeminent threat to the group whom the hero serves.[22] The villain type may actually share traits with the hero type, but they are categorized differently because of either their motivating intent in performing an action or the moral lens through which society views their behavior. A display of physical strength, for example, could be considered either heroic or villainous, depending upon whether it was done in a defensive or an attacking manner.

As with the hero, Klapp uses five categories for the villain type. The first are those who violate or threaten proper social order or status, such as a rebel, rogue, or trouble-maker. Next are usurpers and abusers of power, authority, or privilege, like an oppressor or a "selfish grabber." Outsiders or strangers who violate the cohesiveness of a group are the third category. Those who are traitors, deceivers, or sneaks, or who otherwise sow disloyalty are part of the fourth category, often using information they have in a way to get what they want. The final category consists of those who are variously deemed undesirable within a society for being a drain or otherwise unwilling to contribute to the general welfare. Klapp notes that the villain and hero help to promote a societal theme or value by providing either a negative or positive representation of it in action. By illustrating the break from the rule, the villain can serve society as "a safety valve for aggression."[23]

Amber Roessner notes that Cobb's contractual holdout in 1908 marked the beginning of many sportswriters portraying Cobb as a villain. His combative nature on and off the field for the next few years reinforced the perception. Even when notable writers like F. C. Lane attempted to present more positive, heroic pictures of Cobb, a new incident would occur to renew the villainous image. Some writers offered public praise of Cobb because of their personal friendship with him or in an effort to maintain access to him. Ring Lardner mythologized Cobb as an ideal American worthy of emulation. The result, as Roessner argues, is that Cobb was too complex of a figure and difficult to define, so writers often crafted him as the "quintessential sinner."[24]

In *Busting 'Em*, Cobb devotes the second chapter to his perspective on baseball crowds and what effect they have on the players. The persona he presented on the field was frequently infuriating to fans of the other teams. Cobb thrived on the animosity that opposing crowds displayed toward him. He felt he hit better on the road than he did in front of his own fans. He credited the fans who rooted vociferously against him with helping him break from occasional hitting slumps. Singling out the fans in Philadelphia and St. Louis, Cobb explained that the jeering made him work harder in those cities.[25] He tried to do what he could to encourage crowds to hate him while visiting different ballparks.

Unlike Mike Kelly, Cobb's interactions with the crowds as a player were for the most part adversarial. Taunted and jeered by these crowds, he frequently returned fire with taunts and insults of his own. Near the end of a particularly tough extra-inning game in Boston, Cobb hit a home run to essentially seal the win. After touching the plate, he gestured to the hostile crowd to "sit down and shut up." Even when a crowd was attempting to cheer him for a good play, Cobb admitted that he would rarely acknowledge them by tipping his cap like most players would do. He preferred to maintain a blatant dismissal of their disapproval and an obvious disregard for their approval.[26]

Cobb believed that, as individuals, fans were friendly and generally supportive even of players on the other team, but the anonymity provided by being a member of a crowd allowed more menacing behavior. Among the loudest and most rambunctious fans, Cobb observed, were people who were generally quiet away from the ballpark or who held subservient jobs like that of a waiter or bellhop. The jeering allowed at a game was one of the only ways for a person like this to assert himself.[27] Cobb felt that his persona provided a perfect target for their pent-up hostility, which he could then use to his advantage.

As James L. Smith argues in his work on melodrama, the villain is the most loved of the melodramatic characters because the villain's presence provides the opportunity to boo and hiss at the opposition and obstacle to victory and happiness.[28] The villain functions best as a target for audience frustration and interactions. In Cobb's day, while melodramatic heroes took an audience's admiration, the melodramatic villain reveled in the scorn of both those within the story and those watching from outside of it. Though Cobb reportedly espoused some regret about it later in life, he relished being treated like a villain on the field and in the press.[29]

One of the ways that Cobb could become an easy target for the crowd's hostility was through the spiking of other players on the field. As an element of his status as a threat to the other team, his spikes allowed him to be the aggressor on the base paths when he may have otherwise been at the mercy of the infielders—who by then had the tendency to give Cobb a little more room on close plays at the base.[30] During his career Cobb became known throughout the game for his willingness to spike a man if he was in the way. For the most part, Cobb claimed the incidents were unintentional and oc-curred because the other player entered the base path, which he asserted belonged solely to the runner. He believed that due to the seriousness of such injuries that no player in the league ever tried to spike another with the intention of putting him out of the game.[31] The threat of being spiked was a real concern for players at the time, whether as a runner or a fielder. An ill-placed spike could mean the end of a player's career, and such an injury could mean the difference between continuing to play the game for a living, with its significant financial benefits, or returning to their towns to work in the manual labor jobs that many players had been able to at least stave off for a while. Cobb would often show off the many scars he had received from being stepped on or landed on "accidentally" while on the bases.[32]

After having spiked Bill Bradley of Cleveland, whom Cobb said he had looked up to as a youth, Cobb was exonerated of any wrong doing by the injured player who said it clearly was not Cobb's fault.[33] However, many similar situations did not end so courteously because the injured parties felt that Cobb had gone out of his way to inflict harm. When Philadelphia third baseman Frank Baker was cut on the arm by Cobb's spike while Cobb slid into the base once in 1909, the game was stopped as Baker's arm was bandaged and the Athletics' players demanded that Cobb be removed from the game for dirty play.[34] Though a photograph appeared later showing Cobb attempting to slide away from Baker, Philadelphia's esteemed owner and manager, Connie Mack, accused Cobb of committing the act on purpose and called him the dirtiest player in the game.[35] In the subsequent weeks, stoked by the antagonistic articles written about him in the *Philadelphia Bulletin* by sportswriter Horace Fogel, Cobb received numerous death threats, and there was a visible police presence on his next trip to the city. The incident put his reputation for purposeful spiking and dirty play on national display.

Cobb saw such a reputation as generally useful when not taken to quite the extreme as it was following the Baker spiking. Previously, while in New York in 1908, several Tigers reserve players sat on the bench and used files to sharpen their spikes as the New York players passed by. The prank was meant as a joke to scare the other team. Though Cobb was not present, several sportswriters reported that he was filing his own spikes in full view of the entire New York team in anticipation of getting to slice apart their infielders.[36] This story made its way around the league and helped establish Cobb's reputation as an unscrupulous spike-slashing player. His aggressive base running and his increased involvement in spiking incidents made the story seem more and more believable to fans and, more importantly, to opposing players. For his part, Cobb would never actively deny the spike-sharpening incident during his playing career and only began to refute it during his retirement.[37] The story became another element of the threat he wanted his Crazy Cobb persona to present to the world and another way in which crowds could see Ty Cobb as a villain in the modes of a violator of social order and an abuser of power.

The general animosity among players and fans toward Cobb was evident in a plot launched in 1910 to deny him another of his much-valued batting titles. Late in the season, Cobb had overcome a four-point deficit in batting average to Cleveland's Napoleon Lajoie. With two games remaining in the season and a multiple-point lead in the race, Cobb did not play again that year. Throughout the year he had suffered from eye troubles to the extent that there was speculation that he was going blind. With the team's season standing assured no matter the results of the final games, Cobb eschewed the final two games, he claimed, for the sake of his eyes. Other players around the league, however, felt that Cobb was not playing fairly by sitting on his average and leaving less of a chance for Lajoie to pass him—since, as their averages stood, Lajoie would need a hit in virtually all of his plate appearances during the final doubleheader in St. Louis. Jack O'Conner, the manager of the St. Louis Browns, ordered his young and naïve third baseman to play at the edge of the outfield grass every time that Lajoie came to the plate that day. After the conclusion of the two games, Lajoie had gotten eight hits in nine at-bats, with nearly all of them being bunts toward the deep-playing third baseman. Browns coach Harry Howell even approached the league official scorer for the game with a bribe to see if the result of the remaining at-bat could be changed from a fielder's choice to a hit. Lajoie was mobbed by approximately 10,000 laudatory St. Louis fans and received a telegram from eight of Cobb's Tigers teammates congratulating him on winning the championship. However, when the league's official statistician calculated the totals to determine a winner, Lajoie had an average of .3841 to Cobb's .3848, so Cobb was victorious again. Both O'Conner and Howell were subsequently banished from organized baseball while both Cobb and Lajoie, who had simply taken what the opposition was giving him, each received a brand new Chalmers automobile that had been promised to the winner of the batting race.[38]

The Crazy Cobb image as a member of Klapp's second category of villainous abusers could be extended well beyond Cobb's playing persona. Away from the field, his propensity for violent outbursts not only got him arrested several times, but it also reinforced his image as an oppressor of others through physical means. Due in part to the image he had cultivated on the field, Cobb was often the one seen to be the aggressor or instigator. While he doubtlessly was at fault on many occasions, Cobb nevertheless often claimed to be a victim of circumstance. For the most part, these confrontations revolved around Cobb trying to establish or maintain a level of social status he believed he deserved. Though physical conflict was just one way for him to measure himself against others, he seemed to enjoy it immensely. For example, as a guest referee for a full card of boxing in New Orleans, Cobb allowed one fighter in the first fight to so thoroughly bludgeon the other that the crowd called for Cobb to stop the fight. Ignoring the pleas, Cobb let the beating continue until the local police entered the ring and ended the bout—and he was fired before the second bout began.[39]

Cobb believed that when he or any player had agitated fans enough to become violent, they were much more likely to attack the ballplayer while he was still in his uniform than they were when they would see him later in his street clothes.[40] One fan who ran onto the field to accost Cobb immediately after a game was quickly incapacitated by the ballplayer with a swift knee to the man's groin. Cobb explained to reporters the next day that players were entitled to receive at least some respect while on the field, since "this ball park is our office."[41] Certainly willing to both put up with and encourage the fans' hatred of him, Cobb felt it was permissible to retaliate when his status as a ballplayer was challenged—and he was even more defiant when he felt his personal status was demeaned, as it was in New York during his most renowned fight with a fan.

In May 1912, Cobb was under a barrage of abuse in New York by a particularly belligerent fan whom he had noticed on previous trips to the city. Seated in the stands near Detroit's bench, the fan—Claude Lucker—taunted Cobb from the moment he appeared on the field. After trading insults with the fan like he typically did, Cobb twice attempted to avoid passing near Lucker when returning to the bench. Between the third and the fourth innings (and perhaps goaded into it by teammate Sam Crawford), Cobb leapt the railing and bounded up twelve rows to reach Lucker. Cobb punched him and, once he was knocked down, continued the assault by kicking and stomping on the man with his spikes. When another fan saw that Lucker was missing one entire hand and three additional fingers, fans began to yell that Cobb was beating a man with no hands. While still attacking, Cobb reportedly replied that he did not care if the man had no feet. Eventually Cobb was pulled from the fan by umpires and policemen, and he returned to the field past a line of his teammates who all held bats in case any fan wanted to follow him back onto the field. After being suspended for the incident, Cobb was still supported by his teammates, who became members of the first major league team to strike during the season to protest the abuse that Cobb had to endure and what they felt was mistreatment toward him by league officials.[42]

Cobb's quick temper resulted in many altercations, from yelling arguments to full physical assaults, with many stemming from incidents where he felt his status as Ty Cobb wasn't being respected. Tigers manager Hughie Jennings reported that Lucker had used a particularly odious epithet toward Cobb, questioning his racial purity, immediately before the player jumped into the stands.[43] Such a comment was likely too much for Cobb to bear as he often treated people with darker skin as being beneath him.[44] In fact, there were several reported incidents of physical confrontations between Cobb and African Americans that happened because Cobb perceived some slight toward himself.[45] In 1907, Cobb slapped Henry Cummings, the Black groundskeeper of their spring training park, and chased him around the park because Cummings appeared to be drunk, had gone to shake Cobb's hand,

and had either called Cobb by his first name or as "Carrie." Cobb's teammate Charlie Schmidt intervened in the fracas after Cobb began to choke the groundskeeper's wife, who had begun yelling at Cobb to stop the assault.[46] In June 1908, Cobb assaulted twenty-seven-year-old Fred Collins, a Detroit United Railway worker, who was directing people and traffic around some soft asphalt. Having heard "You can't cross here," Cobb felt that the workman had insulted him, so Cobb punched him in the face and tackled him into the asphalt until others on the street pulled him off.[47] In 1919, he was accused of assaulting Ada Morris, an eighteen-year-old chambermaid at the Pontchartrain Hotel in Detroit, by forcing her out of his room, kicking her in the stomach, and knocking her down the stairs. He was never arrested for the incident; however, he appeared to have paid off the Morris family after they sought to bring charges against him.[48] In 1924, as he neared the end of his career, Cobb once again punched another Black groundskeeper, this time in Philadelphia, as Cobb and the unnamed man argued over the use of the park's telephone.[49] Even when faced with charges, most of these civil offenses were settled quickly given the privileges granted Cobb by his wealth and the standing he held with affluent and powerful white citizens.

Cobb did not restrict his assaults only to Black people, however, as white people who did not properly respect his status were often subjected to the same kind of violent retribution. After hearing that his wife had argued with a Detroit butcher one day in June 1914, Cobb called the man and went to confront him with his revolver in hand. He made the butcher apologize over the phone, but when the butcher's young assistant began to argue, Cobb fought him until the police were called.[50] Cobb argued with a white waitress in 1925 over a bill he thought was wrong. The argument became so heated that a nearby policeman wrestled Cobb to the ground, and the cashier may have hit Cobb over the head with a glass dish to prevent further escalation. At the police station, Cobb acknowledged disagreeing about the bill and posted the $11 bond.[51] He had previously beaten a white student and ballplayer for Wofford College named Rutledge Osborne who argued and taunted the professional player when their teams met as part of a spring exhibition.[52]

Even when litigation was pressed, the practical results of an altercation for Cobb were little more than an inconvenience. While in Cleveland in September 1909, Cobb returned to his hotel at 2:00 a.m. from dinner with some friends. He argued with the elevator operator and slapped the man for being insolent. The hotel's watchman, George Stanfield, hit Cobb with his nightstick. As they wrestled each other to the ground, Cobb cut Stanfield several times with a knife he had in his pocket. Stanfield hit Cobb again in the head with the nightstick and eventually made it back to his room after other hotel employees separated the two.[53] After the team left town the next day, Stanfield filed both criminal and civil charges against Cobb. Though the Tigers' attorney arranged a settlement for Stanfield to drop the charges, the Cleveland police department announced their intention to continue their pursuit of the warrant against Cobb whenever he again came within the Ohio state line. With the Tigers playing the Pittsburgh Pirates in the World Series that year, Cobb was forced to avoid traveling directly between the two cities on the train with his teammates. Instead, his longer route went through Ontario and Buffalo whenever the series changed venues. He eventually appeared in Ohio court in late October and successfully plea-bargained down from felonious assault to simple assault and battery. He paid a $100 fine, and Stanfield received $115 to dismiss his charges.[54] In nearly every case, Cobb contended that he was the aggrieved party and, though he took the punishments doled out to him, he felt he was well within his rights.

Cobb's traits associated with his on-field persona that fit the "selfish grabber" category of villain were evident in his off-the-field life as well. He was greatly motivated by personal gain, and he felt that much of his status was determined through his acquisition of wealth. Cobb cited a watch made with three kinds of gold that was to be awarded to the American League batting champion for 1907 as his primary motivation for achieving that goal.[55] Throughout his career, similar prizes for individual achievements helped to push him, such as the Chalmers touring automobile given to both him and Lajoie following the 1910 batting race controversy. Even when the team was contending for the league pennant, Cobb seemed more concerned about the financial benefits than the achievement itself. He felt that part of his eventual acceptance by his teammates was due to his ability to help get the team toward their "pennant money"—the additional money the players received for their team being in the World Series.[56]

In addition to his frequent association with the traits of abusers of power, Cobb was also easily identified as a stranger or outsider. Part of this categorization was due to his uniqueness as a southern man in professional baseball. Though he was by no means the first southerner, nor was he the only one, he was still vastly outnumbered by players who came from elsewhere in the country. Neither of the major leagues had clubs farther south than St. Louis during Cobb's entire career, so the crowds for whom he played consisted of people much different from him, and the city for which he had to play was the northernmost in his league. With three quarters of Detroit's population either first- or second-generation foreign immigrants when he debuted in the league, Cobb was indeed a stranger as an eighteen-year-old out of the South for the first time in his life.[57] Even his "Georgia Peach" nickname served as a constant reminder of his difference from baseball's primary audience. Cobb believed himself to be different as well. His autobiography wholly identifies him as a southern man, comparing himself to a soldier at Bull Run as a point of pride and calling the depiction of the South in *Uncle Tom's Cabin* a low blow to the region.[58] Teammate Sam Crawford believed that part of Cobb's attitude came from how he saw himself as a lone southerner against a world full of northern Yankees.[59] He included in his autobiography the legacy of the Cobb name, both in his home state of Georgia and throughout the South, and he felt the high status afforded his family name in that region should be respected elsewhere.[60]

Though his career progressed with a villainous reputation with northern crowds, Cobb was received as a hero by numerous southerners since they identified many of his actions as defending personal pride, status, or property. Fans would clamor to greet him whenever he trained in the South or when he toured the region with semi-pro teams to make additional money after the regular season. When Cobb participated in an automobile caravan from New York City to Winston, North Carolina, to help promote a national initiative for "good roads," people throughout the South lined the sides of the road waiting for him to pass, and they would not let him leave Roanoke, Virginia, without giving a short speech.[61] He extolled life in the South versus living in the North.[62] Following allegations late in his career that he had conspired to fix games, 500 supporters gathered at the Confederate monument in his hometown of Augusta to cheer him. There they displayed a banner reading: "TY IS STILL OUR IDOL AND THE IDOL OF AMERICA."[63]

Cobb was indeed held up by many people in power as a model for other southerners. Federal judge William H. Barrett and Augusta mayor William B. White praised him during the Augusta rally. He received a wire from the two senators and ten representatives who made up Georgia's entire congressional delegation commending and defending him following the Claude Lucker incident. Atlanta's police commissioner defended Cobb's action in the fight as the only way to have remained respectable, while Atlanta's mayor commended him for displaying the principles of "Southern manhood." Cobb was asked to address a joint session of the Mississippi legislature after they had voted to adjourn so they could see him play in an exhibition game that ended up being rained out. Most impressive, President William Howard Taft declared Cobb to be the nation's most popular Georgian. When Cobb could not reach a contract agreement for 1913 with Tigers owner Frank Navin, a U.S. representative from Georgia announced his intention to investigate whether baseball violated the Sherman Anti-Trust Act. At the same time, Georgia senator Hoke Smith requested a copy of Cobb's contract to investigate the legality of baseball's reserve clause. Not surprisingly, Navin conceded most of his points to Cobb and a contract between the two was agreed upon—and the congressional inquiries disappeared.[64]

The battle between images presented by sportswriters contributed to the perception of complexity, whether or not it actually existed in Cobb. The melodramatic narrative, according to Heilman, is driven by the simple conflict between heroes and villains. The melodramatic hero eschews complexity. The hero doesn't need to be purely good and free from all vice; the hero only needs to be without the appearance of internal moral conflict.[65] Complexity is the sphere of the villain. Regardless of motivations—because these were ultimately inconsequential anyway—the villain served as the obstacle to the hero's desire and achievement. As such, Cobb could never fit comfortably into the mold of the melodramatic hero, even of his own time.

During the 1911 baseball season, Cobb finalized plans to appear onstage in Vaughn Glaser's touring production of George Ade's popular comedy *The College Widow*. Though he had previously declined a vaudeville tour for a reported $200 a week following his breakout 1907 season, Cobb knew that the opportunity and the money would be there if he changed his mind. He was given a salary guarantee of $10,000 for the play.[66] Glaser could have assumed that excellence on the field and recognition in the papers positioned Cobb to be an excellent theatrical draw. He was indeed famous, and people came to the ballpark to see him, and his abilities seemed to align him at times with a heroic persona. Glaser's tour of the play could highlight Cobb's traits when in the South, as early-twentieth-century rich white southerners like himself saw virtue where others saw vice.

Despite some discussion about changing the sport in the production to match Cobb's own profession, Cobb would play a star football halfback named Billy Bolton as originally written.[67] Though centered on a Thanksgiving football game between rival colleges Atwater and Bingham, the play was constructed as a series of comedic situations with a rather thin plot. Due to the machinations of the Atwater College president's daughter, Jane, the football hero Bolton is lured to enroll at their campus rather than Bingham's.

The contest is won for Atwater by Bolton just as it seemed all was lost. In typical fashion, at the end, Bolton also wins Jane's ever-lasting affection as she breaks away from her role as the titular "college widow."[68]

Though Bolton wins the game and the girl, he certainly falls short of heroic status in the play by Klapp's standards. He is referred to as a great player before he appears, and once he does arrive, his lack of humility shows that he's well aware of the perception when he uses his status to get what he wants. He is shown to be disloyal to his father and to Bingham by forsaking them for Atwater. Then, once enrolled, he professes his disinterest in coursework, studying, or anything not involving Jane or football. The soon-to-be twenty-five-year-old Cobb was physically suited to play the college halfback, with his wiry, muscular frame built from year-round physical activity, and his persona was just as complicated as Bolton's to be the hero of a play. By the time of the production's debut, however, the villainous perception of Ty Cobb had already been well established. Cobb had gained public notoriety for his hard play and aggressive nature, including his fight with the groundskeeper and wife as well as with his own teammate, the spiking of Philadelphia's Baker and the subsequent death threats, the felonious assault charge in Ohio, and the conspiracy hatched against him by other players in the league.

The production opened in Trenton, New Jersey, on October 26, 1911, after the end of the World Series between the New York Giants and the Philadelphia Athletics. In one of the many interviews Cobb gave during the tour, he claimed he had only four days to learn his part and a week's worth of rehearsals before the first performance.[69] Leaving New Jersey, the production visited Richmond on November 6 and continued to Norfolk and other spots in Virginia before performing shows in the Carolinas, Florida, and Georgia over the next ten days. Before the month was out, the production had played in Savannah, Augusta, Atlanta, Birmingham, Chattanooga, Knoxville, and Nashville. It played to big houses throughout the month-long tour of southern cities as Cobb was adored and feted along the way. A newspaper article from Columbia, South Carolina, satirized the reception Cobb received in many southern cities by specifying in bold typeface that there "Will Be No Parade" upon Cobb's arrival in town, and that at later stops in the tour the player "may be given an automobile or two in each of these towns as souvenirs."[70]

In December the tour turned northward, playing a week in Pennsylvania before traveling to Canada for a visit to Toronto for another week-long run which ended on December 16. The latter half of the month was spent in Cobb's professional home of Detroit and four other smaller cities in the surrounding area. Before the week-long run in Chicago to open the new year, Cobb announced that he was leaving the production on January 13 at the conclusion of its presentation in Cleveland, despite having bookings for the remainder of the month in St. Louis and Kansas City. Cobb cited the exhausting schedule as the primary reason for his departure. He told a Grand Rapids reporter that he rarely got into bed before one in the morning and frequently had trouble sleeping even then. The routine of traveling all day then performing once or twice before beginning anew the next day as had happened for the first month had started to affect his conditioning for the upcoming 1912 season.[71] Later in life, in his autobiography, Cobb admitted that actors, not ballplayers, should be considered the iron men of his era due in great part to the near constant travel they had to endure to do their jobs.[72]

The traveling life of an actor likely was more intense than that of a ballplayer at the time. Harold Seymour and Dorothy Seymour Mills asserted in *Baseball: the Golden Age* that major league teams traveled in first class conditions despite a persistent myth to the contrary. Though they spent hours on trains playing poker in coach cars and sleeping in Pullmans, their schedule was fairly consistent as they typically spent several days at a time in a city before having to travel again.[73] Actors and other performers, however, did not necessarily have the luxury of such a consistent routine. While productions might play in one city for an extended run, most followed the pattern that Cobb experienced with Glaser's company, performing in a new city every day or two. As theatre historian Thomas Postlewait points out, traveling was an obligation for actors who had become stars and a requirement for those who had not. From combination companies touring a recent hit play from New York to variety entertainers making their own schedule of small vaudeville houses, everyone toured.[74] While ballplayers were traveling between cities with considerable populations and amenities that were part of their league, actors visited theaters in even the smallest towns. Somewhat fittingly, because of the time of day that each profession worked—ballplayers in the afternoon and actors at night—one was often the other's entertainment while out on the road. It is likely that talk of their frequent travels was a commonplace topic of conversation in the friendships between actors and ballplayers.

The transfer of Cobb's persona to the stage was somewhat more complicated than it was for Anson, Kelly, or Mathewson. Unlike with Anson and Mathewson, the play was not written with Cobb in mind, so it could not showcase certain elements of his persona while dismissing others. Though Kelly's roles were in plays that had been previously produced, he was generally well-liked as a player and had developed a friendly relationship with the audiences he sought to entertain. While these players did not necessarily present an entirely respectable image to audiences, they had also not actively courted the spectators' ill will as Cobb had done. The Crazy Cobb persona Ty Cobb had brought from the ballfield was not something audiences associated with a hero onstage. Glaser's production needed to use Cobb's persona to draw fans—but only select elements of that persona.

Ultimately, the image Cobb presented could not be reconciled with the melodramatic hero. Even as it corresponded at times to elements of a heroic pattern/model, the violent and selfish tendencies shone brighter. By placing Cobb's persona into the role of a melodramatic hero, audiences were robbed of what they most desired. Instead of seeing Cobb as a villain, they had to reckon with being asked to cheer for someone they normally wouldn't and to grapple with the complexities when they were used to only simplicity.

As touring productions entered various towns, the producers would send out informational blurbs or bits for use in the local newspapers to generate interest in the shows. Along with articles usually comprising an interview done by local writers with the stars of the production, these previews, which were essentially puff pieces written by the producers, could help shape how an audience saw a particular production by stressing certain aspects of the production, such as new scenic elements for an old script. Bert Cowan, who served as a theatrical manager for Cobb throughout the tour, compiled a scrapbook of the articles written about Cobb and the production during its run. Many of the previews and articles for *The College Widow* as it came into a town tried to stress the point that the person audiences were going to see onstage was not who he was perceived to be on the field.

One common tactic used early in the tour was to stress Cobb's status as an actor. As one newspaper noted, "an actor and a ballplayer are about as far removed as any two professions possibly could be," and Cobb was known to be a particularly disagreeable ballplayer.[75] Before the production's performance in Norfolk, Virginia, very early in the tour, an article appeared in a local paper that contrasted Cobb's personality with the popular perception of him as a ballplayer. Noting that "he doesn't seem at all different from any other actor," the writer called him "an exceedingly agreeable sort of man." Hardly mentioning the play at all, the article focused on how "pleasant" Cobb was. As if to overemphasize the point, the article's writer asserted "if he were a woman, he's that type you would call loveable."[76]

Frequently, just after referring to Cobb as a champion ballplayer, a great ballplayer, or the world's greatest ballplayer, the previews and articles that advertised the play in each city recontextualized him in theatrical terms. Calling him "a real, first class, finished actor," a preview for his appearance in Athens, Georgia, drew a direct contrast between his being a ballplayer and his stage appearance: "No, he will not hit a home run over the center field wall, nor will he be seen stabbing a line drive while standing on his eyebrows—he will calmly and leisurely act his part in the play, the same as any other stage artist."[77]

In portraying him as "a regular actor," the previews often detailed how dedicated Cobb was in approaching his stage work. In Richmond, Virginia, at the second stop of the tour, Cobb was quoted as saying that he was "learning fast" and was enthusiastic about the work.[78] More than a month later, a blurb for his appearance in Toronto reminded readers that he "is very serious in everything he attempts."[79] Making an implied connection with his notable preparedness on the ballfield, the previews were using an association with his baseball success to predict his stage success. Before the November 16 performance in Jacksonville, Florida, it was written that "his ever present ambition to be the best at everything he attempts causes him a lot of extra work but it lands him the goal he seeks."[80] Another piece previewing the Richmond performance detailed Cobb's record of being a star as a baseball player and a star as a writer about baseball. Recounting the qualities that made him a success in the other two fields, the article naturally concludes that "Mr. Cobb, therefore, has all the qualifications of a star actor."[81]

Even the presentation of Cobb's name in the previews hinted that he should be seen in a different way. Identification with the name "Ty Cobb" was important to draw interest, and his name appeared in that familiar fashion in many previews. Several articles, however, drew distinctions that related to the underlying tension between the audience's recognition of the name and their possible repulsion by it. An article in Richmond began by reporting that the name signed by the man on the hotel register was "T. R. Cobb, actor." The same article introduced another section with "Mr. Cobb—the mister was acquired along with stardom."[82] For many baseball fans, that formality would be as much a marker of difference in how they viewed Cobb as the addition of the word "actor" after his name would have been. This was not going to be "Ty Cobb" on their local stage. The phrasing of a preview used both in Atlanta, Georgia, and Toronto, Canada, implied this more clear distinction of Cobb's separate worlds. Both previews begin with "there are legions of baseball fans who have never seen the great Ty Cobb play ball and there are just as many theater-goers who have never seen Tyrus Raymond Cobb, of Augusta, Ga., on the stage," before providing details about the local production.[83] Again using the formality of Cobb's full name, the previews suggested that the man appearing was a different one than the man who appeared on the field.

Another way these previews communicated the potential difference between Cobb's on-field persona and his stage performances was through their selling of Cobb as an actor. While many reported positively on Cobb's "histrionic ability," it was frequently presented that the ability he showed in acting was surprising. By placing Cobb's performance in these terms, it not only assisted in legitimizing him as an actor but also suggested the presence of a different side of Cobb than what was popularly known. An Atlanta preview stated that Cobb's ability "surprised even those who thought they knew him best."[84] This suggestion that no one should presume how Cobb would appear in the theater was taken even further to the extreme in a preview from Greenville, North Carolina, which stated that Cobb "far exceeded his own expectations."[85]

Other elements of Cobb's persona were highlighted in different areas of the country to give a varying impression of him. Touring through the South for the first month, previews frequently mentioned his southern heritage. A Norfolk preview noted his "southern mannerisms," and one from Chattanooga, Tennessee, claimed he refused to distinguish a particular hometown for himself, preferring to just say he was from Georgia.[86] An article in Richmond left a syllogism unfinished as a way to explain Cobb's charm among women: "Cobb is a Georgian, therefore a Southerner, and—well, but enough of this phase of the actor-ballplayer."[87] The mention of Cobb's heritage was sufficient to frame his persona in a way those audiences would both understand and appreciate and to provide specific appeal to the middle-class women in the audience who may have been hesitant to engage with him.

In Toronto, two separate previews specified that Vaughn Glaser had gone to great lengths to secure actors who were "fitted physically" and who had athletic backgrounds for the roles of the athletes in the play.[88] The articles also noted that each member of the cast, including Cobb, had attended college. While these assertions attempted to enhance the authenticity of the production, particularly for a Toronto audience, the truth was that Cobb had actually never matriculated. Yet, as seen in Christy Mathewson's persona, the association with college gave a player a perception of respectability that people north of the Mason-Dixon Line did not naturally associate with the player. This setting also created an atmosphere in which Cobb wasn't challenged along racial lines. The play depicts a very white college world with no Black or non-white characters presented on the stage. This lack of visible difference allowed white audiences to effectively abandon potential concerns about any racially motivated behavior while watching Cobb onstage.

For the most part, Cobb was sold on only his positive features, with many of his negative traits being effectively removed. However, the story of Cobb's Central Park encounter was actually used to advertise the play when it arrived in Pittsburgh in the first week of December to begin the northern portion of the tour.[89] Though the account resurfaced in Toronto, the use of the story showing Cobb in a potentially unfavorable light may have had real value in Pittsburgh.[90] Since Pittsburgh's ball club was a member of the National League, Pittsburgh was not a city Cobb visited frequently as a player; however, Cobb's Tigers had faced the Pirates just two years earlier in the 1909 World Series. The series went the full seven games, and though the Pirates emerged victorious, it was likely that the city's baseball fans still viewed Cobb as an adversary. With less of a possibility of the city's crowd embracing Cobb in a heroic role, the playing up of his villain persona may have been more convincing in bringing Pittsburghers to the theater. Though the producers may have only intended to stage a photograph of Cobb with a man dressed as a policeman, the story of him punching the man instead only enhanced the perceived villainous behavior.

Friend and producer Vaughan Glaser may have persuaded Cobb to remain just long enough to be able to recoup his investment and return to play Glaser's own hometown of Cleveland.[91] Losing its only notable feature, the production disbanded after just ten weeks of an intended sixteen-week schedule, having only made a slight profit. The reviews of the production largely focused on Cobb, who was the attraction, with brief remarks on some of the other actors or the plot of the already-familiar show. As was written in a Nashville newspaper, other than Cobb there "was nothing in the performance which the people of Nashville have not seen and reseen."[92] Of course, the reviews could not ignore why Cobb was in the production: "the only reason he is playing the part is not because he is an actor, but because he is the brightest star in the national game."[93] Audiences realized, too, that "Cobb was the whole show."[94]

Despite whatever positioning the previews and articles may have done, comparisons between Cobb's acting and his ballplaying were inevitable in the reviews of the play. Trying to describe his performances, reviews made frequent use of the word "hit," with its concurrent meanings for theatre and baseball.[95] An Atlanta newspaper stated that they gave the reviewing assignment to their sporting editor rather than their dramatic critic, and the entire review was written in baseball slang.[96] Given Cobb's history of having high batting averages, a Chattanooga review believed that Cobb hit only "about .230 in the theatrical league," while a Jacksonville comment claimed "he is not destined to hit in the .300 class in the 'theatrical league.'"[97] It was clear to the reviewer in Asheville, North Carolina, that Cobb would "win more shekels on the diamond than he will on the Thespian boards."[98] The Richmond review feared that Cobb was essentially risking all of his greatness by even attempting to act onstage, and his greatness on the field prompted comparisons to stage greats from years past.[99] Intended more as praise than criticism, reviews invoked the names of Booth, Skinner, Irving, Jefferson, and Sothern among others whom Cobb could not claim to be. It was stated, however, that it had never been assumed that he would be an equal to any of them.

Despite the lofty comparisons, expectations for Cobb's ability on the stage were understandably low. Remarked upon by several reviewers, Cobb knew all of his lines, spoke clearly, and did not overtly exhibit any symptoms of stage fright.[100] Though he had some issues, including what to do with his hands, by most accounts Cobb was considered to be a fairly competent actor. Reviewers in Norfolk and Toronto interpreted any awkwardness on Cobb's part to be appropriate imitation of real life, but most understood its origins to stem from a lack of formal training.[101] Several reviewers believed that should Cobb's eyesight fail him or should he otherwise leave baseball, the stage would be a suitable option for him if he received a little formal guidance.[102] Most important to the crowd, in the estimation of the reviewer from Jacksonville, was that Cobb "looked just like his pictures."[103]

A Charlotte review acknowledged the impossibility "to disassociate Cobb the actor from Cobb the player, and to judge how a similar interpretation by a nonentity would be received."[104] This gets at one of the central issues in how a ballplayer's stage work was evaluated. Because what a critic or audience saw a player do onstage was viewed through the lens of the player's persona, it was noticeably tinted. The idea that this was a baseball player and not a trained actor was foregrounded in the performance. Reviewers could focus on a lack of technique or a triumph over stage fright to reflect whether they liked the performance, but, in a large part, criticism was rendered meaningless. The ballplayer simply could not be judged in the same terms as other actors. In Cobb's case, he could not be seen as just another actor because he was not just another actor and never could be just another actor. Furthermore, no amount of aesthetic criticism of the player could dissuade some audience members from attending. As the reviewer in Athens stated, "the people went…to see a ballplayer, not an actor, and were satisfied."[105]

At the heart of a review from Birmingham, Alabama, was that Cobb "never, for a moment, seems to forget that he is Ty Cobb 'playing' at hero."[106] Being a hero for an extended period of time might have been Cobb's intention precisely. While he had stated explicitly that he was only concerned with the money from the tour, the performance offered him a chance to experience a new field while remaining a star. As someone who was then concerned with how people saw him (and later in life obsessed with his legacy), the role onstage was a chance for Cobb to align his persona with the traditional melodramatic hero. In the play, he got to have experiences that eluded him in his regular life. Unlike on the baseball field, his football teammates in the play loved him—and not just because he won them the big game. Moreover, as a player used to always traveling into hostile locations, the production's tour through the southern states saw Cobb return to his home region and receive a hero's welcome in each new city. As the tour turned northward, the celebrations faded away except for in his professional home city of Detroit. While his physical conditioning surely must have suffered and provided a legitimate reason for him to stop performing, he was also facing a schedule that had no more home dates on the tour when he announced he was leaving.

As a Jacksonville review pointed out, "everyone went expecting to see just Ty Cobb," and that is what they got. "Cobb is Cobb all the time and doesn't attempt to be anything else."[107] He was not playing an idealized and softened version of himself like Anson had fifteen years earlier. Nor was the character being played close enough to his own persona that audiences could believe that they were seeing him essentially under a different name as they could have with Mike Kelly. But Cobb had created such a celebrity—and a villainous one at that—that it could not be subsumed into a role that did not share many of the traits of his popular public persona.

Cobb clearly understood what was happening onstage despite stating to Toronto reporters: "I lost myself in my part."[108] He told a Birmingham, Alabama, newspaper before departing the city: "I have a baseball individuality and I can't lose it in the role of actor. What is worse, the public can't lose sight of my identity as a ball player and no matter how good I might ever hope to be as an interpreter of parts, there will be a portion of my audience that will only see me as they have heard of me or thought of me on the diamond."[109]

Cobb had performed his baseball persona so well on the field that nothing he could do would ever make people forget it. His acting performance essentially failed because he had been such a great "interpreter" of the Ty Cobb part that no one could believe he could be anything else. No matter the venue, whether it was on the field or on the stage, in the newspaper or in the streets, he was always performing a version of Ty Cobb that people had come to expect of him.

In many ways, Cobb lives on as a villain long past his death in 1961 through a mix of reality and narrative-reinforcing embellishment enhanced through popular storytelling. This is the ultimate service of the villain to a melodramatic narrative: to stand in persistent contrast to the melodramatic hero. Even as concepts of heroism shift over time, the villain remains both constant and necessary as the opposition that must be surmounted, whether as a reminder of what has been overcome or as an indication of what still must be done.

For most of the run of *The College Widow*, the Cobb that people had come to expect him to perform was played out offstage rather than on.[110] While in Birmingham, another publicity stunt had been arranged so that Cobb would take over as the sports editor for the city's newspaper for a day. Upset by the attitude Cobb displayed toward the task, the paper's managing editor informed his drama critic (who was also the paper's regular sports editor) that he was to give an honest review of that night's production and of Cobb.[111] The reviews from previous stops along the way were largely forgiving of Cobb's theatrical ability, even if they damned the production itself with faint praise. Told to hold nothing back, however, critic Allen Johnson did not. He wrote that the task of criticizing Cobb as an actor could not be done since "there is no actor there" and that Cobb himself was well aware of that fact. Johnson wrote that Cobb was stiff as a stick and "actually embarrassed throughout the performance." Calling his efforts "pitiful," Johnson noted Cobb's inability to look his stage sweetheart in the eye and that he played scenes with her like he would handle a bat which was "hard and strong" because he "didn't try any moderation, gentleness or sentiment." The review ends with Johnson wishing Cobb luck but also proclaiming that Cobb "has hardly a right to foist himself upon the people as an actor."[112]

Upon receiving note of the review nearly a month later while the production was in Detroit, Cobb wrote Johnson a letter in response, though he specified that Johnson's criticism was beneath his notice. He enclosed several much more favorable reviews as he invited Johnson to see what "real critics" had to say about his work. Ending his letter with what was essentially a summary of his feelings toward most people, Cobb wrote: "I am a better actor than you are, a better sports editor than you are, a better dramatic critic than you are, I make more money than you do, and I know I am a better ball player—so why should inferiors criticize superiors?"[113] Ty Cobb believed that "Ty Cobb" was inferior to no one.

Rube Waddell (En)Acting the Fool

GEORGE EDWARD WADDELL was an anomaly in baseball in many ways. He was a strikeout pitcher in an era when most batters rarely struck out. He promoted personal achievements in a time when team achievements took priority. He maintained a sense of amateurism and playfulness toward the game as it was seeking further professionalism and legitimacy as an industry. He stood out due to his odd behavior on and off the field that created an impression for fans beyond the box scores that made him the most talked about figure in the game from 1902 to 1908.[1] These, along with his other idiosyncrasies, created a unique persona that not only lent him his famous nickname—Rube—but also showed how players whose personas weren't neatly confined to hero or villain categories might fulfill a third: the fool. Like others before him, Waddell's persona followed him into the theater, where once again it conflicted with the character he played. The player's inability to be anything other than himself illuminated the limits of acceptability.

Waddell's achievements on the field marked him as undoubtedly one of the greatest pitchers of his era. He led the American League in strikeouts for six consecutive years (1902–1907) while pitching for the Philadelphia Athletics. His record of 349 strikeouts in 1904 was not matched in the major leagues for more than forty years—and not eclipsed until 1965 by Sandy Koufax with

382. Twice during those years Waddell recorded more than 300 strikeouts. He led the American League with twenty-seven wins in 1905 and recorded more than twenty victories four times. Waddell recorded an Earned Run Average of under 2.00 three times in his career and led the league twice. In 1905, he achieved pitching's triple crown by leading the league in wins, strikeouts, and ERA.[2] He was widely recognized as one of professional baseball's best players and was a dominant star in the early years of the American League as a major league.

As notable as Waddell was for his statistical achievements, he was much more renowned due to the behavior he displayed both on and off the field. When he was on the field, Waddell often tried to highlight his dominance over opposing batters. Playing for Louisville in 1899, he intentionally walked the bases loaded in the second inning of a game against Chicago, and then he struck out the next three batters. He would only walk one other batter that game while striking out a total of thirteen.[3] He created an additional layer of toying with the opposition in two other instances, in 1903 and 1906, when he began the final inning by striking out the first two batters, then loading the bases with intentional walks before striking out the final batter to end the game.[4] Displays like these not only emphasized Waddell's dominant ability and created a sense that he was in full control but also served to embarrass and demoralize the opposition.

Another tactic Waddell used to exhibit his superiority over others was by calling his own players off the field to emphasize the batter's inability to make contact with his pitches. He began the practice during his brief stay at Volant College and continued it in a variety of league games and exhibitions throughout his career. When league rules prevented fewer than nine players from being on the field, Waddell had his teammates sit on the ground or had the outfielders stand directly behind the infielders.[5] In one instance, Waddell waved his outfielders off the field and waved the fans onto the field to stand just beyond the infield to see him get the final out with the tying run standing on third base.[6] Unlike providing the opposition with free baserunners and runs, should anyone get a hit off of him, removing the fielders visibly altered the sense of fairness and balance inherent in the game, putting Waddell and his team in the disadvantaged position. The move backfired at least once in an exhibition game against Memphis as a few players made contact with the ball and Waddell had to chase it around the diamond by himself. He eventually secured the victory with a strikeout.[7] Waddell's success in these moments emphasized his individual ability by creating the absence of his teammates. The win might belong to the team, but it created the impression that Waddell could do it on his own.

Even beyond his impressive pitching, Waddell found ways to remain the focus of attention while on the field. He would do various bits of clowning on the field in between moments of play and during the action of the game. He told jokes and stories in between batters or when he stood in the base coaches' boxes on the field. At times he prefaced or punctuated his pitches with odd noises.[8] Most often, Waddell enacted physical clowning, with tumbling like cartwheels, handsprings, somersaults, and walking on his hands as he entered or exited the field. Each of these actions ensured that he stood out on the field and in the game. These were entertaining moments for the fans, but they created an additional layer in his displays of dominance on the field by demonstrating that his performance didn't require pushing himself to physical (or mental) exhaustion. It went beyond displays of physical fitness and became an assertion about how none of the work he performed tired him. The field was a place for playing, not working.

The sense of play Waddell held toward the game led opponents to devise tactics to better their chances of beating him. Detroit Tigers star Sam Crawford recalled later in life that they often tried to keep Waddell laughing and happy on the field so they might be able to distract him from his pitching. If Waddell took the game seriously, they felt they had no chance.[9] Other teams believed it was more effective to distract him through taunting. John McGraw, managing Baltimore in 1902 against Waddell's debut as a member of the Philadelphia Athletics, yelled at the pitcher mercilessly from the bench throughout the game, contributing to an Oriole victory.[10] Other teams used the same tactic with varying results. Waddell charged Brooklyn's third base coach during a game for his taunting, which led to the coach's ejection. Waddell similarly charged the Browns' second baseman in another game, but players stopped the altercation before it got physical.[11] As verbal taunting began to have less effect, teams tried to bunt Waddell's pitches rather than swinging away fully to put pressure on his play in the field.[12] Crawford's Tigers tried several decidedly different approaches by bringing various toys to the game, and once by bringing dogs into the dugout and onto the field to distract Waddell. It didn't work, as Waddell held the Tigers to a single run.[13] His dominance and attitude toward the competition in general required others to engage with him on his terms.

Fans also attempted to taunt Waddell as a way to influence the game's action. At times it was successful, such as when Brooklyn fans yelled so much that Waddell threw to the wrong base on a pickoff attempt, allowing the runner to score.[14] Later in his career, a Chicago fan printed up and distributed 15,000 cards containing a poem. The crowd then chanted at him a portion that read, in part, "you've been drinking; you cannot see the plate."[15] Though not every set of fans was so organized, they did sometimes influence what Waddell did on the field. After being hit by an egg thrown during an Easter Sunday exhibition game, Waddell removed his fielders from the game and struck out the side. One teammate later recalled thinking, "how can a man throw that hard?"[16] Waddell's longtime manager Connie Mack once gave information to a fan to use to taunt Waddell as he began to lose focus during a game.[17] Outside of the bounds of play, fans weren't directly subject to the on-field embarrassment, but such tactics could still be dangerous, however, with a player of Waddell's size and demeanor. He hit the final batter he faced in an inning after being taunted by a particularly vitriolic Brooklyn crowd. Order was restored before the game was ceased due to darkness. Still in Brooklyn two days later, standing at the entrance to the bleachers, Waddell silently and repeatedly threw a large hatchet at one of the fence posts as fans filed by and entered into the park.[18] Taunts by a well-known gambler in the home crowd of Philadelphia (spurred on by players from the St. Louis Browns) prompted Waddell to climb into the stands to punch the man until the crowd eventually managed to separate the two. The game resumed with Waddell continuing to play after consultation with American League President Ban Johnson. Both Waddell and the gambler posted $500 bond, and neither went to jail—although Waddell did receive a five-day suspension.[19]

It wasn't the only time Waddell disregarded the separation from fans. He saw the whole park as his playing area so he would often enter the stands to sit among the fans in a spirit of fun. Absent just before the start of one game, Waddell emerged from the stands and changed into his uniform on the field on his way to the clubhouse. He also ran into the stands to celebrate his success, such as when he ran to the stands several times during a game to have fans slice off a piece of his undershirt for luck after a strikeout. He sat in the stands among the fans occasionally to protest some wrong he felt the club had done to him as well. He sought solace among the fans once when he had been taunted as a bum who didn't know how to pitch. Away from the field, Waddell also made himself the center of attention—and often in a large crowd of people. If a parade went through town, whether it was for the baseball club or not, Waddell was frequently at the head of it. After his death, friends recalled how much he enjoyed the adulation of the fans, from standing in hotel lobbies in order to be worshipped to leading cheers of his own name.[20] Even as Waddell saw himself as exceptional, he wanted to be embraced by the people around him.

People frequently described Waddell as being childlike, whether he thought of himself that way or not. He could often be found playing baseball or marbles with groups of kids. He injured himself on one occasion because he wanted to show a few boys how to throw a curveball—but no one had a ball, so he repeatedly threw a brick instead. Another time, he arrived late to a game he was scheduled to pitch because he had been playing ball with a group of kids. While he played in many sandlot games with kids, he also decided that he would pitch for nearly any team that wanted him. The practice began before he signed a major league contract with its implied exclusivity. While pitching for Franklin, Pennsylvania, in the Oil and Iron League, Waddell agreed to pitch for Volant College. During his one season of college baseball, he was kidnapped and taken to pitch for a team in Mercer, Pennsylvania. They paid him $1 for winning the game. While sitting in the stands at a game in Evans City, Waddell was coaxed into playing for the team after it ran out of pitchers and faced a forfeit. Waddell used this practice as a safety net for when he had a dispute with whomever he believed his primary club to be. While playing primarily for the Detroit Tigers (before the establishment of the American League), Waddell left the team to play for a small club in Chatham, Ontario, after a dispute with the Tigers owner. In Chatham, he was celebrated by the town, and he earned $50 a week from them and $25 a game pitching for other neighboring towns before eventually returning to Pennsylvania. Waddell pitched for a team from Cedar Springs, Michigan, under the name Ole Olesun while already under contract with a team in Grand Rapids. Even after entering the major leagues full-time, Waddell continued to pitch for small town and local teams when he wanted to—despite restrictions against it. After playing in the National League in 1901, he appeared in a barnstorming tour of the West Coast, where teams in Los Angeles, Oakland, and San Francisco each believed they had signed him to a contract for their clubs. Instead of fighting over him, the teams rolled dice to determine his rights. Los Angeles won. He played there a few months before leaving to play for Philadelphia of the American League.[21] Waddell largely saw baseball as a game. He certainly profited financially from his exceptional ability, but his actions were in contrast to the idea of professional competition. His behavior often underscored his desire to play the game of baseball above all other industrial connections to the game.

Waddell also became widely recognized for his impressive physique away from the field as well, which was evident in both virtue and vice. As might be expected from his 6'2" 225-pound size, he excelled at other sports besides baseball, and he had a particular draw to boxers, befriending Jim Corbett, William Rothwell (also known as "Young Corbett"), and Jim Jeffries, whom he impressed with his own boxing technique. Waddell also challenged professional wrestler Frank Gotch, resulting in Waddell being body-slammed on a saloon floor and requiring a few days recovery. Later in life he regularly wrestled with several bear cubs in a Virginia zoo before leaving the area.[22] He was also an expert fisherman and hunter. These actions undoubtedly entertained those watching, and Waddell entered into them with the same spirit of playfulness and a sense of enjoying himself.

If it appeared around baseball that Waddell took very little seriously, one exception was using his physique to help people. Several times he assisted in re-tracking a train or trolley that had become derailed. Most frequently, this help took the form of firefighting. As a three-year-old, Waddell was drawn to the local firehouse and, as he grew older, would regularly throughout his life drop what he was doing at the time to go answer a fire alarm, even while pitching. To save time, he regularly wore red underwear, so he could shed his top layer while on the way to the fire. Several times Waddell's presence was key in protecting people's property. In Wisconsin, he saved a boy's beloved red wagon from a burning building. In Massachusetts, he launched an oil stove out of a window and into a snowbank to prevent it from exploding and engulfing the whole house. While he was on the mound in Los Angeles, a mattress being used as a backstop caught fire. Rushing to it, Waddell pulled the flaming mattress away from the wall and flung it to the ground where it could do little harm. His exuberance, however, was sometimes misplaced. Arriving at the scene of a fire in Kentucky, he took an axe to the roof, without instructions, and chopped it off. Once finished, he learned that it had been unnecessary since the fire was entirely contained in the chimney. He returned later in the week to rebuild the roof. Wherever he went, Waddell befriended the local firefighting corps. His appearance at fires became a regular occurrence. In Dallas for spring training in 1907 as a member of the Philadelphia Athletics, Waddell left the team unannounced and trained with the local fire department's rookies in their drills. The Giants were also in the city for spring training and manager John McGraw saw Waddell in the driver's seat of a hook and ladder truck as it passed by. Though McGraw and his players yelled to get Waddell's attention, he never acknowledged them. McGraw believed he had never seen the man so serious before.[23]

Even with his evident disregard for what professionalism required, for Waddell firefighting was serious business because it was about helping people in trouble, and if his physical abilities could help someone, he offered them up readily with little regard for his personal safety. While out hunting in Illinois, Waddell swam out to rescue a man who was drowning after his boat had turned over. During the flooding that overtook Kentucky in early 1913, Waddell volunteered to move sandbags in the floodwaters despite having battled pneumonia earlier in the winter. The work sparked a relapse. A similar event hastened the end of his life the next year. A rowboat capsized in northern Minnesota resulting in a drowning death, but the body couldn't be found. Waddell repeatedly dove into the cold waters until the body was retrieved. The incident contributed to his declining health; he eventually contracted tuberculosis, which led to his death at the age of only thirty-seven years old.[24]

The other contributing factor to Waddell's early demise was a lifetime of heavy binge drinking. Beginning during his time with the Franklin club, before he reached the major leagues, Waddell would disappear for days at a time—usually just after a successful outing on the mound—missing games and returning either of his own discretion or because someone else had to go find him. When he returned to the mound after these absences, he was just as likely to pitch superbly as he was to pitch terribly. He was, as Connie Mack noted, unpredictable. These events eventually led to tension between the pitcher and the ball club as they tried to reconcile this enormous talent with his adverse tendencies. Managing this balance required deftness and a willingness to tolerate his behavior to a point. After being fined $50 for his drinking by the Louisville club in the National League, Waddell refused to play for them again and threatened to walk away from the game until he was traded to Detroit of the minor Western League. In St. Paul, Minnesota, with Detroit, Waddell, in a stupor, threw a wild pitch, allowing the runner to advance; then he held the ball and allowed the runner to take home. Much later in his career, with the St. Louis Browns, New York players saw Waddell in a saloon with a big mug of beer while on their way to the ballpark. When the game began, he was on the mound ready to pitch. By the fourth inning, watching an opposing player round the bases after a home run, Waddell got dizzy and fell over. The manager removed him from the game to uproarious laughter. Though they may have had only a temporary effect, if any, on Waddell's behavior, Connie Mack tried several methods of emphasizing the negative impact of and the damage caused by Waddell's drinking. One tactic saw Mack demonstrate the lethal effect whiskey had on three live worms in a glass. Waddell acknowledged the damage and concluded that as long as he was drinking, he wouldn't get worms. At the end of his life, however, Waddell produced a letter to young baseball fans citing himself as an example of the destructive effects of alcohol abuse.[25] Even if Waddell's habits were largely unmanageable, teams mostly tolerated his actions as the price for his abilities until the scales eventually tipped unfavorably out of balance.

Waddell also had some violent tendencies, and his drinking and unpredictability only increased the potential for danger. Though an award-winning marksman, he frequently handled loaded firearms in a careless manner, including sitting in the stands playing with a loaded revolver as he watched his team play—and dropping a pistol while walking through a hotel lobby, where it discharged and took out a chunk of the lobby wall. Waddell fought a pair of teammates after their wagon came close to him in the street. The three men were taken to the police station but released by a judge. Even more serious than these examples, Waddell beat his then father-in-law with a flat iron and his mother-in-law with a chair when he attempted to take away his belongings after failing to reconcile with his wife. For years he would not pitch in games in Boston or travel through the commonwealth of Massachusetts due to the warrant seeking his arrest.[26] To those around him, these violent actions offset his impulses for beneficial self-sacrifice, making his persona a complex mixture that was difficult to fully embrace.

Even though each of the above contributed to Waddell's persona, the best descriptor of his style and behavior was simply "odd." That was how Waddell's father described him to the owner of the first major league club to sign his son—and Waddell continually proved the description to be true. Oddness existed as part of nearly all aspects of Waddell's playing persona, and often superseded them as the stories proliferated. He showed off his impressive pitching ability by using it to break planks, which he guaranteed he could do in three pitches. He doused his pitching arm in ice water before a game, explaining that if he didn't take such precautions, his throwing might set the catcher's mitt ablaze. He struck out a player by throwing a lemon instead of a baseball. He fell to his knees as a batter popped up to the shortstop and bemoaned that he didn't get another strikeout. He played in an exhibition skills competition in an Uncle Sam costume. He cut off the button of his own uniform pants when his manager was searching for a replacement for his own. He was forced by his roommate to have a clause inserted in his contract that he was forbidden from eating animal crackers in bed. He wrestled the opposing team's first baseman before a game, and then pitched a complete game while the other player couldn't play at all due to fatigue. He stopped a few feet in front of the plate on what would have been an inside-the-park homerun to kneel and loudly pray that the catcher would drop the throw. He broke all protocols to go shake President William Taft's hand as he entered the park on a visit. He rode ostriches, chased pigs, and kept a bass in a hotel bathtub for several days. He exploded at teammates and the umpire on the field because of a lingering injury to his hand. He stripped off his uniform on the field as he prepared to answer a fire alarm, with no regard to the fact that he wasn't wearing his red firefighting underwear—or any other kind either. He once arrived at the ballpark in the ninth inning, walked to the mound unbeknownst to his manager, announced himself to the umpire, and struck out two batters to win the game.[27] In a symbolically fitting pair of coincidences, he was born on Friday the thirteenth, and he died on April Fool's Day.

Taken alone or in some partial combination, these actions wouldn't be more than colorful footnotes. When taken all together, however, they're illustrative of someone who routinely behaved in a way that did not conform to the dominant behavior in baseball or the larger society. Waddell's playing persona identified him as being exceptional both on the field and off of it. The excellence of his pitching was always infused with the extraordinary and sometimes inexplicable behavior he displayed. He played the professional game with the attitude of fun and play. Other players' similarities to Waddell ended where Waddell went to extremes. In the context of baseball and the context of the level of middle-class society that baseball embraced, Waddell was an anomaly. As a former player recalled about him years later, "In his life, he gave a lot of people a lot of enjoyment."[28] Most of that enjoyment came through laughter as a result of him being an anomaly.

Philosopher Ted Cohen offers up the idea of anomaly as one of the key aspects of why people find things funny. Cohen's attempt to summarize the traditional major theories of humor leads him to identify humorous things as having a basis in the anomalous. An anomaly is something "irregular, unusual, unexpected, and often unsettling." Cohen offers up two reasons why the anomaly is funny: 1) it suggests that we have power over the structures that usually restrain us, and 2) the anomaly exhibits the powerlessness we have to understand and control those structures. The humor of the first part acknowledges that things and people are placed in society or behave in ways that society or nature does not typically tolerate. In the second part, the extremity of the incongruity presents something truly incomprehensible and creates a mood of willing acknowledgement that some things can never be subdued or completely understood.[29]

Waddell indicated both of these ideas for onlookers. His behavior was unusual both within the structure of a baseball game as well as within society as a whole. He violated the expected social norms in both arenas as someone who did not fit neatly, with behavior that people had difficulty figuring out. At the same time, because of his status as a ballplayer in society and as an exceptionally performing player within the world of baseball, what otherwise might have been intolerable was tolerated with a resigned acceptance to the situation that could provoke laughter. Waddell was a comic figure to many, but it wasn't always clear why they were laughing. In either case, Waddell's behavior, and eventually even just his presence, served to illustrate the ridiculous.

Similar to his categories of heroes and villains, Orrin E. Klapp offers up the fool type as the institutionalized means for a society to deal with conspicuous incongruities through ridicule. Societies have used fools to redirect aggressiveness, provide relief from the routine, affirm acceptable standards of behavior, control behavior through means of ridicule, and build a sense of community through laughter. In American society, Klapp identified five types of fools, with each offering a source of ridicule and providing a corrective to improve the structures of society. These types include the incompetent, whose failures illustrate mismatched roles; the claimers of undue status or unearned pretentiousness; nonconformers who deviate from acceptable standards; over-conformers who are too enthusiastic in adhering to standards or seeking group approval; and types that serve as outlets for aggression.[30] A fool may embody the characteristics of multiple categories at once, as an action may be ridiculed for a myriad of reasons. Indeed Waddell's behaviors make him easily recognizable as several types of fools that Klapp has identified.

While on the field and in competition, spectator perspective can be important in how a player like Waddell might be perceived. For fans of his team, the exhibitions of his abilities would align him with the role of the splendid performer variety of the hero type. Those same exaggerated displays of his abilities, however—particularly when set up to make the other players on the field look incompetent or unnecessary—provoked fans to see him as a braggart or a show-off type of fool, whose eventual failure illustrated that his claim of overwhelming superiority was undue (or at least temporary), as the performative displays of his youth became pompous assertions later in his career that led to his comeuppance. These are all examples of Klapp's fools who hold erroneous beliefs about their status, and the deflation of these people leads to ridicule and serves as a lesson against such behavior being emulated by others on the ballfield.[31]

Away from competition, even if still on the field, Waddell's behavior most often resembled a variety of fool type that Klapp identified as nonconformers. This type tends to reaffirm the standards of behavior that they clearly disobey by the ridicule their status as an outlier receives. Klapp makes a fine distinction between the "strange fools," who are ridiculed for the oddness of their personalities and separated somewhat from society, and those who do not conform to society's structure but are still embraced, whom he terms "characters." While still identifying those who do not fit, this latter catch-all category implies a space carved out for oddness to exist, or, as Klapp writes, "toleration with a smile."[32] Of course there must be a reason for the society to deem a character worthy enough to make that space. In Waddell's case, his idiosyncrasies made him strange in a way that would ensure that he wouldn't be fully embraced by society whether he sought it or not. His extraordinary pitching ability, however, required baseball find a way to accommodate those idiosyncrasies. The marker of his place as a character within the game, tolerated with a smile, became the name by which he was popularly known: Rube.

The "rube" is a character that emerged in American popular culture in the nineteenth century, although the character's traits existed in many forms well before that. The nickname is derived from the name Reuben, and both the name and nickname indicate in a mildly derogatory way an unsophisticated person from a rural area. The nickname is usually applied toward others as a clear separation between those who are knowledgeable urban figures and those who are not.[33] The song "When Reuben Comes to Town," written by J. Cheever Goodwin and Maurice Levi in 1901, tells the tale of one such country character arriving in the city where he is promptly fleeced by a cabbie, tempted by a lost lady and her glass of cider, and finds himself with a headache and in a haze facing a judgement of $10 or ten days in jail. The song makes such events seem routine and expected as it repeats that the listener has heard of all these details before. The refrain concludes: "It can't be helped alas/ when a chump's as green as grass/ he'll meet the fate of hundreds who have gone before."[34] Though the title implies that this one particular instance happens to a man named Reuben, the song's lyrics begin with "a Reuben from the country," clearly indicating that the type was already well known and all Reubens are the same.

Mark Evans Bryan traces elements of the rube character in performances to the eighteenth-century portrayals of the unsophisticated by the earnest rural "Stage Yankee" character popular in the United States and the United Kingdom. Bryan notes that early vaudeville managers used "rube" and "Yankee" relatively interchangeably in the description of acts, but that their doing so obscures the influence and incorporation of negative stereotyped caricatures from blackface minstrel performances such as the stump speaker but also elements of the unsophisticated and violent man-child.[35] Bryan further argues that the rube character is an amalgam of the simplistic, clown-like rural laborer and the barbarian with the constant possibility of brutality. These characteristics were already widely acknowledged on vaudeville and variety stages in the United States, where the rube type was a popular and easily identifiable character at the turn of the twentieth century.[36] The character was as popular in film as it was onstage, with the rube a well-known character type recognized by almost all audiences.[37]

At the heart of the comedy of the rube was his ignorance of nearly all elements of contemporary civilized society. Though sometimes having hyperspecific knowledge regarding rural matters that might indicate some practical wisdom or metaphorical lesson for the observer, the rube was put into situations where he was out of place and often confronted with elements of the new society of which he was unaware. The balance of traits in the character meant that each encounter had the possibility of befuddlement or brutality. How would the character answer a challenge—with kindness or cruelty? For audiences, either would provoke laughter, regardless of whether the rube was part of the story or one of their own in the crowd.

The rube concept is often applied to those in the audience whose lack of sophistication doesn't allow them to understand or otherwise makes them misinterpret the artifice of some kind of show or performance by mistaking it for reality. Sometimes referred to as "green 'uns," the rube was often set up as an easy mark to be taken advantage of; but theatre historian David Carlyon argues that stories of these rube moments by audiences were often employed to emphasize and reinforce desired audience behaviors. Nineteenth-century audiences were often vocal and raucous, and interaction with performance was common and accepted as long as it remained within established bounds for whatever the performance dictated. Yelling at performers in order to express approval or displeasure happened as frequently at melodrama play-houses as it did at the ballpark. For Carlyon, the stories of audience rubes—occurring along similar patterns as tales of urban legends—not only help to define the boundaries of acceptable behaviors but also establish quieter and less noisy and disruptive interactions as a middle-class aspiration. Subdued engagement was held up as the ideal for performances courting a higher societal status in contrast to the boisterous popular performances of the lower classes with the rube stories providing a point of ridicule and undesired behavior.[38]

The rube, as a fool, sits in between the hero and the villain, sharing traits of both but not quite adhering to either. In examining the Yankee figure, Richard M. Dorson places it within the realm of the hero, even if it occupies a folk status, because the Yankee transcends the buffoonery which defines the rube.[39] The rube is not quite virtuous enough to be admired as a hero, nor quite serious enough to be taken as a villain. As an in-between, the fool is both and neither. As such, the rube expresses elements of both identities without benefiting from either extreme. Rubes who cannot distinguish fiction from reality don't exist in the same way as villains who are being purposefully disruptive. The rube's inability to acknowledge boundaries or to clearly distinguish fiction from reality clearly indicates that they are not part of the accepted majority and they are regarded as ridiculous. Their limited acceptance by the group is based on not knowing any better, which provokes the smiling tolerance mentioned above. Their presence is tolerated as both a source of humor and as a model of the negative or what shouldn't occur. They are mostly harmless, until they aren't, such as in a "Hey Rube" confrontation at circuses or carnivals where potential for violence becomes actualized.[40]

Waddell's biographer, Alan Levy, finds several anecdotes about how the man who preferred to be called "Eddie" got his nickname, but the most straightforward was from a childhood friend who noted, "We called him Rube because he was a rube."[41] Regardless of how he acquired the nickname, Waddell seemed in many ways to be a perfect embodiment of such a character. He frequently illustrated that although he knew and abided by the rules of baseball, he lacked awareness—or at least adherence—to the propriety of the game. His antics were perceived to be more humorous than harmful. Even though the potential for violence was seemingly ever-present and tempered any conception of him as a hero, Waddell's buffoonish behavior generally prevented him from being seen as a villain.

As a fool and object of ridicule, he served not only as a negative example for other players to heed but he also demonstrated what didn't fall under the expected respectability of the game. While other players would illustrate improper behavior in one aspect or another, Waddell was employed in a multi-faceted way by baseball as a rube fool. His lack of baseball's desired professionalism was cast as his being childlike or lacking the maturity that baseball needed to display as a respectable industry because he preferred to see baseball as a game and approached it with a sense of play. Waddell was particularly valuable as the American League proclaimed its status as a second major league to the longer-established National League. In the AL's early years, Waddell's visibility as a point of conspicuous ridicule showed that the league held to similar standards of respectability that the older circuit claimed. By having him exist as an exception rather than the standard, Waddell's rube-ness further illustrated how the game had grown beyond its rural and pastoral roots into a mature and respectable industry largely populated by players behaving professionally. He provided the contrast that further legitimized the other players and the league.[42] Further, Waddell's interactions with crowds, even when benign or playful, transgressed the typical boundaries between players and fans and provided illustration of why such diversions were necessary. The interactions he had with crowds, whether they were observed in person or existed only in stories, demonstrated to fans what acceptable and desired behavior at the ballpark was by showing what it was not. Though definitely prompted by Waddell's exceptional pitching ability, baseball incorporated the things that made him an outlier into an acceptable, if not fully accepted, character of the game. Waddell effectively became a stage rube with the ballpark as his proscenium. It's clear to see why a theatrical producer saw the potential of Waddell playing on the stage.

Though it wasn't the central focus of a performance, humor was a necessary component in melodrama—much more for the audience's sake than for the story's. James L. Smith argues that the onslaught of trials faced by the victims in a melodrama would be too emotionally overwhelming to an audience without providing moments of laughter. The comic relief didn't even have to necessarily make sense to the story as long as it provided the necessary respite from the melodrama's emotional hold. Michael Kilgariff notes in his book *The Golden Age of Melodrama* that quite a bit of the humor in melodramas depended on the ignorance of rustics.[43]

In the fall of 1902, St. Louis theatre producers John H. Havlin and William Garen contracted Walter Mathews' play *The Stain of Guilt* to be produced at Havlin's Theatre in St. Louis the following spring.[44] Frequently touted in the advertisements and newspaper puff pieces as a great American drama, the play hit many of the standard melodramatic notes popular at the time. The story concerns good, honest, and forthright bank cashier Jim Burford, who has been set up as a thief by bank president Snowden's unscrupulous nephew as a way to remove him as competition for the hand of the lovely Italian street singer Chiquita. Proof of Burford's innocence is sought throughout the play by the famous detective Harry Slade, who appears in each of the four acts initially in different disguises. The play features scenes at the bank undergoing a multi-story construction, the personal home library of the bank president, and a seedy bar and hangout for criminals known as the Menagerie, overseen by Mother Greggin. Chiquita turns out to be Snowden's long-ago kidnapped daughter, and she rushes into Burford's embrace in the final scene as Slade has the nephew taken away by the police. For excitement and action, the play has several fights, an explosion, and a moment where the detective is bound and placed to be crushed under a descending elevator. The story is filled with clear heroes and villains, and the humor of the play during that era depended on popular stereotyped characterizations of the story's foolish characters and on the caricature disguises of the detective.[45]

Havlin and Garen opened the production with two performances on Sunday, March 29, 1903. The production touted St. Louis connections for several of the cast, including Oscar Dane, son of a St. Louis rabbi, as detective Harry Slade and Miss Rachel Acton, the stage name of Rachel Epstein of St. Louis, as Chiquita.[46] Both were mentioned as standouts in a cast that was better than typically seen in a melodrama of the sort.[47] The production ran a full week at Havlin's in St. Louis, closing on Saturday, April 4. It then traveled to Chicago on a short trial tour to play for one week each at the Alhambra Theatre (April 12-18) and the Bijou Theatre (April 19-25) before closing for the season.[48] This production of *The Stain of Guilt* had success and drew pretty well in both cities.

In May, while the Philadelphia Athletics were in St. Louis to play the Browns, William Garen signed Waddell to play an as-yet-unspecified role in *The Stain of Guilt* for the next season.[49] Though the production would begin its 52-week coast-to-coast tour in August, Waddell's contract wasn't set to begin until October 2, after the conclusion of Philadelphia's league season.[50] The production was set up for success. The combination company was touted to be sparing no expense, with two rail cars employed for transporting scenery and effects.[51] Most of the cast was set to return, including Oscar Dane and Rachel Acton, plus another St. Louis performer in the part of the bank cashier's sister, among the 30-person traveling company.[52] Garen believed that adding the pitcher, in this case, would prove valuable due to Waddell's popularity on the field and in the newspapers.[53]

Immediately and through the summer, Waddell's theatrical aspirations were an opportunity for amusement and ridicule, which helped bring attention and interest to the production. The *St. Louis Post-Dispatch* speculated in the initial article announcing the contract that Waddell might be used to throw bricks at the villain, subtly referencing how the pitcher had injured himself only a couple of years before.[54] Several times that summer, sportswriters overloaded game stories on days Waddell pitched with theatrical metaphors and references to his pending acting job.[55] Charlie Dryden of the *North American* in Philadelphia and Frank Hough of the *Philadelphia Inquirer* both ridiculed the situation by imagining what Waddell's participation might look like. Dryden joked about some of Waddell's pay being in real money, the possibility of strange costumes, and that he would likely forget his lines on the trip to Broadway. Dryden added that Waddell would sing a song titled "Where the Heart Is, the Lungs Are Close By." Among other jokes, Hough offered a burlesque that Waddell would take the stage as "Louis the Steenth or Ham, the Doleful Daneheimer," while imagining him and other ballplayers filling out the roles of "Uncle Tom's Caboose." Hough further joked that Waddell was likely to launch into reciting *Hamlet* at an umpire, and that he was already seeking veterinary treatment for a "hoarse voice."[56]

As Waddell's Philadelphia team returned to St. Louis to face the Browns in mid-August, the company had an opportunity to rehearse in person with their featured attraction. After having taken the loss in the second game of a Sunday doubleheader, Waddell arrived at Havlin's Theatre on Monday morning according to the *St. Louis Star*. He conspicuously stood under a poster of himself hanging on the wall before going onstage and reading his lines aloud. Noting a cleaning woman in the gallery, Waddell told her to stop working for a minute because "I'm goin' to act." The stage manager had to tell him not to interrupt the other actors as Waddell began to complain that he should have the romantic role. Waddell lit a cigarette while going over his lines and was told that for safety reasons smoking onstage carried a $2 fine.[57] Charlie Dryden again claimed Waddell was disappointed that the play only had him saying lines and requested that his part be written with a horse and two pistols or he wouldn't go on the road with the show.[58] It is unclear how many—if any—of these anecdotes actually occurred because the stories that circulated about Waddell made the most ridiculous events seem possible. Even if they existed solely as stories not tethered to actuality, they still served the purpose of reinforcing standards of behavior through ridicule of the rube figure's inability to conform.

Waddell joined the *Stain of Guilt* tour nearly a month early in an inauspicious way after having been suspended by his Philadelphia club. On Friday, August 21, Waddell pitched every inning of both games of a doubleheader in Detroit, shutting out the Tigers in the first game and losing 2-1 after a close play at home in the second. He took the train to Cleveland with the team and then couldn't be found for a few days and missed his next planned start. The following morning when he reappeared at 5:00 a.m., Connie Mack released Waddell on the spot. Rather than let another team sign the talented but frustrating left-hander, Mack changed the release to a suspension. Suspecting that Waddell might then join the play tour early, Mack reportedly alerted the minor league teams in locations along the tour route that Waddell was not allowed to play for them.[59] The tour for the play had already begun on Sunday, August 23, in Topeka, Kansas, before it was set to move eastward.[60] Waddell returned home to Camden briefly to tend bar and pitch for the local team.[61] He then joined the tour on Friday, September 4, in Moberly, Missouri, just before it arrived back in St. Louis.

Advertisements for the production noted that Waddell's part was written specially for him, and, indeed, his part does not appear in the extant copy of the play on microfilm at the Library of Congress. Waddell and comedian John Rucker, a Black performer known as "the Alabama Blossom," who was part of the original production as well, were both featured special performers in the production with some bits that could be added or removed at will, as well as some incorporation into the plot. Rather than being added as a caricatured stereotype as Rucker was, Waddell's part was written as a supporting hero. In the first act, Waddell gets introduced in a way that makes it clear to the audience who he is. Appearing as himself, he comes onstage in his Athletics uniform with a glove, bat, and ball to talk to his friend, detective Harry Slade.[62] While there, he argues with the stereotypical stage-Italian character between being a pitcher of baseballs and a pitcher of beer. Using an ethnic slur, Waddell threatens to pitch the man into the river.[63] The next two acts have Waddell physically handling the villains both individually and as a group as he makes a stand with the heroes in the underworld bar. In the final act, he appears as a special police officer, hauling away the villains for good and assuring a happy resolution.[64] Throughout the production, and in the model of other ballplayers onstage at the time, he is essentially seen first as a baseball player and only playing himself to lend a sense of reality to the melodrama's events. Waddell was not portraying a rube character in the play and was much more aligned with the heroes than the comic relief.

The reactions to the production indicate that the play was generally popular and people enjoyed it. The production consistently reported good houses and business throughout Waddell's time on the tour. Critics and audiences received pretty much what they expected from his performance, even if the production had tried to assert "his acting is way above par and will surprise the critics of the East."[65] His line delivery was sometimes wild, but he reveled in the attention he received from those in the gallery, noting "the boys up there can beat any bleacherites that ever collected, and even on the road they're for you."[66] Waddell seemed quite eager to please that portion of the audience as the *New York Clipper* reported that "Rube Waddell handles the villains in a way that makes the gallery gods howl with delight."[67] It was certainly the most notable aspect of his performance as the *Indianapolis Morning Star* wryly observed that his lines "give him ample opportunity to display his physical ability."[68] Another critic from the *Chicago Journal* was more direct, proclaiming that "the stain of guilt for that play will have to rest partly upon the man who wrote it and partly upon who ever hired Waddell."[69] In making Waddell a feature in the production, the producers got the draw they wanted because there were really no expectations for Waddell's acting ability. As the *Sporting Life* printed, "Rube is simply himself in the Havlin-Garen melodrama, but it keeps him busy changing clothes."[70] Yet in the realism the producers sought to add to the story of the melodrama, they didn't account for the melodrama added to the production since the rube character was not in the story. The rube was in the cast.

Waddell continued to embody the rube character throughout the production tour with his odd behaviors. During his time on the road, he played for various local teams as he passed through, including striking out twenty-four batters from Champaign, Illinois, while playing for nearby Mattoon, and he played rugby for Grand Rapids against Detroit.[71] While in Lexington, Kentucky, he played first base for Louisville of the American Association and was knocked unconscious in a collision while clowning around on the bases.[72] Joe Finnigan, a St. Louis sportswriter who was hired to do press for the production, circulated a story that Waddell left the Alahambra Theatre in Chicago between acts while the show was playing and visited another nearby theater where he wrestled with some lion cubs and received a bite to his left hand.[73] He punched a young man in Pittsburgh who was bothering a young woman, and he punched a theater manager in Columbus who said Waddell should be carrying bricks instead of trying to act.[74] In Covington, Kentucky, he nearly fought a street car conductor who didn't acknowledge Waddell's pictures on a four-sheet poster to the pitcher's satisfaction.[75]

With the production itself, Waddell was alternately completely enthralled or completely disinterested. Believing he could do a better job, he offered to rewrite several of his lines to improve them.[76] He tacked up posters for the show in towns while telling people he was going to act in it and even helped occasionally with the scenery.[77] He helped to (over) load the prop guns used in the production, and he reportedly shot castmate George F. Miller through the hand by accident.[78] Seemingly annoyed by a newspaperman's questions, Waddell quietly produced a gun before explaining it was for the show and dashing onstage for the shootout scene.[79] Sometimes, however, Waddell didn't show up at the theater at all, and even when he did, he refused to go onstage or required an immediate enticement of $10 to do so. After having left the production to return to St. Louis to mount a new show, Oscar Dane admitted that more than once they led Waddell to a dressing room and kept him there because he was in no shape to go onstage. The play was adjusted so the company could perform in his absence. Once they attempted to have Waddell sleep it off until his necessary appearance in the final act as the special officer who drags away the villains. When the moment arrived, Waddell was once again absent, so the stage manager walked on in his place believing that something was better than nothing. The audience went wild because they thought it was Waddell himself since the stage manager was wearing clothing most commonly associated with a rube: overalls.[80]

Ultimately, Waddell's inability to adhere to the time, money, and place standards of the theatre led to his departure from the production. On one occasion in Chicago, after drinking all day with friends, Waddell appeared at the theater late while the performance had been held up until his arrival. The stage manager told him the cast was apoplectic and the crowd was mad about the delay. Seeking any excuse to resume his night out, Waddell refused to go on because he insisted he would not appear in front of a mad house, and he immediately left to return to his companions.[81] He frequently demanded advances on his salary from management and then didn't appear onstage after the company had advertised his appearance. As a result of his being denied a $50 advance, he left the production in Wheeling, West Virginia.[82] Joe Finnigan coaxed him to return for engagements a few weeks later in Philadelphia at an increase in salary from $40 per week to $100 per week plus expenses.[83] While in Philadelphia, Waddell again arrived late to one performance, and he invited his teammate and catcher Ossie Schreckengost to come backstage during the Tuesday matinee performance. A fight ensued when the manager refused. Waddell threatened not to go on. Instead, in the grand theatrical tradition, Waddell's trunks were thrown into the alley, and he was barred from the theater. For the rest of the week, a large sign outside the theater advertised that Waddell was no longer a member of the company.[84] In the end, Waddell left he production just like he joined: early and under suspension.

For all of his antics during his run in the production, the way Waddell most conspicuously embodied the rube was in his inability or reluctance to distinguish reality from fiction onstage, leading him to physically harm other actors. In his first rehearsal, Waddell laid his shoulder into George Melville, who played the stereotyped Italian villain. When he was informed that they were just working through things at the moment, Waddell stressed that he wanted "to make the thing look real." Later in a scene he grabbed E. J. Denecke, playing the piece's main villain, by the arm and tossed him across the stage, where he hit the ground and rolled among the footlights. After taking some time to recover, Denecke acknowledged that "it will be into the audience with me if 'Rube' gets excited." While working on one of the play's moments of action during the same rehearsal, Waddell again threw Melville into a pile of stage equipment and lifted up the play's hero like "he was a bunch of straw."[85] Despite being told that the actor would just fall down when touched, Waddell continued to fully commit to the action of the play and roughly handle his fellow actors during performances—to the delight of the crowds.[86] In Chicago, Waddell invited the sporting editors of local papers to the opening performance with the promise of his realistic performance. During the show that night, Waddell dragged the actor playing the villain all around the stage and ended with a punch that landed him among the musicians in the orchestra. Waddell then approached the box where the editors were sitting and, breaking the stage reality he was trying to enact, asked, "Did you see me do him?" The actor quit the show after the performance, but Waddell convinced him to stay.[87]

Playing a heroic role in a melodrama required Waddell to defeat the villains, but the thrashing he gave was absorbed not only by the character but by the actor as well. It is unclear whether Waddell didn't acknowledge his strength in wanting things to seem real onstage or he simply didn't care, but ultimately he failed to distinguish the fiction from the reality. His showing off for his friends or to impress the crowd in the gallery was an activation of the rube's persistent potential for violence in the name of serving an appearance of reality, enacted within the bounds of his perception of fun and play rather than with the more malicious intent of a villain. In this way, by blurring the marker between fiction and reality, Waddell's image as a rube was reinforced and magnified. He didn't take on a rube role in the play, but his behavior in violating the standards of live fictional performance embodied the rube for all in attendance. Rather than watching a rube story, they saw a rube.

Additionally, seeing Waddell embodying the stereotype of the rube and making it reality in a production that had dedicated many resources to presenting an accurate scenic reality created a space where the other stereotypes enacted in the play, mostly those done along ethnic caricature, might also be read (inappropriately) as close to life or authentic as well. This included the portrayal of the Italian villain with dialogue written in eye dialect, such as when he vows "ven-adetta" as he plays with his stiletto, as well as the performance of John Rucker as Rastas Snow, which was described as a "coon specialty" act. Taken separately, these may be acknowledged as typical elements of a melodramatic production of the time. Combined with Waddell playing a version of himself as a character onstage and actually enacting a rube while performing that character, it furthered and reinforced already prevalent and harmful ethnic stereotypes. If the rube stereotype was being displayed as accurate, the audience might assume that the others were as well.

Waddell's rube continued to function as a ridiculous figure and social corrective in a unique way due to the intersection of baseball and theatre. As theatre audiences and critics witnessed the improper behavior and the many violations of accepted standards, they could exhibit tolerance and limited acceptance because Waddell was conspicuously an outlier. As one description of his theatrical endeavor noted, "the critics also treated the pitcher-actor kindly, although they refuse to take him seriously."[88] He wasn't an actor. He was always a baseball player first and foremost. His breaking of the rules, such as talking directly to friends in the audience, reinforced what proper interactions were, even in a genre like melodrama where some interactions were permitted. Audiences could enjoy the sensational deeds onstage because they knew it was all fiction, even as they became engrossed in the story. Waddell's thrashing of the character *and* the actor, however, broke that willing suspension of disbelief. What was supposed to be a semblance of reality became real in front of them, whether they knew it or not.

The assertions of the snarky reviews were that those who held status—those who were "in the know"—saw Waddell as an object of ridicule, and their laughter was directed not at Waddell as a character but at Waddell as a rube. This provided baseball the opportunity to show itself as holding status as well. Ballplayer Mike Donlin, who would eventually transition to stage work himself, laughed so loud at Waddell's performance that it became an entertainment in itself.[89] The response of Donlin and many others, particularly club owners and presidents, along with the satirical sports columns about Waddell, asserted that baseball was in on the joke, too, rather than being taken in by the fiction that Waddell was just like them. Their response was evidence of tolerance of the outlier for his usefulness—but clearly laced with ridicule toward him for not fitting in. They set up Waddell to serve as the visible exception to the norm, which effectively normalized the rest of the profession. One unnamed Cincinnati player spoke in reference to Waddell: "It is pretty tough on the game when an eccentric player poses as a freak, even if it is in a play . . . it does not reflect credit upon his intelligence nor upon the profession in general."[90] Without the contrast provided by those outliers, however, how would anyone know?

After ending with *Stain of Guilt*, neither Waddell nor any theatrical producer thought his involvement with a touring multi-act drama was worth attempting again. The play itself was apparently rewritten to remove both Waddell and John Rucker's roles and included instead an Irish laborer character to fulfill their obligations within the plot. Later, Waddell popped up briefly with vaudeville bits occasionally where his idiosyncrasies could be better put on display with shorter obligation. He was released by the St. Louis Browns in August 1910 after a fractured elbow severely hampered his effectiveness on the mound and he became less of a draw for fans. He never pitched in the major leagues after that, but stories about his exploits on and off the field continued to circulate for decades long after his death in 1914. Though the stories surely both gained and lost something over time, they still served baseball in illustrating the way things used to be in contrast with how the game was at the moment of comparison. However wistful the tales, the contrast reminded the audience how much more respectable the game had become.

CONCLUSION
Babe Ruth and the End of an Era

By the time George Herman Ruth went on his first vaudeville tour in the fall of 1921, he had already become a nationally recognized name. Just the year before, in 1920, he was sold by the team with whom he had won two World Series—from the Boston Red Sox to the New York Yankees; set a new home run record with 54; and starred in a silent movie as a character roughly modeled on himself. Ruth followed that by again setting a new season home run record with 59 in 1921, becoming the all-time leader in home runs in major league history, and leading the Yankees to their first World Series appearance. When he stood on the stage of the Palace Theater to announce a vaudeville tour in the winter season of 1921-22, he was already baseball's biggest star and one of the most identifiable people in the country. Nearly everyone had heard of Babe Ruth. While previous ballplayers may have used theatrical work to keep them in the spotlight while making some additional money in the offseason, clearly Ruth was not lacking in either, since he made the second highest salary in the game in 1921 at $20,000. Vaudeville wasn't necessary for Ruth to distribute his celebrity. Still, he toured twice: in 1921-22 and in 1926-27. Though he wasn't playing in a multi-act scripted drama, Ruth provides an interesting example of how theatrical endeavors worked in the transition phase when theatre began to no longer serve as one of the primary means for spreading a player's persona away from the field as films became more and more widely available.

On the field, Ruth was a uniquely exceptional player as he was one of the major league's best pitchers as well as the era's foremost slugger, even before he moved off the mound full-time, and his achievements were often unable to be matched. Debuting in the major leagues in 1914 at the age of nineteen, Ruth emerged as a star pitcher within only two years, leading the league in Earned Run Average and shutouts pitched in his second full year. Two years after that, he began playing in the outfield regularly and led the league in home runs. Ty Cobb argued that Ruth being a pitcher at first was key to his development as a hitter whose power-based hitting was at odds with the placement-over-power style that dominated the time. Since Ruth was a pitcher, he wasn't expected to contribute at the plate the same way other fielders were, according to Cobb. This allowed Ruth the opportunity to swing freely and powerfully every time without the typical stigma applied to position players when missing the ball completely. When Ruth did connect, the ball went a long way, and Cobb stated that as Ruth learned more consistency, he transitioned to being a full-time outfielder.[1] Excelling at both facets of the game in such a visible way in a relatively short but staggered timeframe not only brought him to the public's attention but also kept him there over an extended period, helping to fix him as a consistent presence at the forefront of baseball consciousness.

Off the field, Ruth's persona was managed to an extent not previously seen in ballplayers, and it led him to a level of celebrity that far exceeded any ballplayer before him. The primary force behind the ubiquity of Ruth's persona was Christy Walsh. Ruth biographer Jane Leavy argues that Walsh was the first sports agent, managing not only Ruth's finances and endorsements but also his public image in a fully coordinated presentation of his persona.[2] Ruth generated plenty of attention from his behavior in public—both good and bad. Walsh sought to nullify the stories of Ruth's recklessness and excesses by enhancing and generating positive ones. Visits with children at hospitals and orphanages were frequent, and the pervasiveness of that image was meant to overwhelm the competing image of Ruth's indiscretions and misbehavior. The goal was not complete eradication of those stories, even if such a thing was possible given Ruth's personality as well as newspapers that were eager for attention-grabbing content. Instead, Ruth's persona was a mixture of the good and the bad with as wide of an appeal as possible without seeming too much to one side. This made him appear admirable but approachable, and it helped shape a sense of reality in his image that made his behavior seem understandable. Unlike a melodramatic character whose glorious, villainous, or foolish deeds were always anticipated and expected, Ruth's image was crafted to seem more true to life. Making him seem like a regular person rather than a mythologized or compulsory figure made his abilities and achievements seem all the more grand. Walsh arranged and publicized Ruth's visit to Columbia University to undergo testing of his motor skills, coordination, and physical abilities. The results announced in the *New York Times* showed that Ruth was "supernormal."[3]

Walsh worked diligently to make sure Ruth's persona was widely available. In addition to the many publicity events, ranging from meetings with anyone who might have a bit of the spotlight themselves to publicity stunts generated to keep Ruth in the public consciousness—accompanied, of course, by plenty of photographs—Walsh helped people with no personal contact with Ruth feel like they really knew the man himself. The Christy Walsh Syndicate hired professional sportswriters to ghostwrite pieces with professional athletes on the bylines. Ruth was his first signee beginning with the 1921 season. Ghostwriting for athletes was not new, but Walsh's Syndicate dependably and steadily produced these pieces like never before, and the consistent presence of Ruth's (purported) thoughts and words in the newspapers made the public feel like they knew him in a personal way. Walsh saw these pieces as entertainments for the fans, and by instructing the ghostwriters to adhere to the temperament and tone of the athlete they were writing for, Walsh kept the image being presented associated at least somewhat with reality.[4] Further, Walsh guided Ruth in his endorsements to enhance Ruth's credibility as a spokesman. Before Walsh took control of his financial arrangements, Ruth agreed to endorsements without a clear plan, which resulted in his sometimes endorsing competing products at the same time. Walsh not only helped limit Ruth's affiliations to only one product in a category—and negotiated the best possible terms for this exclusivity—but he also kept them consistent with a persona that would continue to appeal to children and their parents while also accepting those geared toward adult consumers.[5] Ruth's persona was everywhere, often in a way that made people feel like they knew him, because of Walsh's curation. Ruth's widespread acceptability illustrated how mainstream baseball and its stars had become, as his influence was aimed toward the middle-class family as a whole.

Before Ruth started on the vaudeville stage, his persona was already well known. The public had seen him on-screen the year before his first vaudeville tour as Ruth had filmed *Heading Home* during the summer of the 1920 season. The production filmed in the mornings outside of New York City, and Ruth didn't have to miss a game during filming—although he did occasionally play right field in the afternoon still wearing his makeup. In the silent movie, Ruth played an affable and simple country boy whose baseball skills helped him get the girl by the end. It was a bit of a coincidence that he would play a Stage Yankee on film the first year he played for the Yankees on the field. The movie opened in September to fair reviews, but it disappeared after Ruth sued the producers less than a month later for the remaining $35,000 he was owed.[6] Two other movies featuring Ruth were also released that year, but he had no say in their creation. Educational Films used newsreel footage of his home runs to create *Babe Ruth in Over the Fence* and *How Babe Ruth Makes a Home Run*. Ruth and Walsh eventually sued but lost both at trial and in appeal because Ruth was determined to be a public figure and, therefore, a newsworthy subject.[7] The lawsuits likely influenced Ruth's decision to do the 1921 vaudeville tour, as live performance and his presence gave him more ability to control the product. In vaudeville, the piece would be written specifically for him, and Ruth's act only had to fit the persona he was already known by.

The act was similar to so many others by athletes over the years on vaudeville stages. It was written by Thomas J. Grey, and it paired Ruth with Wellington Cross, a veteran comic and musical performer. To begin the opening performance, the orchestra played "Take Me Out to the Ball Game" before Ruth emerged in a Yankee uniform, which spurred a full minute of applause for the player before Cross came on. Cross sang Irving Berlin's "Along Came Ruth" from the 1914 play of the same name. The pair did some patter jokes back and forth, including a mind-reading bit with Cross playing the straight man to Ruth's punchlines. In a wry acknowledgement of Ruth's recurrent flouting of propriety, one bit played on the fact that he was awaiting word on a possible suspension by the new baseball commissioner for having gone on a barnstorming tour after the 1921 World Series. Ruth also took a turn singing the song "Little by Little and Bit by Bit," which was an English music hall song that had been Americanized and featured in the musical *Go To It* at the Princess Theatre in 1916.[8] Though the musical itself was not a hit, Wellington Cross has been in the original cast, which likely led to the song's inclusion in the act. Overall, the act put a baseball player onstage doing non-baseball things as so many had done before. Though most critics were kind (and others less so), it didn't matter, since being an awkward performer onstage only lent authenticity to the idea that audiences were seeing a real version of Ruth, a man they felt they already knew, in front of them.

Walsh had not yet consolidated all of Ruth's non-baseball activities under his control, so the tour was arranged by Harry Weber and put together through the B. F. Keith circuit of vaudeville houses, which assured that everything would be properly organized—beginning with the press conference announcement of the tour directly from the stage of the Palace Theater in New York City on October 27, 1921. They created a lobby display of Ruth's baseball souvenirs to travel with the act and to greet patrons before seeing the show. The sixteen-week tour began with a lower pressure tryout in Mount Vernon, New York, on November 3, and then officially opened in Boston on November 7 before arriving for two weeks at the Palace on November 14, with other major cities and a few smaller ones down the line into late February. Ruth received $3,000 a week for his two daily performances in the prime spot next to last in the performance bill. Producer E. F. Albee wanted to advertise Ruth as the "Superman of Baseball" but had been advised to get clearance first from George Bernard Shaw, whose play *Man and Superman* had played on Broadway twice by that time. Shaw's response by telegraph—SORRY NEVER HEARD OF HER. WHOSE BABY IS RUTH?—was widely circulated in papers across the country. While the idea that someone would not know Babe Ruth was set up as laughable before he even stepped onstage, Albee seemed to allow that not everyone who knew Ruth would have a proficient understanding of baseball. He provided an explanation as part of the opening billing: "A Satirical Home Run: That's Good."[9] Audiences didn't really need to know anything about baseball to appreciate that Ruth, a baseball player, was out of his element onstage.

Though audiences loved seeing him, Ruth's tour was not much of a success for the producers. Crowds were appreciative but not overwhelming in numbers. While Ruth made nearly $50,000 for the four months of shows, theaters reported that their business didn't increase because of his visit as they were expecting.[10] The *New York Clipper* presented the argument that the age of bringing athletes in to provide a bolster to a bill was coming to an end, citing Ruth's failure, among others, as drawing cards across the country.[11] The practice of adding an athlete to the cast of a touring multi-act production had already nearly ceased, and now even the more manageable vaudeville opportunities were dwindling. Ruth's performance itself didn't do much to contradict the course. Though he certainly was not the first athlete to experience stage fright while putting on a show in a new arena, Ruth admitted to being unusually nervous looking into the crowds on his tour because of who was there. He said, "A vaudeville audience of women is about 60 times harder to face than all the baseball fans in the world. Gosh, I never knew what stage fright was 'til I looked over the footlights and saw two little flappers staring at me from the front row."[12] Nervousness leading to poor performances had led to dwindling interest in ballplayers onstage before. Vaudevillian Joe Laurie, Jr. argued that other vaudeville performers believed it was because people could see him at any time for a quarter or fifty cents.[13] The implication was that Ruth could be seen on the field doing what made him famous or in movie houses where recordings of why he was famous could be seen even in the offseason. There was less appeal in seeing him do something where he wasn't great. It reminded audiences that he was human rather than "super."

That was the persona that Ruth seemed to have to live up to, regardless of how possible it was. Audiences had consistently been presented with an image that had been carefully crafted and managed. The reality of Ruth in person in this alternate arena could not match the one that was readily available elsewhere already. While the vaudeville act wasn't built to be a biography, there wasn't anything it could show audiences that they didn't already know or couldn't find elsewhere. Testifying in a lawsuit unrelated to Ruth, his vaudeville agent Harry Weber made it clear that Ruth's salary for the tour was based on his publicity rather than his talent as an actor.[14] There was no doubt that he was popular. He was Babe Ruth.

Ruth didn't do another vaudeville tour again until after the 1926 World Series, which had ended with him being thrown out while attempting to steal second base, giving the St. Louis Cardinals their first championship. After a two-week barnstorming tour upon the conclusion of the series, Ruth began his twelve-week vaudeville tour on the Pantages circuit of theaters running through the Midwest and the western half of the United States. With nearly all of the cities in the American League located in the east, the tour sites provided a chance for many people to see Ruth in person who could not do so at the ballpark. Additionally, many of the Pantages theaters were combo houses that featured both live vaudeville performances and screened motion pictures.[15]

Unlike his previous tour, Ruth played as a solo act. It began with a seven-minute film featuring him that ended with Ruth seeming to move from screen to stage as he appeared live and in person. Though written by newspaperman Arthur "Bugs" Baer, there wasn't much to the act itself. After a few jokes, Ruth would mainly invite kids to the stage to talk about swinging the bat and to get an autographed baseball. He would then ask them if they wanted to sing or dance or perform a bit of a poem for him and the rest of the crowd.[16] In many ways, he was more of a host than a performer, with the main focus on the man in the short film and then redirected to the kids who wanted to impress him. In contrast to his first tour, and the many baseball player vaudeville turns that had come before him, he wasn't a baseball player set up to do anything else in front of a crowd eager to see novelty. By stepping out from the screen—and by stepping back from the spotlight—Ruth showed that he had moved past having to be a star. He just had to be there. His presence was enough.

In the winter before his legendary 1927 season, Ruth had already reached the zenith of the publicly led life—he only had to appear. As biographer Marshall Smelser noted about Ruth's later life, heroes who don't fade away gain the appearance of stability as part of the ceremony of living in the public eye.[17] More than that, by reaching that status during his playing career while he was still active, Ruth became a slate onto which spectators could write their own story. Since his public persona was a crafted mixture, fans could easily cast him as a hero or a villain or a fool. The biggest star in the melodrama of baseball was whomever fans wanted him to be as they created their own narratives for their teams, their seasons, and their own fandoms.

When Ruth was doing vaudeville, the era of ballplayers onstage for more than a brief novelty was coming to a close—particularly those in full-length multi-act dramas. After their playing days were over, some would jump to brief vaudeville runs until those houses started to close, but most active players of any recognition were earning enough from their season salaries that lengthy and strenuous stage work wasn't an appealing way to spend their offseason—especially if they could make money easier elsewhere. The newer recorded media forms allowed the player's image to be managed and manipulated through editing in a way that live performance didn't permit. Even if it came through different means, Ruth's ascendency as a national media star had its foundation in the era in which theatre was the primary live narrative vehicle for showing a player's persona. Audiences were already used to casting sports players into the hero, villain, and fool roles that had been heavily influenced by the popular melodramatic performances of the day. While the ups and downs of live performance didn't permit a player's image to be as manicured as it might be in the new media, the reputation and requirement of doing it all over again every day created a unique sense of authority for their personas. Crowds saw whom these players really were rather than a carefully managed persona whom they were permitted to see.

· · ·

One observation about baseball notes that a batter who fails six of every ten times to get a hit at the plate over his career would be considered the best batter of all time. Failure is integral to the game that is described as "designed to break your heart." Players experience it, and fans feel it. It is fitting then that the experience of professional baseball players in multi-act dramas in the late nineteenth and early twentieth centuries was largely one of failure—at least from a theatrical perspective. As actors, the players generally failed to conform to the accepted conventional aesthetic of contemporary performance. The productions with which they were involved were often considered failures both critically and financially, with runs for the player or the entire production that ended before they were scheduled to close. The sense of failure extended beyond the players as well. For playwrights like Rida Johnson Young and Charles Hale Hoyt, the plays they wrote about baseball were considered the largest failures in their careers.[18]

Yet for the players themselves, as well as baseball as an industry, these diversions into theatre were profitable in ways beyond their financial compensation. Each player examined here used his stage performances to create or maintain the persona he was known for from what he had done on the field before appearing on the stage, even if it might have been done unwittingly. Appearing as himself onstage, Cap Anson was presented as a man worthy of respect by Hoyt in *A Runaway Colt*, which highlighted a duality that existed in the man of which the late nineteenth-century general public was unaware—he was both baseball player and gentleman. Anson's limited ability to perform in an aesthetically pleasing way actually helped to foreground his presence in the theater as a baseball player, and it served to show that ballplayers could be respectable to the dominant middle-class sentiments of the age.

While Anson's presence onstage required that audiences see him as a baseball player, Mike Kelly's presence transcended being seen as only a baseball player. An exception to the standard player's persona of just being a celebrated ballplayer, Kelly was seen as an embodiment of wealth and success. His participation in multi-act dramas capitalized on that perception. Kelly was a celebrity in popular culture and an excellent showman. He had a reciprocal relationship with his two performance venues. Just as theatrical audiences were still aware that he was a baseball player, Kelly performed as much during ball games as he did on the stage, frequently alluding to his theatrical work while on the field. As his success on the field began to wane, he was able to maintain his public association with success while onstage in vaudeville houses with frequent references to his value and wealth. For audiences, Kelly's appeal was that he could be conflicting things at once: success and failure, extraordinary and everyday.

Rather than appearing onstage himself, the play that Christy Mathewson co-wrote, *The Girl and the Pennant*, featured a proxy of his baseball persona within a thinly veiled representation of current baseball events. Fitting the social type of a hero in American culture in an ideal way, Mathewson's persona easily transferred to a hero in the melodramatic mode. Using that melodramatic hero based on Mathewson's persona, the play showed how baseball could be reformed amidst persistent corruption and how the game could safely embrace the ever-encroaching feminine influence on American society. Mathewson's absence from the stage put the focus of the production on the content but may have also doomed it to only twenty performances.

Ty Cobb's involvement with a tour of *The College Widow* was faced with the issue of how to effectively repackage a player's persona to diminish some of the negative qualities he had acquired through his on- and off-field activities. By creating a persona that would intimidate the other players on the field, Cobb was viewed by some as a prime example of a villainous social type. The production tried to contextualize the player by reinforcing traits that had helped to build his stardom and made an effort to distance the player from the "Crazy Cobb" persona he had built. The efforts were somewhat for naught as, though he was playing a football hero onstage, the baseball persona Cobb had created had become so dominant that neither he nor the audience could ever forget who he was.

Renowned throughout baseball for his antics, Rube Waddell was widely enjoyed as one of the sport's entertaining fools before taking on a specially written role in *The Stain of Guilt*. Not quite virtuous enough to be heroic, nor taken seriously enough to truly be thought of as a villain, Waddell's fool was a target of ridicule as the means to display what was not acceptable, even if tolerated to a point. While the role he played tried to take aspects of his popular persona to make them heroic, the qualities that marked him as a rube superseded the role he was playing and blurred stage reality and actuality as he treated his fellow actors like the villains they were portraying.

Baseball itself was the de facto partner that each of these players performed with onstage. The theatrical work of Anson, Mathewson, and Waddell was concerned with baseball's respectability at different points in the game's history. Anson's presence in the theater gave a body and voice to a baseball player whose profession had not been seen in a favorable light before the turn of the century. More than a decade later, baseball had become enough of an establishment that it faced the danger of losing some of the ground it had gained. While Waddell illustrated the negative examples and boundaries that must be respected, the light comedy fantasy written by Mathewson and embodied by his proxy onstage showed how the industry could make gains instead of losses in the face of looming social threats. How baseball remained tied to the players' personalities that it had made into stars evolved as the professional game grew beyond its nineteenth-century beginnings. While Kelly's persona oscillating from the stage to the field illustrated how baseball could propel a person upward in society in the late nineteenth century, Cobb's inability to be seen as anything else showed how prominent baseball celebrities had become in American culture after the turn of the century. As such, Ruth's final turn in vaudeville required little more than his mere presence itself.

In many ways, baseball's utilization of the melodramatic social types of heroes and villains as seen with the personas of Mathewson and Cobb paved the way for the industry to profit from the American theatre's transition away from melodramas toward social realistic dramas beginning in the 1910s. Given clear heroes for whom to cheer (the home team) and clear villains to boo (the visitors), the game of baseball became an opportunity for audiences to emotionally invest in the contest on the field as they had traditionally emotionally invested in the trials and tribulations of melodramatic characters on the American stage. As content in the theater began to slowly change to more nuanced portrayals of protagonists and antagonists who caused audiences to consider their own relationship to the world around them, many patrons preferred to keep their worldview in black and white rather than shades of gray. Later writers who have waxed poetic about the game focus on the emotions that arise from its playing, from A. Bartlett Giamatti's "Green Fields of the Mind" that states the game is "designed to break your heart" to Roger Angell discussing the "business of caring" as part of his review of the 1975 World Series in *The New Yorker* article titled "Agincourt and After."[19] This emphasis on emotion is due in part because we are used to seeing the game through the framework of melodrama.

Even into the twenty-first century, Buster Olney crafts the players from the 1990s and early 2000s Yankees team in his book *The Last Night of the Yankee Dynasty* into these easily identifiable roles. Olney details how Roger Clemens was cast as a clear villain by other teams who competed against him—and even by the Yankees themselves until his arrival on the team in 1999. Left-handed pitcher David Wells is presented as a kind of rube figure who takes the game as an opportunity to play rather than to dominate as a professional would.[20] This makes him seem unserious as he's contrasted in the same chapter with the depiction of team-oriented, religious family man Andy Pettitte. By adding nuance and depth to certain figures, Olney's portrayals soften the edges of long-time owner George Steinbrenner and re-contextualize the outward displays of frustration of Paul O'Neill so that the traits that cast them as villains to the opposition become traits to be honored and recognized by those who cheer for the pinstripes.

The game of baseball began, developed, and flourished while melodrama was the most ubiquitous performance form in the United States. Players and owners, journalists and writers, and fans themselves were familiar with seeing narrative through a melodramatic frame. Significant for a game that embraces its history like no other, the framework for how to create stories with good guys and bad guys as part of the traditions of baseball since its beginnings has been passed down through generations of fans. Well-versed in the narrative tropes of melodrama, these fans could impose a dramatic narrative that had meaning specifically to them onto the events on the field. Fans willingly (if subconsciously) borrowed those elements of melodramatic performance for their engagement with the game. Baseball fans today still emotionally invest in the melodramatic mode of the heroes on the hometown team the same way they did more than 100 years ago.

Notes

INTRODUCTION

1. Heywood Broun, "Baseball Upsets Bad for Stage," *New York Tribune*, October 16, 1914. P8.

2. This book uses "theater" to refer to physical spaces of theatrical production and "theatre" to refer to non-physical concepts such as the theatre industry or artistic movements. Place names appearing in the text for specific theater buildings reflect whichever spelling they used.

3. Harold Seymour and Dorothy Seymour Mills, *Baseball: The Golden Age* (New York: Oxford Press, 1960), 117–18.

4. Jules Tygiel, *Past Time: Baseball as History* (Oxford: Oxford University Press, 2000), x–xi.

5. The emergence of professional baseball did not eliminate the presence of local amateur and semi-professional teams, which remained popular well into the middle of the twentieth century.

6. Productions on the road were not restricted to the standard multi-act melodramas and comedies from New York, but included other popular forms such as minstrelsy, Uncle Tom shows, and variety entertainments that primarily crisscrossed the eastern half of the United States entertaining crowds in cities and smaller towns alike.

7. Robert Bechtold Heilman, *The Iceman, the Arsonist, and the Troubled Agent: Tragedy and Melodrama on the Modern Stage* (Seattle: University of Washington Press, 1973), 49.

8. James L. Smith, *Melodrama, The Critical Idiom*. Edited by John D. Jump. 28. (London: Methuen & Co, 1973), 9–11.

9. Warren Susman, *Culture as History* (Washington: Smithsonian Institution Press, 2003), 111.

10. LeRoy Ashby, *With Amusement for All: A History of American Popular Culture Since 1830* (Lexington: University of Kentucky Press, 2006), 51.

11. Robert B. Ross, *The Great Baseball Revolt* (Lincoln: University of Nebraska Press, 2016), 27.

12. Amber Roessner, *Inventing Baseball Heroes* (Baton Rouge: Louisiana State University Press, 2014), 4.

13. Richard Schechner, *Performance Studies: An Introduction*, 2nd ed. (New York: Routledge, 2002), 26.

14. For an exploration of the performative aspects in the presentation of a modern baseball game, see Sean Bartley "'You're Out!' Presence and Absence in the Ballpark," 17–29 in *Sporting Performances: Politics in Play*, edited by Shannon L. Walsh.

15. Tygiel, *Past Time*, 22–30.

16. See Roessner, *Inventing Baseball Heroes*.

17. Cormac Power, *Presence in Play: A Critique of Presence in the Theatre* (Amsterdam: Rodopi, 2008), 47. Power develops the term by using "aura" to refer to the possession of a presence that is extraordinary beyond just physically being present.

18. Chris Rojek, *Celebrity* (London: Reaktion, 2001), 17–20. As the nature of celebrity is not universal, three different categories of celebrities are described by Rojek's classification system featured in *Celebrity*. The first is "ascribed celebrity," in which a person is a celebrity primarily due to their heredity. Traditionally, this has been most evident in celebrities of royal lineage; however, the offspring or relatives of celebrities established by other means may indeed qualify. One of these other means may be the public acknowledgement by cultural intermediaries that the person is somehow noteworthy. Rojek calls this category "attributed celebrity" and notes that it is primarily a result of mass media's use of sensationalism. The remaining category, "achieved celebrity," is of most importance for the purpose of this study. Achieved celebrities have gained their recognition through open competition where success and failure was apparent to the audience. Neither a lineage of previous celebrity nor verification by a social mediator is needed to be an achieved celebrity.

19. The benefit offered by the nature of the celebrity held by the players who appeared onstage was somewhat limited by geography, however. The player's value to the producer was easiest to expect in the player's home cities—both his birthplace/residence and the home city for whom he played. While there would likely have been some attraction in cities in the league where the player visited during the season, it would not have been as great. The player may actually have had more value in locations where there was no league team. For people lacking consistent opportunity to see games in person, the physical presence of a professional baseball player in these non-league cities would have had its greatest appeal. In these cases, the audience was more reliant on the producer as cultural mediator to promote the baseball player as a celebrity. The player's presence was still auratic as audiences were likely aware of the player's baseball persona from national and local newspaper reports.

20. Orrin E. Klapp, *Heroes, Villains, and Fools: The Changing American Character* (Englewood Cliffs, NJ: Prentice-Hall, 1962).

21. Roger R. Rollin, "The Lone Ranger and Lenny Skutnik: The Hero as Popular Culture," in *The Hero in Transition*, edited by Ray B. Browne and Marshall W. Fishwick (Bowling Green, OH: Bowling Green Popular Press, 1983), 14.

22. Rollin, "Hero as Popular Culture," 25. Klapp, *Heroes, Villains, and Fools*, 13, 17.

23. Robert Bechtold Heilman, *Tragedy and Melodrama* (Seattle: University of Washington Press, 1968), 76–78. Heilman, *Iceman*, 46–47.

24. Daniel J. Watermeier, "Actors and Acting," in *The Cambridge History of American Theatre: Volume II 1870–1945*, edited by Don B. Wilmeth and Christopher Bigsby (Cambridge: Cambridge University Press, 2001), 448, 452.

25. Though Edwin Booth's name had been widely acknowledged as the pinnacle of American acting excellence for years, he was not largely associated with the popular melodramatic theatre of the time. Instead, as Robert M. Lewis notes, Joseph Jefferson III was the American actor who garnered the most respect in popular theatre for his decades-long portrayal of Rip Van Winkle. Though the melodramatic form allowed for and even encouraged full-throated and overt sentiment, Jefferson offered blends of subtlety and the ability to land the humor as part of his performance that marked him as excellent. Despite reviews meaning specifically to deride or mock players onstage, invoking names like Booth as the measuring stick, audiences would have readily recognized Booth as belonging to a different kind of theatre with different aims. Performers in melodrama had styles, aims, and audience expectations that were unique. With that said, these players were certainly no Jeffersons onstage either. Robert M. Lewis, *From Traveling Show to Vaudeville* (Baltimore: Johns Hopkins University Press, 2003), 15–16.

26. Gunther Barth, *City People: The Rise of Modern City Culture in Nineteenth-Century America* (New York: Oxford University Press, 1980).

27. Harold Seymour and Dorothy Seymour Mills, *Baseball: The Early Years* (New York: Oxford University Press, 1960), 326–27.

28. Richard L. Miller, "The Baseball Parks and the American Culture," in *The Cooperstown Symposium on the American Culture (1990)*, edited by Alvin L. Hall (Westport, CT: Meckler, 1991), 176.

29. Richard Butsch, *The Making of American Audiences: From Stage to Television, 1750–1990* (Cambridge: Cambridge University Press, 2000), 121–38.

30. Butsch, *Making of American Audiences*, 137–38.

31. Ross, *The Great Baseball Revolt*, 42.

32. Ashby, *With Amusement for All*, 47.

33. Ashby, *With Amusement for All*, 49.

34. Butsch, *Making of American Audiences*, 71.

35. John E. Dreifort introducing Leverett T. Smith, Jr., "The Changing Style of

Play: Cobb vs. Ruth" in *Baseball History from Outside the Lines: A Reader* (Lincoln: University of Nebraska Press, 2001), 123–24.

36. Richard Piorcek, "Baseball and Vaudeville and the Development of Popular Culture in the United States, 1880–1930" in *The Cooperstown Symposium on Baseball and American Culture, 1999* (Jefferson, NC: McFarland, 2000).

37. This excludes players like the aforementioned "Turkey" Mike Donlin, an outfielder for the New York Giants, who quit professional baseball for a time in order to tour the vaudeville circuit with his wife, actress Mabel Hite. Additionally, not all players in the Hall of Fame who appeared onstage are represented here either, as the study is focused specifically on players with theatrical pursuits in multi-act productions who created, embraced, or attempted to reject their on-field personas.

38. Thomas Postlewait, *The Cambridge Introduction to Theatre Historiography* (Cambridge: Cambridge University Press, 2009), 85.

CHAPTER 1

1. A portion of this chapter appeared as "At Play: Cap Anson's Performance of 'Cap Anson' in *A Runaway Colt*" in *Sporting Performances: Politics in Play*, edited by Shannon L. Walsh (London: Routledge, 2021), 165–76.

2. Adrian Constantine Anson Player File, A. Bartlett Giamatti Research Center, National Baseball Hall of Fame and Museum, Cooperstown, NY.

3. All statistical information from http://www.baseball-reference.com.

4. John Thorn and Pete Palmer, eds., *Total Baseball* (New York: Warner, 1989), 2286.

5. Howard W. Rosenberg, *Cap Anson 4: Bigger Than Babe Ruth; Captain Anson of Chicago* (n.p.: Tile Books, 2006), 285.

6. Howard W. Rosenberg, *Cap Anson 2: The Theatrical and Kingly Mike Kelly, U.S. Team Sport's First Media Sensation and Baseball's Original Casey at the Bat* (n.p.: Tile Books, 2004), 282–85.

7. David L. Fleitz, *Cap Anson: The Grand Old Man of Baseball* (Jefferson, NC: McFarland, 2005), 221.

8. Fleitz, *Cap Anson*, 12, 20. Howard W. Rosenberg, *Cap Anson 3: Muggsy John McGraw and the Tricksters; Baseball's Fun Age of Rule Bending* (n.p.: Tile Books, 2005), 332.

9. Howard W. Rosenberg, *Cap Anson 1: When Captaining a Team Meant Something; Leadership in Baseball's Early Years* (n.p.: Tile Books, 2003), 126.

10. Rosenberg, *Cap Anson 1*, 202, 75–76.

11. Rosenberg, *Cap Anson 1*, 120.

12. Rosenberg, *Cap Anson 3*, 245, 254–56.

13. John Rickards Betts, *America's Sporting Heritage: 1850–1950* (Reading, MA:

Addison-Wesley, 1974), 186, 116. Though unfinished, Betts' work was one of the first to address the rise of sports in America.

14. David Quentin Voigt, *American Baseball: From Gentleman's Sport to the Commissioner System* (Norman: University of Oklahoma Press, 1966), x-xi.

15. Mike Kelly, *Play Ball: Stories of the Diamond Field* (Boston: Press of Emery & Hughes. Repr. Jefferson, NC: McFarland, 2006), 34–35.

16. Voigt, *American Baseball* vol. 1, 185.

17. Rosenberg, *Cap Anson 4,* 74–77.

18. Rosenberg, *Cap Anson 1,* 96.

19. Rosenberg, *Cap Anson 4,* 15.

20. Rosenberg, *Cap Anson 1,* 98–99.

21. *Sporting Life,* August 8, 1888. Rosenberg, *Cap Anson 1,* 112.

22. Rosenberg, *Cap Anson 1,* 36.

23. Rosenberg, *Cap Anson 1,* 98.

24. Seymour and Mills, *Early Years,* 330–32.

25. Seymour and Mills, *Early Years,* 211, 261.

26. Rosenberg, *Cap Anson 2,* 321, 352. Rosenberg found that Anson bet on his team fifty-seven times between 1876 and 1900. This was by far the most bets made by any player, manager, or owner associated with baseball, beating second place by forty-eight bets.

27. Rosenberg, *Cap Anson 2,* 297.

28. Rosenberg, *Cap Anson 1,* 35.

29. Rosenberg, *Cap Anson 4,* 68.

30. Rosenberg, *Cap Anson 1,* 65, 68.

31. Voigt, *American Baseball* vol. 1, 278.

32. Adrian Burgos, Jr., *Playing America's Game: Baseball, Latinos, and the Color Line* (Berkeley: U of California Press, 2007), 55.

33. Burgos, *Playing America's Game,* 60–1. Adrian C. Anson, *A Ballplayer's Career* (Chicago: Era Publishing, 1900), 148–50.

34. Stow Persons, *The Decline of the American Gentility* (New York: Columbia University Press, 1973), vi, 3.

35. Benjamin McArthur, *Actors and American Culture, 1880–1920* (Philadelphia: Temple University Press, 1984), 141.

36. Richard Bushman, "The Genteel Republic," in *Wilson Quarterly*, 38:1, Winter 2014.

37. Richard Bushman, *The Refinement of America* (New York: Knopf, 1992), 446.

38. *New York Sun,* January 30, 1898. Rosenberg, *Cap Anson 1,* 90.

39. Rosenberg, *Cap Anson 1,* 58.

40. John Frick, "A Changing Theatre: New York and Beyond," in *The Cambridge History of American Theatre, Volume Two: 1870–1945,* edited by Don B. Wilmeth and Christopher Bigsby (Cambridge: Cambridge University Press, 1999), 200–292.

41. *New York Times,* December 23, 1890; *Chicago Evening Post,* October 23, 1891.

42. Gerald Bordman, *American Theatre: A Chronicle of Comedy and Drama, 1869–1914* (New York: Oxford University Press, 1994), 298–99, 337, 339, 367.

43. *Chicago Daily News,* October 6, 1888; *Chicago Daily Tribune,* October 6, 1888.

44. *New York Tribune,* October 6, 1888.

45. *Chicago Daily Tribune,* October 6, 1888.

46. *Chicago Daily News,* October 6, 1888; *Chicago Daily Tribune,* October 6, 1888; *New York Tribune,* October 6, 1888.

47. Rosenberg, *Cap Anson 2,* 58.

48. Douglas L. Hunt, introduction to *Five Plays by Charles H. Hoyt* (Princeton: Princeton University Press, 1941), xi-xii.

49. Charles Hale Hoyt, *A Runaway Colt,* in *The Dramatic Works of Charles H. Hoyt,* 8, 11, 16.

50. Hoyt, *A Runaway Colt,* 17, 19, 20.

51. Hoyt, *A Runaway Colt,* 76.

52. Biographer Howard Rosenberg finds Anson reportedly using profanity in arguments on the field—and concedes that Anson likely had several favorite profane expressions—but doubts that the majority of the time they were used in a voice above a whisper. *Cap Anson 1,* 94–96.

53. Hoyt, *A Runaway Colt,* 41, 59.

54. Hoyt, *A Runaway Colt,* 99.

55. Hoyt, *A Runaway Colt,* 41 (emphasis original).

56. Hoyt, *A Runaway Colt,* 80, 91.

57. Hoyt, *A Runaway Colt,* 51, 52, 56, 78. It is later implied in the play that Rosie feigned drowning in order to get Anson to jump in to save her.

58. Hoyt, *A Runaway Colt,* 62.

59. Hoyt, *A Runaway Colt,* 26–27.

60. Hoyt, *A Runaway Colt,* 26, 61.

61. Hoyt, *A Runaway Colt,* 90. The scorecard vendor mentions that it is a pity that Mr. MacDonald could not join him at the ballpark. MacDonald played Little John in the production. Hopper had become famous for reciting Earnest Thayer's famous baseball poem "Casey at the Bat" as part of his act with Bell.

62. Rosenberg, *Cap Anson 2,* 61.

63. Fleitz, *Cap Anson,* 243.

64. Rosenberg, *Cap Anson 2,* 65–66.

65. *New York Clipper,* January 4, 1896. It is likely that it was the three-week run in New York City that doomed the play financially. Though it was never well received critically, the novelty of having Anson onstage made the production successful at several locations.

66. Rosenberg, *Cap Anson 2,* 63.

67. *Oswego Daily Times,* November 16, 1895.

68. Rosenberg, *Cap Anson 2*, 64.

69. Rosenberg, *Cap Anson 2*, 66. *Washington Post,* February 12, 1896.

70. *New York Sun,* December 16, 1895.

71. *Syracuse Standard,* November 12, 1895, and November 14, 1895.

72. Fleitz, *Cap Anson*, 244. The players decided on some impromptu retribution for being cast as the losers in the final scene, and as Anson rounded third base after his game-winning hit, one of the players tripped him, causing him to crash to the stage floor.

73. *Brooklyn Eagle,* November 26, 1895.

74. *Syracuse Herald,* November 10, 1895.

75. *New York Clipper,* January 4, 1896.

76. Fleitz, *Cap Anson*, 246.

CHAPTER 2

1. A portion of this chapter appears as "Mike Kelly's Performance of Success and Failure on the Field and on the Stage" in *Theatre Symposium*, vol. 27, 2019, 39–52.

2. Kelly does not mention the precise source material for the play. Although likely suspects include W. T. Moncrieff's *Jack Sheppard, the Housebreaker, or London in 1724* from 1825, William Harrison Ainsworth's novel *Jack Sheppard*, or the John Buckstone stage adaptation of the novel from 1839, the version performed was probably a bastardized version of the story.

3. Kelly, *Play Ball*, 8–9.

4. *Boston Herald,* March 27, 1888. Rosenberg, *Cap Anson 2*, 45.

5. Marty Appel, *Slide Kelly Slide: The Wild Life and Times of Mike "King" Kelly, Baseball's First Superstar* (Lanham, MD: Scarecrow Press, 1996), 42.

6. Kelly, *Play Ball*, 25.

7. Rosenberg, *Cap Anson 2*, 7.

8. Rosenberg, *Cap Anson 2*, 218.

9. Kelly, *Play Ball*, 92.

10. Rosenberg, *Cap Anson 2*, 264.

11. Voigt, *American Baseball,* vol. 1, 178.

12. *Chicago Daily Tribune,* September 6, 1886.

13. Kelly, *Play Ball*, 166. *Boston Globe,* March 29, 1887.

14. Rosenberg, *Cap Anson 2*, 173.

15. *New York Telegram,* November 20, 1894.

16. Rosenberg, *Cap Anson 2*, 4.

17. *Chicago Daily Tribune,* September 22, 1881. Rosenberg, *Cap Anson 2*, 4.

18. Kelly, *Play Ball*, 34–35.

19. Appel, *Slide Kelly Slide*, 32.

20. Kelly, *Play Ball*, 6.

21. Rosenberg, *Cap Anson 2*, 106.

22. "Murnane Recalls Great Generalship of Mike Kelly," in *The Evening Mail*, December 1912, located in Michael J. Kelly player file, A. Bartlett Giamatti Research Center, National Baseball Hall of Fame and Museum, Cooperstown, NY.

23. *Chicago Daily Tribune*, August 18, 1886. *Chicago Herald*, August 18, 1886.

24. *Brookfield [NY] Courier*, November 9, 1894.

25. Rosenberg, *Cap Anson 2*, 29.

26. *New York World*, September 15, 1889. Rosenberg, *Cap Anson 2*, 82–3.

27. Voigt, *American Baseball*, vol. 1, 178.

28. Rojek, *Celebrity*, 12.

29. "Ed Williamson on Kelly's Release," Kelly player file, National Baseball Hall of Fame.

30. http://www.baseball-almanac.com/teams/cubsatte.shtml. Figures accumulated from *Sporting News* and *New York Times* reports.

31. *Chicago Daily Tribune*, April 10, 1881.

32. *Chicago Daily Herald*, January 9, 1887.

33. Alfred H. Spink, *The National Game*, second ed. (National Game Pub., 1911; repr. Carbondale: Southern Illinois UP, 2000), 28. *New York Times*, October 18, 1885, in *Early Innings: A Documentary History of Baseball, 1825–1908* (Lincoln, NE: University of Nebraska Press, 1995), 139–40.

34. Appel, *Slide Kelly Slide*, 99.

35. Rosenberg, *Cap Anson 2*, 110.

36. Seymour and Mills, *Early Years*, 109.

37. Appel, *Slide Kelly Slide*, 102.

38. Kelly, *Play Ball*, 46.

39. Appel, *Slide Kelly Slide*, 104. Anson reported that Kelly had received a total of $12,700 for his seven years of work for Chicago. In 1887 alone, Anson reportedly received $12,000 from the club through various ownership agreements. "Kelly a Spendthrift," Kelly player file, National Baseball Hall of Fame.

40. www.retrosheet.org. John Clarkson, who was sold from Chicago to Boston the year after Kelly, was also effectively released for $10,000, but typical of these transactions did not receive any of the money for the release, nor a salary increase from his new club. Seymour and Mills argue that by selling him for such a high price over his salary, the Chicago team essentially received two and a half years' worth of Clarkson's services for free, plus they made money from the transaction. Seymour and Mills, *Early Years*, 110.

41. Robert A. Margo, "Annual Earnings in Selected Industries and Occupations: 1890–1926," in *Historical Statistics of the United States*, vol. 2, Millennial Ed. (New York; Cambridge Press, 2000), 2–271.

42. http://www.senate.gov/artandhistory/history/common/briefing/senate_salaries.htm; http://www.usgennet.org/usa/topic/preservation/gov/usgov.htm.

43. Martin Murray, *Circus: From Rome to Ringling* (New York: Appleton-Century-Crofts, 1956), 252.

44. Appel, *Slide Kelly Slide*, 105.

45. *New York Herald,* February 16, 1887.

46. Rosenberg, *Cap Anson 2*, 132–33.

47. *New York Clipper*, April 9, 1887.

48. *Boston Globe*, August 15, 1887.

49. Michael T. Isenberg, *John L. Sullivan and His America* (Urbana: University of Illinois Press, 1994), 13, 26, 42.

50. G. C. Duggan, *The Stage Irishman: A History of the Irish Play and Stage Characters from the Earliest Times,* (Dublin: Talbot Press, 1937), 290.

51. Isenberg, *John L. Sullivan,* 22.

52. Judy Scully, "'A Stage Irish Identity'—an Example of 'Symbolic Power,'" in *Journal of Ethnic and Migration Studies,* 23:3, 397.

53. Rosenberg, *Cap Anson 2*, 11.

54. *Boston Globe*, April 11, 1887.

55. *Boston Globe*, June 30, 1887.

56. *New York Herald*, February 16, 1887.

57. http://www.baseball-almanac.com/teams/bravatte.shtml.

58. *New York Evening Telegram,* March 25, 1887.

59. Rosenberg, *Cap Anson 2*, 11.

60. Kelly, *Play Ball*, ix.

61. *Sporting Life*, April 27, 1887.

62. *Boston Globe*, June 30, 1887.

63. Rosenberg, *Cap Anson 2*, 41–42. Kelly, *Play Ball*, 83.

64. *New York Clipper,* March 31, 1888.

65. *New York Clipper,* March 31, 1888.

66. Kelly, *Play Ball*, 86. Rosenberg, *Cap Anson 2*, 45.

67. *New York Clipper,* March 31, 1888.

68. *New York Clipper,* April 14, 1888.

69. Kelly, *Play Ball*, 84–85.

70. *New York Clipper,* April 14, 1888.

71. Rosenberg, *Cap Anson 2*, 30, 116, 143, 156, 161, 168, 180. The parrot is featured in a humorous tale from the November 10, 1886, issue of the *Sporting Life* concerning Kelly and his wife as they were hosting Rev. Thomas Green of Chicago's St. Andrews Church.

72. *Chicago Daily Tribune*, June 25, 1887. Rosenberg, *Cap Anson 2*, 130, 133.

73. *New York Sun*, June 2, 1889.

74. *Boston Globe*, May 10, 1887. Rosenberg, *Cap Anson 2*, 128.

75. *Buffalo Daily Courier*, November 6, 1886.

76. Rosenberg, *Cap Anson 2*, 146.

77. *Boston Globe*, November 4, 1888. *Boston Globe*, December 22, 1888. The two Kellys were not related to each other.

78. Rosenberg, *Cap Anson 2*, 124.

79. *New York World*, December 17, 1888.

80. *New York World*, December 23, 1888.

81. Charles Hale Hoyt, *A Tin Soldier*, in *The Dramatic Works of Charles H. Hoyt*, 39.

82. *New York World*, December 23, 1888.

83. *New York Herald*, December 25, 1888.

84. *New York World*, December 25, 1888.

85. *New York Clipper*, January 5, 1889.

86. Rosenberg, *Cap Anson 2*, 172.

87. Rosenberg, *Cap Anson 2*, 2. Kelly, *Play Ball*, 143–44.

88. Appel, *Slide Kelly Slide*, 136–37.

89. Seymour and Mills, *Early Years*, 221–50.

90. *Buffalo Express*, December 2, 1889.

91. "Setting the Pace," Kelly player file, National Baseball Hall of Fame.

92. Rosenberg, *Cap Anson 2*, 185.

93. *Pittsburgh Press*, June 23, 1890. *St. Louis Post-Dispatch*, August 13, 1890. Rosenberg, *Cap Anson 2*, 187–89.

94. Rosenberg, *Cap Anson 2*, 215.

95. *Sporting Life*, December 17, 1892.

96. *New York Clipper*, December 31, 1892. *New York Clipper*, January 7, 1893. *New York Clipper*, January 14, 1893.

97. *New York Clipper*, January 21, 1893.

98. *New York Clipper*, March 25, 1893.

99. Rosenberg, *Cap Anson 2*, 229.

100. Rosenberg, *Cap Anson 2*, 51.

101. Eugene C. Murdock, *Mighty Casey: All American* (Westport, CT: Greenwood Press, 1984), 5–6.

102. Murdock, *Mighty Casey*, 22–26.

103. Jim Moore and Natalie Vermilyea, *Ernest Thayer's "Casey at the Bat": Background and Characters of Baseball's Most Famous Poem* (Jefferson, NC: McFarland, 1994), 237- 9. Thayer would later maintain that there was no one player who was the basis for "Casey."

104. Rosenberg, *Cap Anson 2*, 228.

105. Rosenberg, *Cap Anson 2*, 50.

106. Asa Bordages, "2 Things Kelly Could Do, Play Smart Baseball and Drink Straight Whisky," *New York World-Telegram*, May 13, 1939, located in Kelly player file, National Baseball Hall of Fame.

107. *New York Daily Tribune*, June 11, 1893.

108. Appel, *Slide Kelly Slide*, 165.

109. Anson, *A Ballplayer's Career*, 115.

110. Rosenberg, *Cap Anson 2*, 230.

111. *Chicago Daily Tribune*, July 11, 1888. *Boston Globe*, July 14, 1888. "His Tribute to Kelly," Kelly player file, National Baseball Hall of Fame.

112. Rosenberg, *Cap Anson 2*, 246.

113. *Chicago Daily Herald*, November 10, 1894.

114. Rosenberg, *Cap Anson 2*, 160.

115. *Boston Globe*, April 28, 1893. Rosenberg, *Cap Anson 2*, 189.

116. Rosenberg, *Cap Anson 2*, 46.

117. Rosenberg, *Cap Anson 2*, 49.

118. Rosenberg, *Cap Anson 2*, 220.

119. *New York Sun*, November 16, 1893.

120. *Boston Globe*, March 11, 1894.

121. He reportedly used the watch given to him by the Elks as security for the players on the Allentown team to return home via rail after the club went broke in Buffalo in 1894. Rosenberg, *Cap Anson 2*, 319.

122. Rosenberg, *Cap Anson 2*, 1.

123. Rosenberg, *Cap Anson 2*, 244.

124. Alfred P. Cappio, *'Slide Kelly Slide': The Story of Michael J. Kelly The 'King' of Baseball* (Passaic County Historical Society, 1962), 15, located in Kelly player file, National Baseball Hall of Fame.

CHAPTER 3

1. A portion of this chapter appeared as "Staging a Feminist Movement in Baseball: Rida Johnson Young's *The Girl and the Pennant*," in *Baseball/Literature/Culture 2008–2009,* edited by Ronald E. Kates and Warren Tormey (Jefferson, NC: McFarland, 2010), 64–71.

2. "Mathewson a Playwright," *New York Times*, April 8, 1913.

3. Klapp, *Heroes, Villains, and Fools*, 11–12.

4. Klapp, *Heroes, Villains, and Fools*, 27–28.

5. The Giants won the National League in 1904, but no World Series against the American League champion was held.

6. Ray Robinson, *Matty: An American Hero* (New York: Oxford UP, 1993), 118.

7. As of this writing, Mathewson stands tied for third in wins, ninth in ERA, and thirty-ninth in strikeouts for his career.

8. Roessner, *Inventing Baseball Heroes*, 12, 35.

9. Christy Mathewson, *Pitching in a Pinch* (1912; repr., New York: Stein and Day, 1977), 64.

10. Mathewson, *Pitching*, 57.

11. Robinson, *Matty*, 157.

12. Michael Hartley, *Christy Mathewson: A Biography* (Jefferson, NC: McFarland, 2004), 77–78. Philip Seib, *The Player: Christy Mathewson, Baseball, and the American Century* (New York: Thunder's Mouth Press, 2003), 60-1, 73.

13. *Playthings*, March 1922, 61. Clipping from Christopher Mathewson player file, A. Bartlett Giamatti Research Center, National Baseball Hall of Fame and Museum, Cooperstown, NY.

14. Hartley, *Christy Mathewson*, 27.

15 Seib, *Player*, 85, 91.

16. Hartley, *Christy Mathewson*, 24.

17. Seymour and Mills, *Golden Age*, 359. The municipal restrictions on playing baseball on Sundays were lifted slowly through the early part of the 1900s until half of the teams in the major leagues could legally play at home on that day of the week. However, most teams continued to play in defiance of such blue laws and would undergo periodic arrests and fines with little to no effect as the popularity of Sunday baseball financially outweighed the possible negative social aspects. Chicago, St. Louis, Cincinnati, Detroit, Cleveland, and Washington allowed Sunday ball by the end of World War I, but it took an additional fifteen years for the practice to become legal league-wide.

18. Seymour and Mills, *Early Years*, 290.

19. Seymour and Mills, *Golden Age*, 140–42. Robinson, *Matty*, 47–48.

20. Robinson, *Matty*, 48.

21. Seib, *Player*, 35.

22. Seib, *Player*, 35. Seymour and Mills, *Golden Age*, 99.

23. Robinson, *Matty*, 95.

24. Frank Deford, *The Old Ball Game: How John McGraw, Christy Mathewson, and the New York Giants Created Modern Baseball* (New York: Atlantic Monthly Press, 2005), 36–37.

25. W. J. MacBeth, "In All Fairness," *New York Tribune*, September 26, 1921. Seib *Player*, 51.

26. Hartley, *Christy Mathewson*, 146. Robinson, *Matty*, 127. Roessner, *Inventing Baseball Heroes*, 70.

27. Mathewson, *Pitching in a Pinch*, xv.

28. Robinson, *Matty*, 25.

29. Christy Mathewson, "How I Became a Big-League Pitcher," *Boston Globe*, January 17, 1926. Repr. in C. H. Claudy, *The Battle of Base-ball* (1912; Jefferson, NC: McFarland, 2005), 197.

30. Hartley, *Christy Mathewson*, 74–75.

31. Located at A. Bartlett Giamatti Research Center, National Baseball Hall of Fame.

32. Robinson, *Matty*, 114.

33. Mathewson player file, National Baseball Hall of Fame.

34. Robinson, *Matty*, 166.

35. Robinson, *Matty*, 18.

36. John "Red" Murray, "Personalities Presented by a Personality," *The Sporting News,* January 25, 1934, 5.

37. Robinson, *Matty*, 102, 149.

38. The perfect game remains one of baseball's rarest feats as of this writing, with only twenty-four having been pitched in the more than 145 years of major league baseball.

39. Robinson, *Matty*, 32.

40. Roessner, *Inventing Baseball Heroes*, 153.

41. Klapp, *Heroes, Villains, and Fools*, 13, 17. Rollin, "The Lone Ranger and Lenny Skutnik," 14, 25.

42. Klapp, *Heroes, Villains, and Fools*, 21.

43. Ashby, *With Amusement for All*, 151.

44. Joan M. Thomas, *Baseball's First Lady: Helene Hathaway Robison Britton and the St. Louis Cardinals* (St. Louis: Reedy Press, 2010), 151. Thomas asserts from her biographical research on the Robison family that despite appearing variously as De Haas, de Hass, and de Haas, that De Hass is the correct spelling for Frank Robison.

45. "St. Louis' Club," *The Sporting News,* April 8, 1911.

46. Thomas, *Baseball's First Lady*, 58, 69–70, 76, 108–9. Gai Ingham Berlage, *Women in Baseball: The Forgotten History* (Westport, CT: Praeger, 1994), 67. "A Court's Help," *The Sporting Life,* April 27, 1912.

47. "'Card' Control," *The Sporting Life,* June 15, 1912. Thomas, *Baseball's First Lady*, 63, 67. Marguerite Martyn, "Baseball Better Mental Exercise for Women Than Bridge," *St. Louis Post-Dispatch,* April 14, 1912.

48. Thomas, *Baseball's First Lady*, 70. "The Woman Magnate," *The Sporting Life,* August 31, 1912. "Bresnahan Out," *The Sporting Life,* November 2, 1912.

49. Seymour and Mills, *Golden Age,* 31.

50. "Bresnahan Out," *The Sporting Life,* November 2, 1912.

51. "Mrs. Britton Has Reasons," *The Sporting Life,* November 2, 1912.

52. "Roger Didn't Try Hard," *New York Times,* November 26, 1912. Thomas, *Baseball's First Lady*, 73.

53. Thomas, *Baseball's First Lady*, 73.

54. Rida Johnson Young and Christopher Mathewson, 1913, *The Girl and the Pennant* typescript, Performing Arts Library, New York Public Library, New York, 26.

55. *Baseball Encyclopedia: The Complete and Definitive Record of Major League Baseball*, Ninth ed., (New York: Macmillan, 1993). www.baseball-reference.com

56. Mathewson also had a brother, Henry, who joined him on the Giants for a brief time.

57. David Grimsted, *Melodrama Unveiled: American Theater and Culture 1800–1850* (Chicago: University of Chicago Press, 1968), 180–81.

58. Seymour and Mills, *Golden Age,* 101–6, details some of the players of the era who became known for their involvement with women and/or alcohol.

59. Though drinking was a concern with many players in the league, the real-life player to whom Punch was an allusion, Rube Marquard, claimed in an interview well after his playing career that he never drank during his career. However, Marquard's name was often involved in scandal in the newspapers during the years just before the play's debut for his tempestuous romance with married actress Blossom Seeley. They were married after her divorce became finalized in March 1913. Lawrence S. Ritter, *The Glory of Their Times: The Story of the Early Days of Baseball Told By the Men Who Played It,* enlarged ed. (1966; New York: William Morrow and Co., 1984).

60. Seymour and Mills, *Golden Age,* chapter 14, describes many instances of dishonesty in baseball during the era, from gambling in general to players being bought to fix games or shape the outcome of both batting and pennant races.

61. Frederick G. Lieb, *The St. Louis Cardinals: History of a Great Ballclub* (1944; Carbondale: Southern Illinois University Press, 2001), 47–8.

62. Young and Mathewson, *The Girl and the Pennant* typescript, 135. The threat of this type of dishonesty to the actual game was not just one of sportsmanship or fair play. It spoke to a larger issue in the economic structure of the game.

63. Michael S. Kimmel, "Baseball and the Reconstitution of American Masculinity, 1880–1920," in *Baseball History 3: An Annual of Original Baseball Research,* edited by Peter Levine (Westport, CT: Meckler, 1990), 98–109.

64. Young and Mathewson, *The Girl and the Pennant* typescript, 55–56.

65. Young and Mathewson, *The Girl and the Pennant* typescript, 42–43.

66. Young and Mathewson, *The Girl and the Pennant* typescript, 80.

67. Young and Mathewson, *The Girl and the Pennant* typescript, 23.

68. Young and Mathewson, *The Girl and the Pennant* typescript, 85.

69. Young and Mathewson, *The Girl and the Pennant* typescript, 40–41.

70. Young and Mathewson, *The Girl and the Pennant* typescript, 87.

71. Young and Mathewson, *The Girl and the Pennant* typescript, 24.

72. Young and Mathewson, *The Girl and the Pennant* typescript, 42.

73. Young and Mathewson, *The Girl and the Pennant* typescript, 34.

74. Grimsted, *Melodrama Unveiled,* 181.

75. Young and Mathewson, *The Girl and the Pennant* typescript, 34.

76. Young and Mathewson, *The Girl and the Pennant* typescript, 66.

77. Young and Mathewson, *The Girl and the Pennant* typescript, 35.

78. Young and Mathewson, *The Girl and the Pennant* typescript, 79.

79. Young and Mathewson, *The Girl and the Pennant* typescript, 89.

80. Young and Mathewson, *The Girl and the Pennant* typescript, 39.

81. *New York Sun,* October 15, 1913.

82. *New York Clipper,* November 1, 1913.

83. "The Girl and the Pennant," *New Rochelle Pioneer*, November 1, 1913.

84. "Cheers and Laughs for Baseball Play," *New York Times*, October 24, 1913.

85. "The Girl and the Pennant in for a Winning Run," *New York Herald*, October 24, 1913.

86. *Auburn Citizen*, October 25, 1913.

87. "'Matty' Does a Play," *New York Tribune*, October 24, 1913.

88. *New Rochelle Pioneer*, January 3, 1914. *New York Sun*, January 6, 1914. The new leading man for "America's Premier Stock Company" was named Harrison Ford.

89. Helen Christine Bennett, "The Woman Who Wrote 'Mother Machree,'" *American Magazine,* December 1920, 186.

CHAPTER 4

1. Ty Cobb with Al Stump, *Ty Cobb: My Life in Baseball* (New York: Doubleday, 1961), 185–6. Rob Edelman, "Ty Cobb, Actor," in *The National Pastime: Baseball in the Peach State*, edited by Ken Fester and Wynn Montgomery (Cleveland: Society for American Baseball Research, 2010), 103. Charles Leehrsen, *Ty Cobb: A Terrible Beauty* (New York: Simon and Schuster, 2015), 246, 254.

2. Charles Alexander, *Ty Cobb* (New York: Oxford UP, 1984), 101. Tim Hornbaker, *War on the Basepaths* (New York: Sports Publishing, 2015), 321n58.

3. "At the theatres," *Birmingham News,* December 1, 1911.

4. Cobb with Stump, *My Life in Baseball*, 47–48. Alexander, *Ty Cobb*, 17–8. Howard Rosenberg, *Ty Cobb Unleashed* (n.p.: Tile Books, 2018), 12.

5. Cobb with Stump, *My Life in Baseball*, 41.

6. Alexander, *Ty Cobb*, 3.

7. It was believed at the time that Cobb's total stood at 4,191 on September 11, 1985, when Pete Rose was celebrated for breaking the record. Since then, Cobb's official total has been revised to the 4,189 number and his career batting average has been amended to .366 instead of the previously acknowledged .367.

8. Cobb with Stump, *My Life in Baseball*, 66.

9. Ty Cobb, *Busting 'Em and Other Big League Stories* (New York: E. J. Clode, 1914; Jefferson, NC: McFarland & Co., 2003), 9.

10. Cobb, *Busting 'Em*, 19.

11. Cobb, *Busting 'Em*, 109–12. Alexander, *Ty Cobb*, 99. Cobb with Stump, *My Life in Baseball*, 275. Rosenberg, *Cobb*, 124.

12. Alexander, *Ty Cobb*, 141.

13. Cobb, *Busting 'Em*, 9–10; Alexander, *Ty Cobb*, 144. Hornbaker, *War*, 84.

14. Cobb, *Busting 'Em*, 21.

15. Cobb with Stump, *My Life in Baseball*, 83.

16. Cobb, *Busting 'Em*, 37.

17. Cobb, *Busting 'Em*, 107.

18. Cobb with Stump, *My Life in Baseball*, 157. Alexander, *Ty Cobb*, 56. Leerhsen, *Cobb*, 11. Rosenberg, *Cobb*, 263.

19. Cobb with Stump, *My Life in Baseball*, 176–77. Hornbaker, *War*, 123.

20. Cobb with Stump, *My Life in Baseball*, 94.

21. Alexander, *Ty Cobb*, 90–91, 157. Cobb with Stump, *My Life in Baseball*, 157.

22. Klapp, *Heroes, Villains, and Fools*, 50.

23. Klapp, *Heroes, Villains, and Fools*, 51–66.

24. Roessner, *Inventing Baseball Heroes*, 41, 50, 55, 82, 108, 121, 123.

25. Cobb, *Busting 'Em*, 17, 26, 130.

26. Alexander, *Ty Cobb*, 67. Cobb, *Busting 'Em*, 27.

27. Cobb, *Busting 'Em*, 32.

28. Smith, *Melodrama*, 20.

29. Roessner, *Inventing Baseball Heroes*, 99. Smith, *Melodrama*, 20.

30. Cobb, *Busting 'Em*, 122.

31. Cobb, *Busting 'Em*, 153. After his retirement, Cobb admitted that he had, indeed, intentionally tried to spike men on the field; he limited the number, however, to only two occasions through his entire career and insisted that both times it was done as retribution for previous wrongs done to him. Cobb claimed to have missed in his attempt at the first man—a catcher for Cleveland named Harry Bemis who had once used the ball clenched in his hand to beat Cobb's head while he was on the ground—but he acknowledged connecting with the other. The second man was Boston pitcher Dutch Leonard. Cobb had been hit by one of Leonard's pitches already in one game and believed that Leonard had been throwing at his head. During his next at bat, Cobb bunted down the first base line, forcing the first baseman to field the ball and forcing Leonard to cover the base. Leonard received the ball, made the out, and continued into foul territory. Ignoring the base completely, Cobb veered toward him and jumped at the pitcher's legs. Cobb's spikes sliced through Leonard's uniform but did not cut his skin. With the pitcher having just barely missed a possibly significant injury, Cobb claimed it was the last time Leonard ever threw at him. Though Cobb's autobiography tries to set these two instances off as justified acts of vengeance, which he couches in lines from Shakespeare's *Hamlet* about being obliged to win a fight when forced to do so, Cobb knew his spikes were weapons on the base paths and, with a mindset that every player was an enemy, he wielded them in a way that made his "Crazy Cobb" even more villainous. Leerhsen notes that Cobb repeated the "only" a small number of players he intentionally tried to spike throughout his life with both the number of players and list of names changing from time to time. Alexander, *Ty Cobb*, 122. Cobb with Stump, *My Life in Baseball*, 125. Leerhsen, *Cobb*, 211.

32. Rosenberg, *Cobb*, 77–80.

33. Alexander, *Ty Cobb*, 77.

34. Alexander, *Ty Cobb*, 79. Leerhsen, *Cobb*, 213. Christy Mathewson (or the ghostwriter under his name) even called Cobb guiltless in the slide. Hornbaker, *War*, 313n62.

35. Alexander, *Ty Cobb*, 79–80. Leerhsen, *Cobb*, 214. Hornbaker, *War*, 89–90.

36. Alexander, *Ty Cobb*, 67. Cobb with Stump, *My Life in Baseball*, 122. Hornbaker, *War*, 278. Rosenberg, *Cobb,* 290. Hornbaker notes Cobb's former teammate Davy Jones identified the Philadelphia Athletics as the target of the prank rather than New York.

37. Rosenberg notes several times when Cobb even admitted in casual conversation that he had done it. Rosenberg, *Cobb*, 69–71.

38. Alexander, *Ty Cobb*, 95–96. Cobb with Stump, *My Life in Baseball*, 95–99. Subsequent analysis of the 1910 season from years later has shown that Cobb was initially credited with two more hits than he had actually achieved. Lajoie is now credited as having won the batting title over Cobb. Leerhsen, *Cobb*, 239–44. Hornbaker, *War*, 109–11.

39. Alexander, *Ty Cobb*, 75. Hornbaker, *War*, 311n10.

40. Cobb, *Busting 'Em*, 33.

41. Alexander, *Ty Cobb*, 145. Hornbaker, *War*, 178–79.

42. Alexander, *Ty Cobb*, 105–7. Cobb, *Busting 'Em*, 28–30. Hornbaker, *War*, 132–3. Alexander had previously reported the man's last name as "Lueker."

43. Alexander, *Ty Cobb*, 105. Hornbaker, *War*, 132, 323n8. Leerhsen, *Cobb*, 258. Jennings said Lucker called Cobb a "half-n*****" while Lucker admitted to hearing someone else call Cobb a "half coon."

44. He toured once with several other major league players to Cuba. Though he was quite pleased with the money made from the trip, he never returned due in part to the number of dark-skinned Cubans on the opposing team. Never again did Cobb play on the same field as a Black player. Alexander, *Ty Cobb*, 98–99. Rosenberg, *Cobb*, 139–40.

45. Rosenberg cites an article by Wesley Fricks that argues each of the altercations occurred because of an action that was committed rather than Cobb seeking out a Black person specifically to assault. Rosenberg, *Cobb*, 103.

46. Alexander, *Ty Cobb*, 50. Hornbaker, *War*, 54–55. Rosenberg, *Cobb*, 148–49. Leerhsen, *Cobb*, 151. Leerhsen offers that "Carrie" may have been a reference to hatchet-wielding temperance advocate Carrie Nation.

47. Cobb with Stump, *My Life in Baseball*, 94. Alexander, *Ty Cobb*, 68. Hornbaker, *War*, 73–74.

48. Hornbaker, *War*, 177–78. Leerhsen, *Cobb*, 302–4. Rosenberg, *Cobb*, 26, 107, 191.

49. Alexander, *Ty Cobb*, 171–72. Hornbaker, *War*, 212.

50. Alexander, *Ty Cobb*, 119. Hornbaker, *War*, 145–46.

51. Alexander, *Ty Cobb*, 174. Hornbaker, *War*, 217–18. Rosenberg, *Cobb*, 200.

52. Alexander, *Ty Cobb*, 112. Hornbaker, *War*, 137–38.

53. Both hotel employees as well as the butcher's assistant had previously been identified as Black, but evidence discovered in contemporary census data has revealed that each of these three were white. Stanfield's name had also been presented as "Stansfield." Hornbaker, *War*, 90–91, 326n7. Leerhsen, *Cobb*, 219–20, 281. Rosenberg, *Cobb*, 104.

54. Alexander, *Ty Cobb*, 80–86. Hornbaker, *War*, 91–93, 103. Leerhsen, *Cobb*, 217–20, 226.

55. Cobb with Stump, *My Life in Baseball*, 29. Leerhsen, *Cobb*, 190–1. Cobb took the item on the road with him the next season to show off to people.

56. Cobb with Stump, *My Life in Baseball*, 60.

57. Alexander, *Ty Cobb*, 31. Cobb with Stump, *My Life in Baseball*, 21. Leerhsen, *Cobb*, 118.

58. Cobb with Stump, *My Life in Baseball*, 31, 131.

59. Alexander, *Ty Cobb,* 39.

60. Cobb with Stump, *My Life in Baseball*, 21, 32–37.

61. Alexander, *Ty Cobb,* 74.

62. Rosenberg, *Cobb*, 198.

63. Alexander, *Ty Cobb*, 189.

64. Alexander, *Ty Cobb*, 87, 107, 109, 112–3, 118.

65. Heilman, *Iceman*, 46–47. Heilman, *Tragedy*, 77–79.

66. Alexander, *Ty Cobb,* 101.

67. Edelman, "Ty Cobb, Actor," 103.

68. The term was used to denote a young woman who would date successive college men until they each graduated and moved away, leaving her behind.

69. "Ty Don't Believe in This Acting Business," TyCobb Scrapbook 33, A. Bartlett Giamatti Research Center, National Baseball Hall of Fame and Museum, Cooperstown, NY.

70. "Called 'the Georgia Peach'; Great American Here to Visit Columbia," Scrapbook 33, Baseball Hall of Fame. Tour schedule gleaned from issues of *the New York Clipper*.

71. T. H. Kline, "Interviewing Ty Cobb, Here as Actor, Proves to be Decidedly Pleasant Task," Scrapbook 33, Baseball Hall of Fame.

72. Cobb with Stump, *My Life in Baseball*, 186.

73. Seymour and Mills, *Golden Age*, 42, 100.

74. Thomas Postlewait, "The Hieroglyphic Stage: American Theatre and Society, Post-Civil War to 1945," in *The Cambridge History of American Theatre, Volume 2: 1870-1945*, edited by Don B. Wilmeth and Christopher Bigsby (Cambridge: Cambridge University Press, 1999), 150–51.

75. "'Ty' Cobb in College Widow," Scrapbook 33, Baseball Hall of Fame.

76. "'Ty' Cobb a Modest Actor, Talks Baseball and Stage," Scrapbook 33, Baseball Hall of Fame.

77. "Mighty Tyrus is in the City," Scrapbook 33, Baseball Hall of Fame.

78. "Cobb Greeted by Women and Men," Scrapbook 33, Baseball Hall of Fame.

79. "Ty Cobb Arrives," Scrapbook 33, Baseball Hall of Fame.

80. "Cobb Making Good as a Star in College Widow," Scrapbook 33, Baseball Hall of Fame.

81. "Mighty Tyrus is in the City," Scrapbook 33, Baseball Hall of Fame.

82. "Cobb Greeted by Women and Men," Scrapbook 33, Baseball Hall of Fame.

83. "Tyrus Cobb (at the Atlanta)" and "Ty Cobb in 'The Village Widow,'" Scrapbook 33, Baseball Hall of Fame.

84. "Ty Cobb Next at Bat," Scrapbook 33, Baseball Hall of Fame.

85. "The College Widow," Scrapbook 33, Baseball Hall of Fame.

86. "Ty Cobb a Modest Actor, Talks Baseball and Stage" and "Just from 'Georgia,'" Scrapbook 33, Baseball Hall of Fame.

87. "Cobb Greeted by Women and Men," Scrapbook 33, Baseball Hall of Fame.

88. "Ty Cobb with 'The College Widow'" and "Ty Cobb and 'The College Widow,'" Scrapbook 33, Baseball Hall of Fame.

89. "Cobb was Taken in by a Motion Picture Man," Scrapbook 33, Baseball Hall of Fame.

90. "When Cobb was Pinched," Scrapbook 33, Baseball Hall of Fame.

91. According to details in the *New York Clipper,* Glaser mounted a production of David Belasco's *The Girl of the Golden West* in the city just two weeks after *The College Widow*'s end.

92. "Vendome," Scrapbook 33, Baseball Hall of Fame.

93. "Large Audience sees Cobb in College Play," Scrapbook 33, Baseball Hall of Fame.

94. "Vendome," Scrapbook 33, Baseball Hall of Fame.

95. The Oxford English Dictionary shows that these multiple meanings of "hit" had been in popular use since the mid-nineteenth century.

96. "Ty Cobb Scores a Home Run in Ade's College Widow," Scrapbook 33, Baseball Hall of Fame.

97. "Large Audience sees Cobb in College Play" and "Sport Comment," Scrapbook 33, Baseball Hall of Fame.

98. "'The College Widow' Seen at Auditorium," Scrapbook 33, Baseball Hall of Fame.

99. "Ty Cobb Has a Pleasing Voice," Scrapbook 33, Baseball Hall of Fame.

100. "Ty Cobb Scores Hit," "The Lyceum," and "The College Widow—Duval," Scrapbook 33, Baseball Hall of Fame.

101. "Tyrus Raymond Cobb No Slouch as Thespian," "At the Grand: Ty Cobb with 'The College Widow,'" and "Ty Cobb at the Grand," Scrapbook 33, Baseball Hall of Fame.

102. "Ty Cobb Whole Show By Himself" and "Large Audience Sees Cobb in College Play," Scrapbook 33, Baseball Hall of Fame.

103. "The College Widow—Duval," Scrapbook 33, Baseball Hall of Fame.

104. "Amusements," Scrapbook 33, Baseball Hall of Fame.

105. "Capacity House to Hear Ty Cobb in College Widow," Scrapbook 33, Baseball Hall of Fame.

106. "At the theatres," *Birmingham News*, December 1, 1911.

107. "The College Widow, with Ty Cobb," Scrapbook 33, Baseball Hall of Fame.

108. "Great Ty Cobb in Town," Scrapbook 33, Baseball Hall of Fame.

109. "Ty Don't Believe in this Acting Business," Scrapbook 33, Baseball Hall of Fame.

110. The villainous traits that had been scrubbed from the stage did eventually emerge elsewhere in the course of the production. When a stagehand was being questioned by Glaser and the production staff during a performance about some missing sweaters, the confrontation became heated. Previously uninvolved in the conversation, Cobb walked over to the stagehand and knocked him down with a punch to the head. Cobb then proceeded to walk onto the stage for his scene. Ron Thomas, "Toronto Man Recalls Ty Cobb as an Actor," *Toronto Daily Star*, July 19, 1961. Baseball Hall of Fame Player File.

111. "Ty Cobb, Poor Actor, Good Ballplayer," *New York Times*, June 13, 1915.

112. "At the theatres," *Birmingham News*, December 1, 1911.

113. "Ty Cobb, Poor Actor, Good Ballplayer," *New York Times*, June 13, 1915.

CHAPTER 5

1. "The Passing of Waddell," *The Sporting Life*, April 11, 1914, 16.

2. www.baseball-reference.com

3. Alan H. Levy, *Rube Waddell: The Zany, Brilliant Life of a Strikeout Artist* (Jefferson: McFarland, 2000), 43.

4. Levy, *Waddell*, 126, 192.

5. Levy, *Waddell*, 17, 31, 44, 114.

6. Levy, *Waddell*, 154. In this case, the game ended as the runner was out trying to steal home before Waddell struck out the batter.

7. Connie Mack, "The One and Only Rube," *Saturday Evening Post*, March 14, 1936, 106.

8. Levy, *Waddell*, 25, 28, 34, 259.

9. Ritter, *Glory of Their Times*, 51.

10. Levy, *Waddell*, 102.

11. Levy, *Waddell*, 72, 112.

12. Levy, *Waddell*, 116, 133, 238–9.

13. Levy, *Waddell*, 252. Ritter, *Glory of Their Times*, 51.

14. Levy, *Waddell*, 51.

15. Levy, *Waddell*, 217.

16. Ritter, *Glory of Their Times*, 25.

17. Levy, *Waddell*, 61.

18. Levy, *Waddell*, 65.

19. Levy, *Waddell*, 140–41.

20. Ritter, *Glory of Their Times*, 25. Levy, *Waddell*, 18, 30, 34, 78, 127. Mack, "Rube," 108, 110. John Dell, "Here's the 'Real' Rube Waddell Story," *Philadelphia Inquirer*, May 5, 1962, 18.

21. Ritter, *Glory of Their Time*, 25. Levy, *Waddell*, 13–17, 30–31, 37, 40–41, 53, 94–100.

22. Levy, *Waddell*, 83, 96, 100, 193–94, 296.

23. Levy, *Waddell*, 11, 62, 96–99, 117, 162, 188, 208, 290–91.

24. Levy, *Waddell*, 252, 292, 296–97.

25. Levy, *Waddell*, 26, 30, 129–30, 256, 297.

26. Levy, *Waddell*, 6–7, 78, 133, 162–63, 230–31.

27. Levy, *Waddell*, 12, 31, 38, 64, 69, 110–11, 123, 125, 129, 136, 146, 177, 211, 260, 265, 290–91, 293.

28. Ritter, *Glory*, 89.

29. Ted Cohen, "Humor," in *Routledge Companion to Aesthetics* 2nd Ed., edited by Berys Gaut and Dominic McIver Lopes (London: Routledge, 2005), 474–5.

30. Klapp, *Heroes, Villains, and Fools,* 68–91.

31. Klapp, *Heroes, Villains, and Fools,* 76–77.

32. Klapp, *Heroes, Villains, and Fools,* 80–81.

33. *Oxford English Dictionary*, "Rube" and "Reuben," updated December 2020.

34. "When Reuben Comes to Town," New York Public Library Digital Collections, Music Division, The New York Public Library, https://digitalcollections.nypl.org/items/510d47e0-c064-a3d9-e040-e00a18064a99.

35. Mark Evans Bryan, "Yeoman and Barbarians: Popular Outland Caricature and American Identity," *The Journal of Popular Culture*, 46, no. 3 (2013): 464–68.

36. Bryan, "Yeoman," 468–69.

37. Thomas Elsaesser, *Film History as Media Archaeology* (Amsterdam University Press, 2016). Chapter title "Archaeologies of Interactivity: The 'Rube' as Symptom of Media Change," 199. Thomas Elsaesser presents that the "rube" film is almost as old as cinema itself.

38. David Carlyon, "'blow your nose with your fingers': The Rube Story as Crowd Control," *New England Theatre Journal* 7 (1996): 7–8. Carlyon goes on to argue that the rube stories may have also been used to disrupt any critiques by the audience regardless of their appropriateness. Butsch, *Making American Audiences*, 57–8.

39. Richard M. Dorson, "The Yankee on the Stage—A Folk Hero of American Drama," *The New England Quarterly* 13, no. 3 (September 1940), 476.

40. The "Hey Rube" was a disputed but popularly acknowledged sign around

circuses in the nineteenth century that a fight was occurring between circus personnel and locals, which could often become a deadly affair. "What Do Yer Soy?," *Cincinnati Enquirer*, February 23, 1878, 8.

41. Levy, *Waddell*, 12–3. Dell, "Here's the 'Real' Rube Waddell Story,"18. The other anecdotes include the nickname being given to him by a catcher as he warmed up the first time for the Franklin team, and Waddell's own version which Waddell himself told about his extraordinary strength and stamina in pitching both games of a doubleheader and hitting two home runs after having been knocked unconscious for five minutes from taking a line drive to the forehead. Levy notes the latter story as likely being one of Waddell's embellishments.

42. After having started his major league career with four years in the National League, it is notable that he spent the remainder of his career in the American League, which was likely more tolerant of his behavior because of this added benefit, which held less value for the National League.

43. Smith, *Melodrama*, 31, 33. Kilgariff, *The Golden Age of Melodrama*, 24.

44. *New York Clipper*, November 1, 1902, 789.

45. Walter S. Mathews, *The Stain of Guilt*, 1902. Located in the Library of Congress Copyright Office drama deposits, 1901–1977.

46. "Havlin and Garen's New Production Will Have Decidedly St. Louis Flavor," *St. Louis Post-Dispatch*, March 26, 1903, 15.

47. *New York Clipper*, April 11, 1903, 161. "Stain of Guilt Done at Havlin's," *St. Louis Post-Dispatch*, March 30, 1903, 6.

48. *New York Clipper*, April 11, 1903, 162.

49. "Rube Waddell to be an Actor," *St. Louis Post-Dispatch*, May 18, 1903, 3. "Rain Prevents Ball Game," *Louisville Courier-Journal*, May 22, 1903, 6.

50. "Waddell an Actor," *The Sporting Life*, May 23, 1903, 5.

51. *New York Clipper*, August 8, 1903, 561.

52. "Garden Bills for the Week Promise First Class Entertainment," *St. Louis Post-Dispatch*, May 31, 1903, 6B.

53. "Rube Waddell to be an Actor," *St. Louis Post-Dispatch*, May 18, 1903, 3. "Rain Prevents Ball Game," *Louisville Courier-Journal*, May 22, 1903, 6.

54. "Rube Waddell to be an Actor," *St. Louis Post-Dispatch*, May 18, 1903, 3. Levy, *Waddell*, 53.

55. "Two Hits and No Runs," *Washington Post*, June 2, 1903, 9. "Athletics Take Two," *Washington Post*, July 31, 1903, 9.

56. "Waddell, Actor," *Sporting Life*, June 6, 1903, 26.

57. "Wadddell's [sic] Rehearsal," *Washington Post*, August 23, 1903, 9.

58. "More Thunder for Waddell," *Sporting Life*, September 5, 1903, 24.

59. Levy, *Waddell*, 147. "Century to Cut Minute," *Detroit Free Press*, August 30, 1903, A6.

60. *New York Clipper*, August 8, 1903, 561. *New York Clipper*, August 22, 1903, 609.

61. Levy, *Waddell*, 147.

62. *Sporting Life*, October 24, 1903, 13. *Sporting Life*, November 21, 1903, 7.

63. "Reub Waddell to Save Many Lives," *Indianapolis Morning Star*, August 24, 1903, 8.

64. *Sporting Life*, October 24, 1903, 13.

65. *New York Clipper*, October 3, 1903, 751.

66. "On Dit," *Louisville Courier-Journal*, September 21, 1903, 4.

67. *New York Clipper*, November 21, 1903, 928.

68. "'The Stain of Guilt' at the Park Theater," *Indianapolis Morning Star*, October 8, 1903, 8.

69. *Sporting Life*, October 24, 1903, 13.

70. *Sporting Life*, November 21, 1903, 7.

71. *Sporting Life*, November 14, 1903, 2.

72. *Sporting Life*, October 3, 1903, 4.

73. *Sporting Life*, September 5, 1903, 9. *Sporting Life*, November 14, 1903, 2. *Cincinnati Enquirer*, October 31, 1903, 3. "Rube Waddell Amuck," *Los Angeles Times*, November 29, 1903, 4.

74. "Baseball Gossip," *Washington Post*, December 20, 1903, A2. *Sporting Life*, November 14, 1903, 2.

75. *Sporting Life*, December 12, 1903, 4.

76. "Rube's a Poet," *Indianapolis Morning Star*, January 2, 1909, 9.

77. "Great Waddell with Outlaws," *Louisville Courier-Journal*, September 16, 1906, C3.

78. *Sporting Life*, December 12, 1903, 4. *Sporting Life*, October 3, 1903, 4.

79. "Waddell Says No," *Indianapolis Morning Star*, October 9, 1903, 7.

80. "Cardinals of 1904 Now the Greatest of Baseball Problems," *St. Louis Post-Dispatch*, November 29, 1903, 7B.

81. "Baseball Law is to Figure," *Louisville Courier-Journal*, January 17, 1904, B4.

82. "Five Strenuous Days Rube Waddell Spends Then Goes to Butler," *Wheeling Intelligencer*, November 24, 1903, 7. "Rube Waddell's Many Roles," *Baltimore Sun*, November 25, 1903, 9.

83. "Rube Waddell May Be Released," *Louisville Courier- Journal*, January 17, 1904, B4. Finnigan also asked permission from the Pittsburgh club to have Honus Wagner take the role in the play. The club president would not allow it under any conditions. "$20,000 for Two Players," *Boston Daily Globe*, December 4, 1903, 8.

84. "Baseball Men to Meet To-Day," *Louisville Courier-Journal*, January 4, 1904, 7. *Sporting Life*, December 26, 1903, 5.

85. "Wadddell's [*sic*] Rehearsal," *Washington Post*, August 23, 1903, 9.

86. "Baseball Gossip," *Washington Post*, August 23, 1903, ES12.

87. *Sporting Life*, December 5, 1903, 7.

88. *Sporting Life*, October 24, 1903, 13.

89. *Sporting Life*, November 21, 1903, 7.

90. "Baseball Gossip," *Washington Post*, September 20, 1903, E12.

CONCLUSION

1. Robert W. Creamer, *Babe: The Legend Comes to Life* (New York: Simon and Schuster, 1974, 2005), 109.

2. Jane Leavy, *The Big Fella: Babe Ruth and the World He Created* (New York: Harper, 2018), XXVI.

3. Leavy, *Big Fella*, 305, 562. "Ruth Supernormal, So He Hits Homers," *New York Times*, September 11, 1921, 25.

4. Marshall Smelser, *The Life that Ruth Built* (New York: Quadrangle, 1975), 208–9.

5. Leavy, *Big Fella*, 197, 222.

6. Smelser, *Life*, 200–201. Leavy, *Big Fella*, 111. Leigh Montville, *The Big Bam: The Life and Times of Babe Ruth* (New York: Doubleday, 2006), 118.

7. Smelser, *Life*, 201–2. Leavy, *Big Fella*, 229.

8. Leavy, *Big Fella*, 205. Smelser, *Life*, 233. Creamer, *Babe*, 251. Montville, *Big Bam*, 145–6. IBDB.com. folksongandmusichall.com, Archive of Popular American Music, UCLA.

9. Creamer, *Babe*, 250–1. Smelser, *Life*, 232. Montville, *Big Bam*, 145. Leavy, *Big Fella*, 61, 207.

10. "Babe Didn't Draw," *New York Clipper*, January 18, 1922, 6. Creamer, *Babe*, 257.

11. "Athletes Fail as Drawing Cards," *New York Clipper*, December 18, 1921, 8.

12. Leavy, *Big Fella*, 206–7.

13. Laurie, *Vaudeville*, 126.

14. "Shubert Suit Against Smith and Dale Tried in U.S. Court," *New York Clipper*, November 9, 1921, 4, 28.

15. Smesler, *Life*, 346. Leavy, *Big Fella*, 127. Montville, *Big Bam*, 248.

16. Leavy, *Big Fella*, 126–7. Ruth faced a lawsuit in San Diego for having broken child labor laws while in the city because he failed to obtain a permit from the commissioner of the Bureau of Labor Statistics for having a child recite a poem after 10:00 p.m. The suit was dismissed. Leavy, *Big Fella*, 129–30.

17. Smelser, *Life*, 517.

18. Despite many attempts, a scripted drama centering on baseball would not actually become a hit in the theatre until *Damn Yankees* in 1955. Likely among the reasons for its success was that the ball-playing in the musical did not have the expectation by the audience of being portrayed realistically.

19. A. Bartlett Giamatti, "Green Fields of the Mind," in *A Great and Glorious Game* (Chapel Hill: Algonquin Books, 1998). Roger Angell, "Agincourt and

After," *New Yorker,* November 17, 1975. Though not directly presented in the piece, Angell's title offers an allusion to Shakespeare's *Henry V.*

20. Olney even details a plan for dealing with Wells that is reminiscent of Rube Waddell. When in Detroit, Tigers manager Sparky Anderson told Wells he could do what he wanted for three out of every five days, but the other two belonged to the team.

Bibliography

Primary Sources

BOOKS AND PLAYS

Anson, Adrian C. *A Ball Player's Career*. Chicago: Era Publishing, 1900.

Cobb, Ty. *Busting 'Em and Other Big League Stories*. New York: E. J. Clode, 1914. Reprint Jefferson, NC: McFarland, 2003.

———. *My Twenty Years in Baseball*. Edited by William R. Cobb. Mineola, NY: Dover, 2009.

——— with Al Stump. *My Life in Baseball: The True Record*. New York: Doubleday, 1961. Reprint Lincoln, NE: Bison Books, 1993.

Hoyt, Charles Hale. *A Runaway Colt*. Microfilm. *The Dramatic Works of Charles Hale Hoyt*.

———. *A Tin Soldier*. Microfilm. *The Dramatic Works of Charles Hale Hoyt*.

Kelly, Mike. *Play Ball: Stories of the Diamond Field*. Boston: Press of Emery & Hughes, c1888. Reprint, Jefferson, NC: McFarland, 2006.

Mathews, Walter S. *The Stain of Guilt*. 1902. Library of Congress Copyright Office Drama Deposits, 1901-1977.

Mathewson, Christy. *Pitching in a Pinch*. 1912. Reprint, New York: Stein and Day, 1977.

Young, Rida Johnson. *The Girl and the Pennant*. New York: Samuel French, 1917.

——— and Christopher Mathewson. *The Girl and the Pennant*. 1912 Typescript. Performing Arts Library, New York Public Library, New York.

NEWSPAPERS

Auburn Citizen
Boston Globe
Boston Herald
Brookfield Courier
Brooklyn Eagle
Buffalo Daily Courier
Buffalo Express

Chicago Daily News
Chicago Evening Post
Chicago Daily Herald
Chicago Daily Tribune
New Rochelle Pioneer
New York Clipper
New York Herald
New York Sun
New York Telegram
New York Times
New York Tribune
New York World
Oswego Daily Times
Philadelphia Inquirer
Pittsburgh Press
St. Louis Post-Dispatch
Sporting Life
Syracuse Herald
Syracuse Standard
Washington Post

PLAYER FILES

Located at the A. Bartlett Giamatti Research Center, National Baseball Hall of
    Fame and Museum, Cooperstown, NY:
    Adrian Constantine Anson
    Michael Joseph Kelly
    Christopher Mathewson
    Henry Mathewson
    Tyrus Raymond Cobb

Secondary Sources

Alexander, Charles C. *Our Game: An American Baseball History*. New York: Henry
    Holt, 1991.
———. *Ty Cobb*. New York: Oxford UP, 1984.
Angell, Roger. "Agincourt and After," *New Yorker*, November 17, 1975.
Appel, Marty. *Slide Kelly Slide: The Wild Life and Times of Mike "King" Kelly,*
    Baseball's First Superstar. Lanham, MD: Scarecrow Press, 1996.
Ashby, LeRoy. *With Amusement for All: A History of American Popular Culture*
    Since 1830. Lexington: University of Kentucky Press, 2006, 2012.

Baldwin, Davarian L. *Chicago's New Negroes: Modernity, The Great Migration, and Black Urban Life*. Chapel Hill: University of North Carolina Press, 2007.

Barth, Gunther. *City People: The Rise of Modern City Culture in Nineteenth-Century America*. New York: Oxford UP, 1980.

Bartley, Sean. "'You're Out!' Presence and Absence at the Ballpark." In *Sporting Performances: Politics at Play*, edited by Shannon L. Walsh, 17-29. London: Routledge, 2021.

Baseball Encyclopedia: The Complete and Definite Record of Major League Baseball. Ninth ed. New York: Macmillan, 1993.

Bennett, Helen Christine. "The Woman Who Wrote 'Mother Machree.'" *American Magazine*, December 1920.

Berlage, Gai Ingham. *Women in Baseball: The Forgotten History*. Westport, CT: Praeger, 1994.

Bernheim, Alfred L. *The Business of the Theatre: An Economic History of the American Theatre, 1750-1932*. New York: Benjamin Blom, 1932.

Betts, John Rickards. *America's Sporting Heritage: 1850-1950*. Reading, MA: Addison-Wesley, 1974.

Bordman, Gerald. *American Theatre: A Chronicle of Comedy and Drama 1869-1914*. New York: Oxford UP, 1994.

Braudy, Leo. *The Frenzy of Renown: Fame & Its History*. New York: Oxford UP, 1986.

Browne, Ray B. and Marshall W. Fishwick, eds. *The Hero in Transition*. Bowling Green, OH: Bowling Green University Popular Press, 1983.

Bryan, Mark Evans. "Yeoman and Barbarians: Popular Outland Caricature and American Identity," *The Journal of Popular Culture* 46, no. 3: 463-80.

Burgos, Adrian Jr. *Playing America's Game: Baseball, Latinos, and the Color Line*. Berkeley: University of California Press, 2007.

Burk, Robert F. *Never Just a Game: Players, Owners, and American Baseball to 1920*. Chapel Hill: University of North Carolina Press, 1994.

Bushman, Richard L. "The Genteel Republic," *Wilson Quarterly* 38:1 (Winter 2014).

———. *The Refinement of America*. New York: Knopf, 1992.

Butsch, Richard. *The Making of American Audiences: From Stage to Television, 1750-1990*. Cambridge: Cambridge UP, 2000.

Carlyon, David. "'blow your nose with your fingers': The Rube Story as Crowd Control," *New England Theatre Journal* 7 (1996): 1-22.

Claudy, C. H. *The Battle of Base-ball*. 1912. Reprint, Jefferson, NC: McFarland, 2005.

Cobb, William R. "The Georgia Peach: Stumped by the Storyteller." In *The National Pastime: Baseball in the Peach State*, edited by Ken Fester and Wynn Montgomery, 84-101. Cleveland: Society for American Baseball Research, 2010.

Cohen, Ted. "Humor." In *Routledge Companion to Aesthetics*, 2nd ed., edited by Berys Gaut and Dominic McIver Lopes. London: Routledge, 2005.

Creamer, Robert W. *Babe: The Legend Comes to Life*. 1974. Reprint, paperback edition, New York: Simon & Schuster, 2005.

Deford, Frank. *The Old Ballgame: How John McGraw, Christy Mathewson, and the New York Giants Created Modern Baseball*. New York: Atlantic Monthly Press, 2005.

Derks, Scott, ed. *The Value of a Dollar: Prices and Incomes in the United States 1860-1999*. Lakeville: Grey House Publishing, 1999.

Di Salvatore, Bryan. *A Clever Base-Ballist: The Life and Times of John Montgomery Ward*. New York: Pantheon Books, 1999.

Dorson, Richard M. "The Yankee on the Stage—A Folk Hero of American Drama," *The New England Quarterly* 13, no. 3 (September 1940): 467-93.

Dreifort, John E., ed. *Baseball History from Outside the Lines: A Reader*. Lincoln: University of Nebraska Press, 2001.

Duggan, G. C. *The Stage Irishman: A History of the Irish Play and Stage Characters from the Earliest Times*. Dublin: Talbot Press, 1937.

Edelman, Rob. "Baseball, Vaudeville, and Mike Donlin." *Base Ball*, Spring 2008, 44-57.

———. "Mike Donlin, movie actor: roll 'em!" *The Baseball Research Journal* (2000): 73-6.

———. "Ty Cobb, Actor." In *The National Pastime: Baseball in the Peach State*, edited by Ken Fester and Wynn Montgomery, 102-110. Cleveland: Society for American Baseball Research, 2010.

Elsaesser, Thomas. *Film History as Media Archaeology*. Amsterdam UP, 2016.

Engle, Ron and Tice L. Miller, eds. *The American Stage: Social and Economic Issues from the Colonial Period to the Present*. Cambridge: Cambridge UP, 1993.

Fleitz, David L. *Cap Anson: The Grand Old Man of Baseball*. Jefferson, NC: McFarland, 2005.

Frick, John. "A Changing Theatre: New York and Beyond." In *The Cambridge History of American Theatre, Volume Two: 1870-1945*, edited by Don B. Wilmeth and Christopher Bigsby, 196-232. Cambridge: Cambridge UP, 1999.

Gelzheiser, Robert P. *Labor and Capital in 19th Century Baseball*. Jefferson, NC: McFarland, 2006.

Giamatti, A. Bartlett. "Green Fields of the Mind." In *A Great and Glorious Game*. Chapel Hill: Algonquin Books, 1998.

Gieskes, Edward. *Representing the Professions: Administration, Law and Theater in Early Modern England*. Newark: University of Delaware Press, 2006.

Goffman, Erving. *The Presentation of Self in Everyday Life*. New York: Doubleday Anchor, 1959.

Goldstein, Warren. *Playing for Keeps: A History of Early Baseball*. Ithaca: Cornell UP, 1989.

Green, Abel and Joe Laurie, Jr. *Show Biz: From Vaude to Video*. New York: Holt, 1951.

Grella, George. "The Actor as Ballplayer, the Ballplayer as Actor." In *The Cooperstown Symposium on Baseball and American Culture, 2001*, edited by William M. Simons, 156-66. Jefferson, NC: McFarland, 2002.

Grimsted, David. *Melodrama Unveiled: American Theater and Culture1800-1850*. Chicago: University of Chicago Press, 1968.

Hapgood, Norman. *The Stage in America, 1897-1900*. New York: Macmillan, 1901.

Hartley, Michael. *Christy Mathewson: A Biography*. Jefferson, NC: McFarland, 2004.

Hays, Michael and Anastasia Nikolopoulou, eds. *Melodrama: The Cultural Emergence of a Genre*. New York: St. Martin's Press, 1996.

Heilman, Robert Bechtold. *The Iceman, the Arsonist, and the Troubled Agent: Tragedy and Melodrama on the Modern Stage*. Seattle: University of Washington Press, 1973.

———. *Tragedy and Melodrama: Versions of Experience*. Seattle: University of Washington Press, 1968.

Hewitt, Barnard. *Theatre U.S.A. 1665-1957*. New York: McGraw-Hill, 1959.

Honig, Donald. *Baseball America: The Heroes of the Game and the Times of their Glory*. New York: MacMillan, 1985.

Hornbaker, Tim. *War on the Basepaths: The Definitive Biography of Ty Cobb*. New York: Sports Publishing, 2015.

Hornblow, Arthur. *A History of the Theatre in America: From Its Beginnings to the Present Time*. Three volumes. 1919. Reprint, New York: Benjamin Blom, 1965.

Hoyt, Charles. *Five Plays*. Princeton: Princeton UP, 1941.

Hughes, Glenn. *A History of the American Theatre 1700-1950*. New York: Samuel French, 1951.

Hunt, Douglas L. Introduction to *Five Plays by Charles H. Hoyt*. Princeton: Princeton UP, 1941.

Isenberg, Michael T. *John L. Sullivan and His America*. Sport and Society Series, edited by Benjamin G. Rader & Randy Roberts. Urbana: University of Illinois Press, 1994.

Kimmel, Michael S. "Baseball and the Reconstitution of American Masculinity, 1880-1920." In *Baseball History 3: An Annual of Original Baseball Research*, edited by Peter Levine, 98-112. Westport, CT: Meckler, 1990.

Klapp, Orrin E. *Heroes, Villains, and Fools: The Changing American Character*. Englewood Cliffs, NJ: Prentice-Hall, 1962.

Laurie, Joe, Jr. *Vaudeville: From the Honky-Tonks to the Palace*. New York: Holt, 1953.

Leavy, Jane. *The Big Fella: Babe Ruth and the World He Created*. New York: Harper, 2018.

Leerhsen, Charles. *Ty Cobb: A Terrible Beauty*. New York: Simon & Schuster, 2015.

Levy, Alan H. *Rube Waddell: The Zany, Brilliant Life of a Strikeout Artist*. Jefferson: McFarland, 2000.

Lewis, Robert M. *From Traveling Show to Vaudeville: Theatrical Spectacle in American, 1830-1910*. Baltimore: Johns Hopkins UP, 2003.

Lieb, Frederick G. *The St. Louis Cardinals: History of a Great Ballclub*. 1944. Reprint, Carbondale: Southern Illinois UP, 2001.

Lott, Eric. *Love and Theft: Blackface Minstrelsy and the American Working Class*. 20th Anniversary Ed., New York: Oxford UP, 2013.

Mack, Connie. "The One and Only Rube," *Saturday Evening Post*, March 14, 1936, 11-2, 106-10.

Margo, Robert A. "Annual Earning in Selected Industries and Occupations, 1890-1926." In *Historical Statistics of the United States*. Vol 2. Millennium Ed. New York: Cambridge, 2000.

McArthur, Benjamin. *Actors and American Culture: 1880-1920*. Philadelphia: Temple UP, 1984.

McConachie, Bruce. *Melodramatic Formations: American Theatre & Society, 1820-1870*. Iowa City: University of Iowa Press, 1992.

Miller, Richard L. "The Baseball Parks and the American Culture." In *The Cooperstown Symposium on the American Culture (1990)*, edited by Alvin L. Hall, 168-186. Westport, CT: Meckler, 1991.

Montville, Leigh. *The Big Bam: The Life and Times of Babe Ruth*. New York: Doubleday, 2006.

Moore, Jim and Natalie Vermilyea. *Ernest Thayer's "Casey at the Bat": Background and Characters of Baseball's Most Famous Poem*. Jefferson, NC: McFarland, 1994.

Mordden, Ethan. *The American Theatre*. New York: Oxford UP, 1981.

Moses, Montrose and John Mason Brown, eds. *The American Theatre As Seen By Its Critics, 1752-1934*. New York: W. W. Norton, 1934.

Mrozek, Donald J. *Sport and American Mentality, 1880-1920*. Knoxville: University of Tennessee Press, 1983.

Murdock, Eugene C. *Mighty Casey: All American*. Westport, CT: Greenwood Press, 1984.

Murray, Martin. *Circus: From Rome to Ringling*. New York: Appleton-Century-Crofts, 1956.

Olney, Buster. *The Last Night of the Yankee Dynasty*. New York: Harper Perennial, 2008.

Persons, Stow. *The Decline of American Gentility*. New York: Columbia UP, 1973.

Piorcek, Richard. "Baseball and Vaudeville and the Development of Popular Culture in the United States, 1880-1930." In *The Cooperstown Symposium on Baseball and American Culture, 1999*, edited by Peter M. Rutkoff, 83-100. Jefferson, NC: McFarland, 2000.

Poggi, Jack. *Theater in America: The Impact of Economic Forces 1870-1967*. Ithaca: Cornell UP, 1968.

Postlewait, Thomas. *The Cambridge Introduction to Theatre Historiography*. Cambridge: Cambridge UP, 2009.

———. "The Hieroglyphic Stage: American Theatre and Society, Post-Civil War to 1945." In *The Cambridge History of American Theatre: Volume II 1870-1945*, edited by Don B. Wilmeth and Christopher Bigsby, 107-195. Cambridge: Cambridge UP, 1999.

Power, Cormac. *Presence in Play: A Critique of Theories of Presence in the Theatre*. Amsterdam: Rodopi, 2008.

Rader, Benjamin G. *Baseball: A History of America's Game*. Urbana: University of Illinois Press, 2008.

Rahill, Frank. *The World of Melodrama*. University Park: Pennsylvania State UP, 1967.

Riess, Steven A. *Sport in Industrial America 1850-1920*. Wheeling, IL: Harlan Davidson, 1995.

———. *Touching Base: Professional Baseball and American Culture in the Progressive Era*. Revised ed. Urbana, IL: University of Illinois Press, 1999.

Ritter, Lawrence S. *The Glory of Their Times: The Story of the Early Days of Baseball Told By the Men Who Played It*. 1966. Reprint, enlarged ed., New York: William and Morrow Co., 1984.

Robinson, Ray. *Matty: An American Hero*. New York: Oxford P, 1993.

Roessner, Amber. *Inventing Baseball Heroes: Ty Cobb, Christy Mathewson, and the Sporting Press in America*. Baton Rouge: Louisiana State UP, 2014.

Rojek, Chris. *Celebrity*. London: Reaktion, 2001.

Rollin, Roger R. "The Lone Ranger and Lenny Skutnik: The Hero as Popular Culture." In *The Hero in Transition*, edited by Ray B. Browne and Marshall W. Fishwick, 14-45. Bowling Green, OH: Bowling Green Popular Press, 1983.

Rosenberg, Howard W. *Cap Anson 1: When Captaining a Team Meant Something: Leadership in Baseball's Early Years*. N.p.: Tile Books, 2003.

———. *Cap Anson 2: The Theatrical and Kingly Mike Kelly, U.S. Team Sport's First Media Sensation and Baseball's Original Casey at the Bat*. N.p.: Tile Books, 2004.

———. *Cap Anson 3: Muggsy John McGraw and the Tricksters: Baseball's Fun Age of Rule Bending*. N.p.: Tile Books, 2005.

———. *Cap Anson 4: Bigger than Babe Ruth: Cap Anson of Chicago*. N.p.: Tile Books, 2006.

———. *Ty Cobb Unleashed*. N.p.: Tile Books, 2018.

Ross, Robert B. *The Great Baseball Revolt: The Rise and Fall of the 1890 Players League*. Lincoln: University of Nebraska Press, 2016.

Schaefer, Robert H. "Anson on Broadway: The Failure of *A Runaway Colt*," *The National Pastime* 25 (2005): 74-81.

Schechner, Richard. *Performance Studies: An Introduction*, 2nd ed. New York: Routledge, 2022.

Schwartz, Vanessa R. *Spectacular Realities: Early Mass Culture in Fin-de-Siècle Paris*. Berkeley: University of California Press, 1998.

Scully, Judy. "'A Stage Irish Identity'—An Example of 'Symbolic Power,'" *Journal of Ethnic and Migration Studies* 23, no. 3: 385-98.

S.D., Trav. *No Applause, Just Throw Money, or The Book That Made Vaudeville Famous*. New York: Faber and Faber, 2005.

Seib, Philip. *The Player: Christy Mathewson, Baseball and the American Century*. New York: Thunder's Mouth, 2003.

Seymour, Harold, and Dorothy Seymour Mills. *Baseball: The Early Years*. New York: Oxford UP, 1960.

———. *Baseball: The Golden Age*. New York: Oxford UP, 1971.

Smelser, Marshall. *The Life That Ruth Built*. New York: Quadrangle, 1975.

Smith, James L. *Melodrama: The Critical Idiom*. Edited by John D. Jump. 28. London: Methuen & Co. Ltd., 1973.

Smith, Leverett T., Jr. *The American Dream and the National Game*. Bowling Green, OH: Bowling Green University Popular Press, 1975.

Sotiropoulos, Karen. *Staging Race: Black Performers in Turn of the Century America*. Cambridge, MA: Harvard UP, 2006.

Spalding, Albert G. *America's National Game*. New York: American Sports Publishing, 1911.

Spink, Alfred. *The National Game*. National Game Publishing, 1911. Reprint, second ed., Carbondale: Southern Illinois UP, 2000.

Susman, Warren. *Culture As History*. Washington: Smithsonian Institute Press, 2003.

Stern, Travis. "At Play: Cap Anson's Performance of 'Cap Anson' in *A Runaway Colt*." In *Sporting Performances: Politics in Play*, edited by Shannon L. Walsh, 165-76. London: Routledge, 2021.

———. "Mike Kelly's Performance of Success and Failure on the Field and on the Stage." In *Theatre Symposium* 27 (2019): 39-52.

———. "Staging a Feminist Movement in Baseball: Rida Johnson Young's *The Girl and the Pennant*." In *Baseball/Literature/Culture 2008-2009*, edited by Ron E. Kates and Warren Tormey, 64-71. Jefferson, NC: McFarland, 2010.

Stout, Glenn. *The Selling of the Babe*. New York: Thomas Dunne Books, 2016.

Strang, Lewis C. *Players and Plays of the Last Quarter Century*. Two volumes. Boston: L. C. Page and Co, 1902.

Stump, Al. *Cobb: A Biography*. Chapel Hill, NC: Algonquin Books, 1994.

Sullivan, Dean, ed. *Early Innings: A Documentary History of Baseball, 1825-1908*. Lincoln, NE: University of Nebraska Press, 1995.

Thomas, Joan M. *Baseball's First Lady: Helene Hathaway Robison Britton and the St. Louis Cardinals*. St. Louis: Reedy Press, 2010.

Thorn, John, and Pete Palmer, eds. *Total Baseball*. New York: Warner, 1989.

Trachtenberg, Alan. *The Incorporation of America: Culture and Society in the Gilded Age*. New York: Hill and Wang, 1982.

Tygiel, Jules. *Past Time: Baseball as History*. Oxford: Oxford UP, 2000.

Voigt, David Quentin. *American Baseball: From Gentleman's Sport to the Commissioner System*. Norman: University of Oklahoma Press, 1966.

———. *American Baseball Volume II: From the Commissioners to Continental Expansion*. Norman: University of Oklahoma Press, 1970.

Walsh, Shannon L., ed. *Sporting Performances: Politics in Play*. London: Routledge, 2021.

Watermeier, Daniel J. "Actors and Acting." In *The Cambridge History of American Theatre: Volume II 1870-1945*, edited by Don B. Wilmeth and Christopher Bigsby, 446-486. Cambridge: Cambridge UP, 1999.

White, G. Edward. *Creating the National Pastime: Baseball Transforms Itself 1903-1953*. Princeton: Princeton UP, 1996.

Wilson, Garff B. *Three Hundred Years of American Drama and Theatre: From Ye Bare and Ye Cubb to Chorus Line*. Second ed. Englewood Cliffs, NJ: Prentice-Hall, 1983.

Woods, Alan. "James J. Corbett: Theatrical Star." *Journal of Sport History* 3, no. 2 (Summer 1976): 162-75.

Woodward, Kath. *Boxing, Masculinity, and Identity: The "I" of the Tiger*. London: Routledge, 2007.

WEBSITES

http://www.baseball-almanac.com
http://www.baseball-reference.com
http://www.ibdb.com
http://folksongandmusichall.com
http://www.retrosheet.org
http://www.senate.gov
http://usgennet.org

Index

Page numbers in **boldface** refer to illustrations.